PRAISE

Sonia has written a beautiful, wise, and much-needed guide for anyone involved in raising or supporting children. Her decades of clinical experience is combined with both spiritual and lived wisdom, and her work has helped countless families, mine included, to parent from a place of deep connection and intuition. Raising Empowered Humans is both soulful and practical – a rare combination, which makes this book feel like a trusted companion. A truly transformative read.

Maha Corbett – Speaker, Author, Co-Founder of SWIISH

Sonia is a bright light in this world. Her work is a beautiful blend of insight, inspiration and grounded guidance. Raising Empowered Humans is a treasure trove of wisdom from a trusted voice in the space of conscious parenting and human development. A gift for all of us to benefit from Sonia and her work to create meaningful lasting impact.

Amy Pocsik – Founder of Bold Moves

Sonia is an exceptional human, gifted with insight, intuition, and wisdom. Born to guide, she has accumulated vast experience and authority in understanding humanity. Trust her every word – this book will serve you well!

Julia Scott – CEO of Jane Wealth & Founder of Love Luck Wealth

Sonia leads with intuitive brilliance and wholehearted presence. She sees the whole person – child or adult – and gently unlocks their potential with compassion, wisdom, and joy. Her ability to bring lightness to even the most challenging moments is a rare and powerful gift. As both a gifted writer and hands-on practitioner, Sonia's work is a true invitation to flourish.

Vanessa Bell – Champion of Australian Wool, Sustainability Advocate & Host of Fashion to Farmer

Sonia brings a rare depth to everything she does. With a strong foundation in clinical knowledge and a beautifully intuitive approach, she speaks with the kind of clarity and heart that makes you stop and really listen. Raising Empowered Humans is more than a book; it's an invitation to rethink how we show up for the children – our future – in our lives. Grounded, wise and refreshingly real, Sonia's work is something the world truly needs right now.

Sophie Bretag – CEO, Metta Leaders, Senior HR Consultant & Kindness Expert

Sonia has a wonderful way of making big ideas feel grounded and real. Whether she's writing, speaking, or simply connecting with others, she brings insight that feels both clear and genuinely caring. Her words have stayed with me and continue to shape how I lead, listen, and show up.

Dave Jereb – Paediatric Occupational Therapist, Author, Co-Founder of MoveAbout & The Allied Health Sanctuary

Sonia Bestulic is an extraordinary individual dedicated to improving the world through her impactful work and the lives she inspires. I deeply admire her commitment to fostering positive change – this book beautifully reflects her humble, curious, and empowering nature.
Si Ning Koh – Head of Organisational Growth and Development, Orchard Early Learning Centres

As a heart-led leader and father of two beautiful daughters, I found this book to be a breath of fresh air. It invites children to rediscover the joy of fun, adventure, imagination, and deep connection – with their family, with nature, and with their community.

Most importantly, it nurtures the courage to embrace their unique gifts in a world that so often asks them to fit in. When children learn to truly love and value who they are, they not only flourish – they create a ripple effect, making a meaningful impact on their own lives and on everyone they touch.

I wholeheartedly encourage every parent to receive the gifts this book offers, for themselves and for their children.
Stephen Pisani – Director, Pisani Group, Founder of A Million Dreams Foundation

5 GOLDEN KEYS TO

RAISING **EMPOWERED** HUMANS

UNLOCK KIDS' SELF-LEADERSHIP & LIFELONG FLOURISHING

SONIA BESTULIC

AWARD-WINNING AUTHOR OF *FLOURISH FOR MUMS*

First published in Australia in 2026
by KMD Books
Waikiki, WA 6169

A catalogue record for this work is available from the National Library of Australia

National Library of Australia Catalogue-in-Publication data:
5 Golden Keys to Raising Empowered Humans / Sonia Bestulic

To you, the reader:

You hold the golden keys.

Use them to unlock a flourishing future – now.

Sonia xo

To you, my children:

Zara, Cleo, and Maximus.

Embrace infinite love and light as your guide; for this is the truth of who you are.

Love you always, Mum xo

Disclaimer

The information contained within this book is not intended as a substitute for professional medical and health advice. It is recommended that you seek professional advice from a trusted practitioner with regards to adopting any lifestyle changes and advice related to your individual (or your family's) health and wellbeing circumstances.

CONTENTS

ACKNOWLEDGEMENTS

To the Divine Creative Source of all wisdom, and to my *Sparkle Self* – thank you for guiding the energy, essence, and expression within these pages.

To my children and empowered flourishing humans: Zara, Cleo, and Maximus … yes, you've done it again … you've helped inspire much wisdom for me to embody and share throughout this book and far beyond. What a wild and honourable ride it is to share in this lifetime together.

To my siblings, with special mention to my brother Sergio (because I know you love special mentions) – and you are also a very much appreciated pillar of support; my brother Adriano because your sensitive support, although quiet, is felt; and to my sister Bianca, for your fiery, dedicated, and unwavering support.

To my parents – thank you for the gifts, the guidance and the growth that only you both could offer.

To all my ancestors – across all timelines – thank you for your unseen hands and hearts, ever guiding the rewriting of our collective story into one of empowerment, light, and infinite love.

I also share deep gratitude to my 'heart sparkle' friends, who I deem my *family of frequency* … high vibe, authentic, bright, brilliant, and fiercely supportive, who have journeyed with me through poignant chapters in this school of life. With special mention to Alice, Stephen,

Sophie, and Dave.

To my mentors, coaches, and teachers throughout the years – thank you for helping to guide my path of integration and alignment.

To Karen Weaver – you are quite literally the weaver of magic and miracles; and to the team at KMD books, thank you for birthing this book into flourishing form and sparking this collective movement to raise empowered humans. Your belief in me, your patience, your encouragement, and your solid support are held with deep heart felt gratitude.

To my podcast guests who helped bring to life the *Raising Empowered Humans* series on the *Chatabout Children* podcast – what an absolute joy and privilege it was to share time together and co-create a flourishing frequency to share with the world. Thank you … David Meltzer, Sonia Choquette, Karen Weaver, Kim Woods, Tory Archbold, Anna Dutton, Robyn Saranah, Stephenie Rodriguez, Vanessa Bell, Julia Scott, Paul Sullivan, and Carrie Kwan. And big hugs of gratitude to the wonderful producer, Amelia Rees, from Pretty Podcasts for your brilliance and creativity.

To all those I've had the honour of working with: as your intuitive coach, your holistic speech pathologist, or through the beautiful integration of both … thank you. You've helped shape the person I am today, and the world is truly brighter because of your presence.

And to every heart-led changemaker, innovator, and difference maker – whether you're a parent, caregiver, educator, health or medical professional, CEO, entrepreneur, creative … no matter your titles – your essence is a gift to the world, and you weave light into the fabric of humanity and beyond.

Thank you for saying *yes* to flourishing.

An Empowered Humanity …

Embraces their infinite genius.
Lives in their creative power.
Lives in harmony.
Lives in reverence.
Lives in celebration.
Lives in gratitude.
Lives in expanded presence.
Lives in INFINITE LOVE.
Lives in the nourishment of NOW.
Lives in PEACE, with themselves, with others and …
with everything.

To raise an empowered human is to embrace a flow of graceful trust and divine support that liberates a dance of pure and miraculous magnificence.

-Sonia Bestulic-

LET THE FLOURISHING BEGIN …

This book may sound different from my last.

This is intentional – and essential.

Since my previous work, I've moved through a profound deepening.

As a speech pathologist of nearly three decades, I've worked alongside thousands of children and their families, learning and teaching the language of human development – not just through science, but through soul. I founded and led a reputable speech pathology company for over 18 years, building systems and services designed to hold humans, not just manage them; whilst expanding my personal growth and training within the broader realms of human health and potential, as an intuitive life coach and Reiki master.

And, most importantly as a mother of three, the evolution has continued through life chapters of joy, loss, growth, and becoming; whilst applying years of spiritual study and practice. So today, I don't just speak from a place of learning but of integration; having been initiated again and again into the sacred rhythm of remembering … and this has allowed me to embrace the multi-layers that shape our human experience and our ability to flourish.

So yes – my 'voice' has changed.

Because I have and will continue to.

And because the world has and will continue to, as will you.

In this era of accelerated change there is a felt sense of collective disorientation (to various degrees). Children are growing up in systems that were not necessarily designed for their brilliance. Families are stretched thin, trying to reconcile intuition with external expectations. Meanwhile, disconnection, overwhelm, loneliness, youth mental health issues, and burnout have become the baseline norm. Not because there's something 'wrong' with our kids; but perhaps because something is deeply misaligned in the environments, and structures we've expected them to adapt to. This is *especially so* for families with children deemed neurodivergent.

From my many years working across countless classrooms, therapy rooms, and kitchen tables, I've seen what happens when children are truly seen, not just in their challenges, but in their essence. I've also witnessed the limitations of conventional approaches when they ignore the full spectrum of who a child is: physically, emotionally, mentally, spiritually – intuitively.

If you are reading this … know you are part of a growing wave of conscious parents, educators, carers, and changemakers, who know in the depths of their heart that there is more to raising a child than ticking developmental boxes.

You are being called into deeper connection. Into remembering that you already hold the wisdom needed to raise empowered humans; and that this book is your living companion that honours your presence; and invites you to trust it.

We are both singing the same song – living the intention to raise children in truth – whilst guiding and shaping a future aligned with clarity, compassion, and courage.

Put simply, this is a return to the art and science of self – through play, intuition, communication, and conscious care.

That's why this book doesn't just speak to parenting strategies or developmental milestones. It weaves together lived experience, spiritual insight, clinical wisdom, and energetic truth, informed by both evidence-based practice and embodied knowing. Together with this I share powerful stories of wisdom through conversations with various heart-led leaders and changemakers across the globe.

In essence, this book invites us to spark not just our children's potential, but our own; as a response to that remembering, and a reimagining of what it means to raise, guide, and walk beside empowered humans in these changing times.

No, you won't find a rigid prescription here. Instead, you'll discover a rhythm – five golden keys – that open the doors to lifelong flourishing. These are not tools to impose on your child, but frequencies to activate in your family field. This is about co-creating a foundation that embraces the divine intelligence within every human being.

And, at the core of it all, *5 Golden Keys to Raising Empowered Humans* is not about fixing children.

It is about ...

Honouring their natural frequency.

Unlocking their self-leadership – not someday, but now.

And remembering what we've forgotten ... that joy is our original and natural state, and that connection and play is the soul's first language.

Moving through this Book. A Gentle Guide.

This book is intentionally designed to feel rhythmic.

Move through it sequentially or open to the chapter your heart is drawn to in the moment. You can use this as a personal practice companion, a family tool, or a shared resource in educational and therapeutic settings.

There's no one way to experience this book. Let it meet you where you are. Let it move with you. Whichever way you are drawn to it is perfect.

You'll notice it's divided into five sections representing the Five Golden Keys:

Foundations, Freedom, Fun, Fulfilment, and Flourishing.

Each of these represents more than a theme. They are frequencies; energetic fields you're invited to attune to and explore within yourself, your child, and your shared experience of growth.

You'll also notice that each chapter carries a specially designed symbolic imprint, which energetically mirrors the essence of that chapter's content. These are designed to reflect the energy of each chapter and spark your own inner knowing.

Each chapter flows with a blend of science and spirituality, gently leading into practical activities; aligned to nurture your child's heart-led self-leadership and lifelong flourishing. And, to deepen the experience, I've included a chapter summary and journal prompts; offering you a space to explore your own inner world if you feel called.

Finally, each chapter ends with a powerful **Truth Statement**. These can be:

- used in meditation
- held in reflective journalling
- chosen intuitively to set the tone of your day
- written on your (or your kid's) mirror as a soul-level mantra … to be removed when it feels embodied.

You'll be excited to discover a **Resources** section too; offering visual representations to support some of the key frameworks and concepts shared throughout the chapters.

And, for all the curious minds, the evidence-lovers, and anyone wanting to explore some of the topic areas and themes more thoroughly, I've included a list of **References** at the back of the book.

My role is to translate soul-aligned wisdom, together with a spectrum of sciences, into practice. So that you feel supported in raising humans who are empowered, attuned, sovereign, and happily themselves.

Know that my words don't come from a place of perfection; they come from a pulse, of bedtime stories and belly laughs, of meltdowns and miracles, of deep rekindled remembrance.

So, take what resonates.

Let go of what doesn't.

And trust your own deep knowing above all else.

May the words throughout these pages be a mirror.

May they nourish your intuition.

May they awaken the flourishing that is your present and your future.

Welcome home …

May we flourish together,

Sonia xo

GOLDEN KEY ONE

THE FREQUENCY OF FOUNDATIONS

The Art & Science of Self

foundation: noun
/faʊnˈdeɪʃən/

The root system of beliefs, values, and experiences that ground an individual, providing stability, nourishment, and the potential for growth.

OWN YOUR CREATORSHIP

Awaken the Power of Human Purpose

"What if the greatest act of parenting isn't to shape our children into something… but to remember, with them, what it truly means to be human?"

I was in a meeting with a heart-led CEO of a global company, when he remarked,

'Sonia, the mental health of our young people in the world has been declining rapidly. Suicide rates globally are staggering – impacting younger and younger children.' Exasperated, he asked, 'What do you think is going on?!'

My response was immediate and clear: **'What's going on is that we are all born creators … yet trained to be consumers.'**

Children are brought into this world fluent in the language of creativity. They sing without needing a tune, build without plans, imagine without boundaries. But as they grow, many are quietly distanced from their innate nature.

We see it in the rise of childhood anxiety, depression, and ADHD diagnoses. I believe, beneath the labels, lies a deeper truth – *a spiritual crisis.* A misalignment of the inner compass.

I recall the day, at seven years old, when I made a decision that shaped the trajectory of my life. Whilst walking past the TV one afternoon, I was stopped in my tracks by a news update. As the scenes of suffering played out before me, I didn't have words for all that stirred inside of me, but I did know there was a quiet breaking of my heart.

I was both confronted and confused. Questions swirled within me; but what rose even more strongly was the realisation of how deeply I cared for humanity, and how much love I held for the world. This brought with it contemplation and revelation. And from this place, I made the immediate decision that I wanted to be part of the solution to make the world a happier and more harmonious place. … Quite the mission to carry for a seven-year-old!

But I followed that spark. I began journalling every day; recording my observations of the world, writing out what my heart wished for it, and imagining all the ways I might contribute. I didn't know it then, but I was activating my purpose – owning my creatorship. And this activation – this inner orientation – is what our systems so often overlook.

As a professional, I've witnessed this firsthand with countless children; and as a parent, I've witnessed this firsthand with my own children. It was clear my son, from a young age, didn't think in conventional ways. His lens was (and still is) one of deep curiosity, layered exploration, and unapologetic expression. His questions weren't rebellious; they were deeply honest …

'Why should I wear a stiff school uniform with a tie? It doesn't feel comfortable.'

'Why is art class about copying someone else's style when I have my own?'

'Why can't I play the guitar in my own way?'

'Why was my answer marked wrong on the test when I got the right answer, just through a different method?'

'Why aren't all cars working on solar power?'

The list goes on.

These are the questions of children who haven't forgotten their creatorship.

They don't want to replicate – they want to originate. And many of them are struggling not because they're deficient, but because they are deeply aware, and the world around them hasn't made space for that awareness.

Traditional systems were not designed with visionaries in mind. They reward compliance over curiosity and standardisation over soul. But children with higher levels of consciousness can feel this misalignment. They live in a world that asks them to dim their light just to fit in.

Research in education and developmental psychology now confirms what many of us instinctively know: divergent thinking, creativity, and emotional authenticity are foundational to long-term wellbeing and resilience. When we suppress a child's voice or force them into narrow pathways, we don't just inhibit learning, we dampen their life force.

That's why I've long championed **holistic school readiness** – or more aptly, **school of life readiness**. Through masterclasses, workshops, and ongoing dialogue with families and educators, I advocate for the kind of preparation that doesn't just focus on academic ability but honours the multidimensional being of each child.

In recent years I remember reading research by the World Economic Forum regarding the future of jobs. It ranked creative thinking as the top skill for the future, even outpacing analytical thinking. 'Finally!' I said aloud with a mix of joy and relief. It felt like long-overdue recognition; for the many kids I'd watched over the years with extraordinary ways of seeing and experiencing the world.

And the raising of **authentically creative humans** is one of the **keys to truly flourishing in our ever-evolving landscape called life**.

Now … when I talk about creativity, I don't just mean it in the traditional sense. It's about something deeper – about bringing your *true self* to the table, about thinking in expansive, divergent ways, and expressing ideas that are rooted in purpose and individuality.

In a world that's calling for more innovation and authenticity, creativity isn't a luxury; it's a lifeline. We're not simply helping our children develop skills here; we're honouring their soul's expression. In this new landscape, authenticity is fast becoming a kind of professional currency. And creativity – when it's aligned with self-trust and a clear sense of who we are – becomes the foundation for empowered contribution.

It's important to remember from a quantum perspective, everything is energy … and everything is frequency. When we align our own frequency with the truth of who we are – aka creators – we access our innate power. And when we don't? That's often when we feel disconnection creep in … with a sense of disharmony, and eventually, even dis-ease.

At the heart of it all, as caregivers, we want the same things: for our children to be healthy and happy. So, I invite you, gently … to pause and reflect on this …

True health is the expression of **wholeness**.

Wholeness is born through **alignment**.

Alignment is the **harmony** of spirit, soul, mind, and body (our natural design).

Harmony is when children attune to their **true essence** and **unique potential**.

The expression of unique potential comes from how deeply

creatorship is honoured.

Heart-Powered Self-Leadership

So how can we help children own their creatorship?

Creatorship is not about becoming an artist – it's about embodying inner authority and expressing your soul's language in whatever form it takes.

We help children reclaim this when we:

Reflect Their Natural Creative Intelligence

Use a wide range of creative expressions in your everyday language, such as:

- *I love how you chose those ingredients for dinner.*
- *Your outfit for today shows your style – how do you feel wearing it?*
- *That game you made up shows such creative thinking.*

These reflections help children feel seen and valued for who they are; not for just conforming to a set task or outcome.

Invite 'Everyday Expression' as Creative Contribution

Remind children that creativity isn't limited to art class. It shows up in how they:

- solve a problem in a way no one else would
- set the table with intention and care
- choose clothing to express how they feel
- move their body spontaneously or design a Lego world in their own way.

By valuing everyday expression, we normalise creativity as a way of being, not just doing.

Use Language That Activates Inner Ownership

Words can ignite self-leadership. Use phrases that affirm the origin of their ideas and efforts:

- *That idea came from inside you.*
- *You're making this moment really special.*
- *What would feel fun to explore next?*

This language reinforces trust in their inner compass, not external validation.

Value Process Over Product

Shift the focus away from perfection and performance.

Go from *What is it?* to:

- *How did you feel whilst creating/doing that?*
- *What surprised you about what you made?*
- *Was there a part that felt really exciting or challenging?*

This builds emotional awareness, curiosity, and resilience.

Reframe Everyday Tasks as Creation

Encourage children to see daily life as an opportunity to create.

- *Let's co-create a morning flow that feels good for everyone.*
- *You've made your room feel so calm by how you set it up.*
- *What would you change about how we do this together?*

Even routines can become a space for agency and self-expression.

Let Children Lead

When we step back and allow kids to take the lead, it opens the door for them to grow their problem-solving skills and trust their unique perspective.

Follow their plan, story, or idea. Empower them to create outcomes and evaluate them. Ask:

- *What's your vision for how this could work better?*
- *How would you solve this your way?*
- *Want to be in charge of how we do this today?*

Leading doesn't mean always being right; it means being invited to try, adjust, and grow.

Lifelong Flourishing

Daily Rituals & Rhythms for Families, Educators & Therapists

Creativity thrives when it's normalised as *part of life*; not reserved for special projects or artistic activities. Here are some ways in might look in the day to day:

The 'Creation Zone'

Create space (not just physical) where freedom of expression is welcome.

This could be a bench in the garden, a spot on the fridge, or a moment after dinner. What matters is presence and permission.

Family Creation Hour (Weekly)

Everyone does something expressive at the same time: cooking, writing, building, planning outfits, designing gardens.

Wonder Walks

Let curiosity guide the way as you go on a walk without a structured plan of where to walk.

What feels inspiring today?

What's something ordinary that holds extraordinary beauty?

Soul Sparks Journal (or Board)

Keep a shared or individual space to capture inspired thoughts, dreams, and creations. This could be drawn, written, or collaged. For many years, we had a collage on an entire lounge room wall and corridor wall with all the kids' paintings and drawings.

Themed Days or Moments

Magic Monday: Everyone creates something new.

Freedom Friday: Dress differently, try new combinations, remix the rules.

Soul Sunday: Reflect on what you created, felt, or grew through.

Micro-Creation Moments in Learning/Therapy Settings

Choose how you'd like to share what you learnt; draw it, act it, teach it.

If this concept were a character or colour, who or what would it be?

When creativity is honoured as our universal language, children don't just feel seen, they feel sovereign.

Legacy in Motion

Reflect. Integrate. Empower.

When honouring a child's innate creatorship, we do more than support their self-expression; we ignite their purpose. We shift the narrative from *What do you want to be?* to *Who are you becoming, and what are you here to create?*

The legacy we leave is not only built through achievements but also shaped through moments where children feel seen for their essence and trusted in their process.

Ultimately, the owning (or reclaiming) of our creatorship invites us, and our children, to live life not as a checklist, but as a canvas.

A canvas that dances with presence and purpose.

And what's beautiful is that when we own our creatorship, we notice how it shapes our connections too … how we relate, respond, and ripple into the lives around us.

So, next, we'll explore that space more deeply … because empowered humans don't grow in isolation. They flourish in relationships rooted in respect, safety, and truth.

Journal Prompts

- *What does a flourishing family mean to me?*
- *In what areas of life have I silenced my own inner creator; and what would it mean to welcome it back?*
- *How can I honour my child's sovereignty while still guiding them?*
- *What does my child teach me about creativity, freedom, and self-trust?*

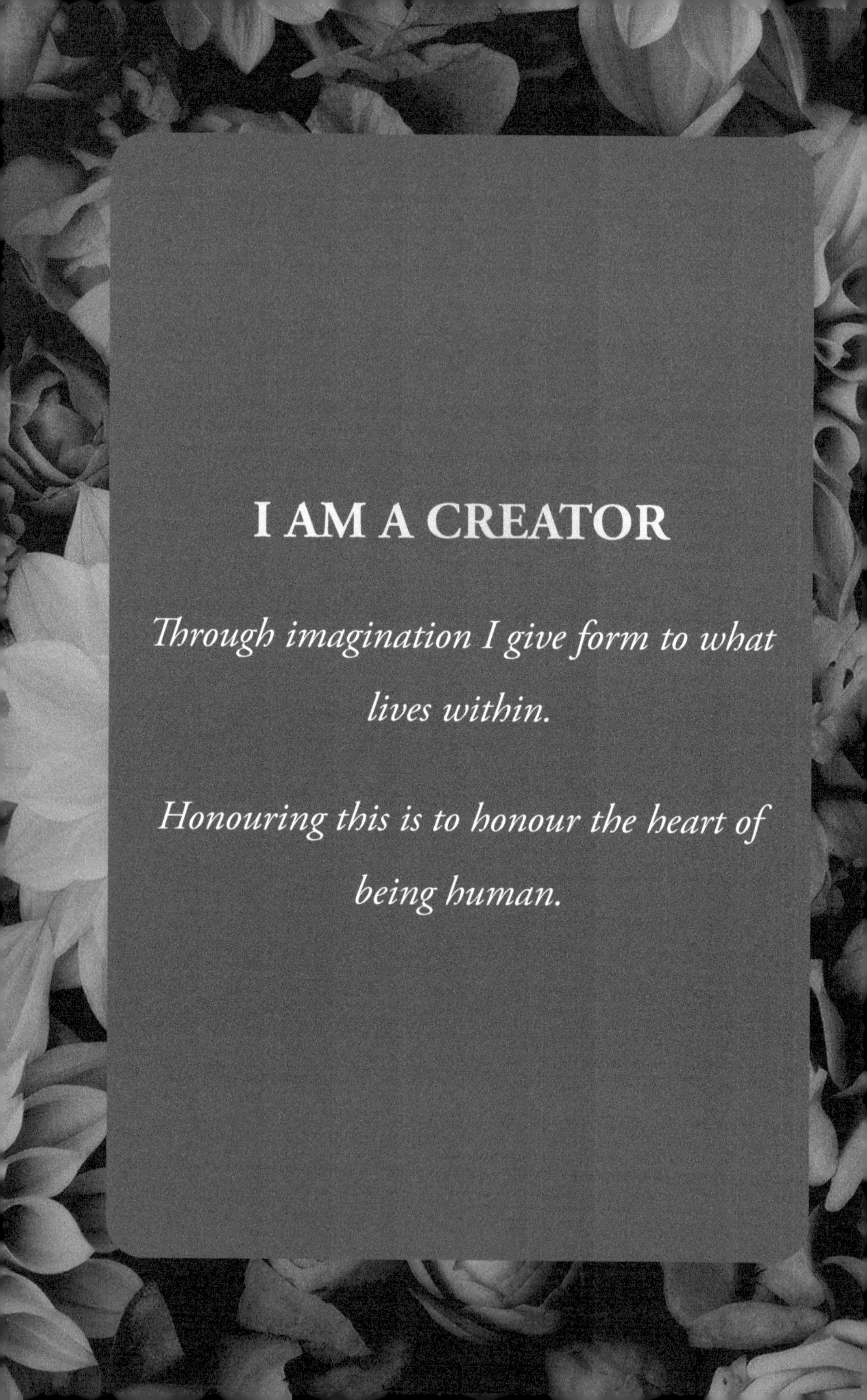

I AM A CREATOR
Through imagination I give form to what lives within.
Honouring this is to honour the heart of being human.

RELISH IN RELATIONSHIPS

The Seeds for Lifelong Flourishing

What if the way we relate – to ourselves, others, the world, and the unseen – was a mirror, reflecting how deeply we honour our own essence?

At the heart of every child's growth, beneath learning, behaviour, and development, is one quiet, foundational truth:

We are always in relationship.
Not just with people, but with breath, sound, rhythm, movement, food, story, and space.

From the moment a child arrives Earthside, they are forming a web of connection; each thread shaping how they see the world, and how the world mirrors them in return.

Relationship is not something we have. It is a dynamic we are part of.

In this chapter, we explore four foundational relationships that nourish empowered humans: our relationship with **Self**, **Others**, **the World**, and **the Sacred**.

Each one offers a mirror … a path back to wholeness.

Relationship with Self: The First Home

This is where it all begins.

When children learn to tune into their body, feel their feelings, and trust their inner voice, they build a relationship with the most important guide they'll ever have … themselves.

But 'self' is not just one thing.

It's a whole spectrum.

It includes the voice of fear and the voice of knowing.

The part that doubts, and the part that remembers.

I recall a moment with my son that etched this truth deeply into my heart.

We were building a tower with Lego blocks, aiming to use every piece to construct the tallest tower possible. As we reached the final block, he eagerly prepared to place it on top, then paused. His hand hovered above the tower, his body tense.

'I don't trust myself,' he said to me softly. 'Can you do it?' he asked.

I met his eyes and gently responded, 'How about you trust yourself – and you do it. Place that last block … and know that even if the tower falls, you can *still* trust yourself.'

He placed the block.

The tower stood tall.

That instance is a reminder, that our relationship with ourselves is the foundation.

It is not built through perfection, but through wholeness.

We can teach children that their *ego* (the part of them that wants to stay safe) is not bad. It's just part of them. And that their *truth self* – the inner wisdom that knows who they are – is part of them too. They need both. We all do.

As parents, we support this sacred relationship by modelling how we speak to ourselves in moments of challenge; how we listen to our own needs, without guilt or justification; and how we honour that our inner world matters.

Empowered humans aren't perfect; they are in relationship with all parts of themselves. Without erasing fear but walking with it whilst listening deeply.

Relationship with Others: The Dance of Empathy

Our relationships with others begin long before we're aware of them. From our earliest moments – how we're held, spoken to, responded to – we're learning how to relate. Not just how to act around others … but how to *feel* with them. And that's the part that matters most.

When children are raised in environments where empathy, repair, and boundaries are modelled with consistency and care, something powerful happens. They don't just learn to get along. They learn how to *stay connected* to themselves and to others, even when things get a little messy or challenging.

So, in the scenario when a child comes home and quietly says, 'Someone at school was mean to me today,' we might feel the pull to jump in, to fix, to advise, to protect. But these moments … they're gold. They're invitations to hold space for what's real.

To nourish connection, you might say: 'That sounds really hard. Do you want to tell me about it, or would a hug feel good first?' or 'Have you ever felt like being unkind when something inside you was hurting?'

These aren't about excusing bad behaviour. They're about helping our kids build the muscles of relational wisdom, where self-respect and compassion can live side by side. And we do this through how we *respond*, not just what we *say*.

Ultimately, we activate this by:

- co-regulating during the big feelings
- having open conversations about fairness, voice, and making things right
- letting our kids see us apologise, forgive, and reconnect from the heart.

Strong relationships with others aren't built on control. They grow in the soil of mutual respect, and that begins in childhood.

This came to life during a conversation I shared on my podcast with Anna Dutton, co-founder of *The CEO Magazine*. Anna carries a grounded strength, shaped by her upbringing and her deep love for family.

'I can't go past the two main women in my life – my mother and my grandmother,' she shared. 'They were both strong-minded, independent women. My grandmother always looked after herself financially, and I think I inherited that drive. My mum also ran her own advertising business, so I grew up surrounded by entrepreneurship and publishing energy.'

From her father, she learnt the value of health and showing up for others. 'He coached people in our local area to be the best runners they could be,' she reflected. 'Both my parents were really social and community driven. That's stayed with me.'

And now, as a parent herself, she brings that into the everyday.

'I use what I call an *impact thermometer*,' Anna explained. 'I ask: Is this affecting my daughter's health, wellness, or learning? If yes, it's a priority. And if something keeps recurring – that's a sign to go deeper.'

She also shared the beautiful reminder that, '*Golden time* matters.'

For Anna and her daughter, that might look like a dinner chat, a weekend walk, or a café catch up ... it's those everyday moments where connection becomes the anchor.

And really, that's what empowered relationships are all about, knowing every connection holds the potential for love, learning, and healing.

Relationship with the World: Wonder as a Compass

As a child, I was blessed to grow up with a wild, abundant garden as my playground. I'd climb mulberry trees and eat the fruit straight from the branches, legs swinging in the air. I helped rescue injured wildlife, collected cicada shells like treasure, and picked herbs from the garden for dinner. I watched trees regrow after bushfires and planted new ones with quiet reverence. And whenever I saw rubbish, I instinctively picked it up. Not because anyone told me to, but because I felt part of something larger.

That kind of relationship with the world is more than 'being in nature'; it's a lived feeling of *belonging to it* and experiencing the Earth as alive, responsive, and connected to us. Children flourish when they know they're not separate from the world but woven into its tapestry. They become caretakers – through love.

So how do we nurture this?

By giving kids space to explore, to get messy, to witness the cycles of life, and to take small actions that honour the living world around them. Because the more immersed they are in nature's rhythms, the more naturally they learn to respect, protect, and celebrate the world they're a part of; with wonder as their compass and presence as their sacred teacher.

Relationship with the Sacred: Belonging Beyond the Seen

As a child, I loved stargazing and cloud watching. I would marvel at the shapes and stories in the sky, feeling both tiny and infinite at once. The cosmos reminded me there was more than what was happening in my daily life; more beauty, more story, more mystery.

As we know, our children are more than physical, emotional, and relational beings, they are deeply spiritual too. Even before they have words for the sacred, they feel it. They are drawn towards something greater – something deeper – with wonder and remembrance.

Whether we call it Creator, Divine Intelligence, God, Source, or simply Love, this relationship is the wellspring of trust, purpose, and belonging.

Children often ask sacred questions – I know I did, and no doubt you did too – like:

'Where was I before I was born?'

'Why am I here?'

'What happens when we die?'

These aren't just curiosities. They're soul whispered moments of sacredness.

In my children's book, *Kisses in Your Heart*, I shared this very message (being sacred and being connected to it) in a way that children can feel in their hearts, with a knowing that there is a great, great love that lives inside them. A love that stays with them – even when they feel nervous, scared, or sad. It's a book that's travelled across the world, whispered into bedtime routines, and placed into classrooms as a tool for helping children build emotional resilience.

Why?

Because it reminds them of this truth: *You are always held. You are never alone.*

And that's the essence of being in relationship with the sacred. It's the foundation of true resilience. Because when a child knows they're held by something bigger, whatever name we give it, they meet the world with a deeper peace and a greater courage.

We don't need to give them all the answers. In fact, it's often more powerful to hold the space for questions. To wonder with them. For a child connected to the sacred, is not just learning about faith – they're remembering the essence of who they really are.

Heart-Powered Self-Leadership

So how can we help children relish relationships?

Raising children through the lens of relationship means to help them form a life where they feel:

- grounded in who they are
- safe with others
- connected to the planet
- aligned with something greater.

These practices help children build inner awareness, emotional strength, and spiritual connection from within:

Emotion Naming & Validation

Help children identify and name their feelings using feeling charts, mirroring language, or creative expression. Validating these feelings teaches them that all emotions are acceptable and informative.

Mindful Breathing Exercises

Introduce short breathing practices (e.g. 'balloon belly') to help children self-regulate, especially before transitions, tests, or social challenges.

Reflective Journalling (Age-Appropriate)
Support older children in keeping a journal with prompts like *What made me feel proud today?* or *When did I feel calm?*. Journalling deepens their capacity to notice and process inner experience.

Active Listening Practice (Peer-Focused)
Engage in turn-taking games or 'feelings circles' where children listen and reflect what another said. This builds empathy and attention.

Conflict Resolution Role-Play
Use scenarios with toys or scripts to help children learn to express needs, set boundaries, and find win-win solutions.

Gratitude Drawing or Lists
Invite children to draw or write about things they are grateful for regularly. This helps cultivate emotional resilience, joyfulness, and spiritual attunement.

Storytelling & Symbolic Mythology
Share stories with archetypal characters or metaphors that explore bravery, kindness, or mystery. This helps to encourage imagination as a bridge to deeper truth.

Lifelong Flourishing

Daily Rituals & Rhythms for Families, Educators & Therapists

We're wired for connection; not just in our biology, but in our energy.

Every moment we connect, we're picking up on something more subtle – a tone, a vibe, a frequency. It's less like a transaction and more like a dance; sometimes in harmony, sometimes off-beat. But always, it's an exchange that shapes us.

The following ideas help support children's development across all four relationship layers:

Co-Regulation Rituals

Intentional pauses for breath or physical connection (like holding hands or a shared mantra) during emotionally charged moments nurtures safety in connection. Name the unseen love that surrounds them: *Even when you can't see it, something wise and loving is walking with you.*

Golden Time (Presence-Focused Rituals)

Scheduled daily or weekly, windows of one-on-one, screen-free time. Doing something led by the child signals: *You matter. I see you.*

I had my three children within a two-and-a-half-year window, so *Golden Time* with them one to one was super important. For us it took the form of scheduled 'mum dates' and 'dad dates' that the kids always looked forward to ... and still do!

Community Service or 'Kindness Days'

Participating in neighbourhood clean-ups, food drives, or making cards for others fosters a sense of purpose and belonging. Being open to opportunities to be kind – just because – is incredibly powerful.

Invite Awe

Invite awe through nature, music, art, or quiet time, whether walking barefoot, cloud watching, feeling the energy of music or gardening; this helps children feel grounded and interconnected.

Shared Family Rituals (e.g. Before Meals or Bedtime)

Sharing simple family rituals of gratitude, reflection, prayer, honouring ancestors – whatever feels true for your values.

We have a before bedtime ritual of coming together, lighting our 'gratitude candle' and taking turns to share gratitude. Each person ends their gratitude 'segment' by sharing one aspect of themselves they are grateful for.

Household Energy Check-ins

This family ritual is about sharing 'what my energy feels like today' with colours, words, or drawings. It is helpful in normalising emotional honesty and attunement.

Rituals of Repair

After conflict, model and practise repair through sincere apology, listening, and mutual reconnection. This is important in reinforcing that relationships can mend and grow stronger. When we embed these practices into our homes, therapy rooms, and classrooms, we give children the tools to navigate life with grounded confidence and heart-led clarity.

Legacy in Motion

Reflect. Integrate. Empower.

Relationships are the threads that weave a life of wholeness.

They're not just about getting along; they're how we grow, how we feel seen, how we make sense of the world around us.

Relational empowerment starts with presence.

It deepens with empathy.

And it lasts when we root it in truth.

As we nurture relationships built on safety and truth, we raise kids moving through life with both groundedness and glow … and we also begin to see how deeply our children's sense of connection is tied to their inner rhythm.

Next, we'll explore exactly that – the power of human rhythm – and how restoring flow in the body, through breath, movement, and presence is vital for helping children feel regulated and fully at home in their humanness.

Journal Prompts

- *What kind of relationship do I currently have with myself?*
- *Where do I tend to over-give or disconnect in relationships?*
- *What does a safe, empowering relationship feel like for me and my child?*
- *What energetic boundaries or rituals could support our family dynamic?*

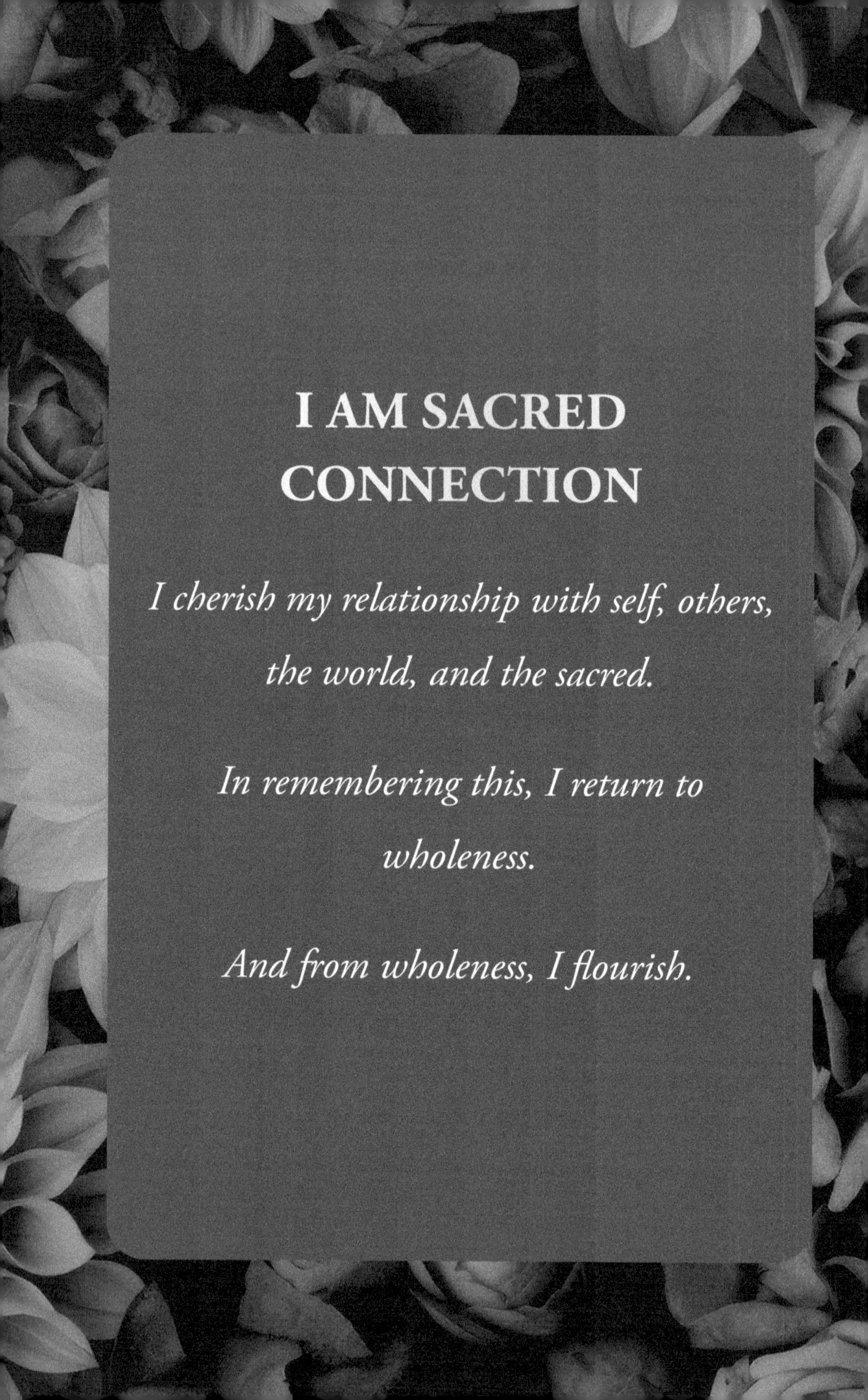

I AM SACRED CONNECTION

I cherish my relationship with self, others, the world, and the sacred.

In remembering this, I return to wholeness.

And from wholeness, I flourish.

REINSTATE THE RHYTHM OF HUMANNESS

Restore Flow and Reclaim Nervous System Wisdom

What if the rhythm of your child's wellbeing isn't something they learn, but something they return to?

I have always been an early riser. Even as a child, I'd wake before my siblings, relishing the quiet moments that felt entirely mine. Me, my own rhythm, uninterrupted.

I was blessed to grow up with lots of unstructured outdoor play. There were no checklists or timers, just time to *be* in my own nature. And by that, I mean *our* own nature. Because we are not separate from it; and when we are truly present in nature, it is experienced as a whole other timeline than what modern urban living offers.

This truth came alive during a surfing lesson with my kids in Middleton, South Australia. As we entered the water, time began to dissolve. We were fully immersed in the power of presence. At what seemed like we'd be nearing the final part of our surf session, we asked our instructor how much time was remaining.

'We're *almost* halfway through,' he said, smiling.

My kids and I paused and looked at one another exasperated; you could 'hear' our collective thought and sense our shared joy – *Not even halfway through?? … YES!!*

The rhythm of the ocean synced with the rhythm of our bodies. We weren't just learning to surf – we were remembering what it meant to *feel* our natural state of rhythm.

Later that evening my kids reiterated how much they enjoyed their surfing experience, noting it seemed like time was going really, really slow.

My daughter commented, 'Time felt "stretched out" mum …'

Their hearts were full, and their deep sense of fulfilment was palpable.

'Why did it feel like that mum?' my daughter wondered.

To which I responded, 'What you felt was the true rhythm of being a human *being*. Being fully in the moment. That is what *aliveness* feels like. That is what truly *living* feels like.'

Before routine was scheduled by clocks and calendars, there was rhythm. Breath, heartbeat, sunlight, tides … the quiet intelligence of the body. We are *rhythmic beings*!

To restore the natural flow of life, we must first remember: *we are nature*. Rhythm is life, and life is rhythm.

And on that note (excuse the pun!), neuroscience confirms something many of us have long felt intuitively. That when a child is upset or overwhelmed, it's not just words that help; it's the *calm presence* of a regulated adult. This is called **co-regulation**.

When we stay steady, warm, and emotionally present, our children's nervous systems receive the message: *you are safe, you're not alone.* Over time, this helps them develop the ability to calm themselves.

***Rhythm* is a subject expansive enough to warrant its own book**

… spanning across traditional human sciences, quantum science, nature-based science, and ancient philosophy.

From the cellular to the cosmic, rhythm is the invisible thread that underpins all living systems – a vital foundation for human functioning, thriving, and flourishing.

I had the honour of co-founding The Allied Health Sanctuary with my incredible colleague Dave Jereb, an occupational therapist whose leadership and work I deeply respect. Throughout our coaching and masterclass sessions, we often found ourselves arriving at the same core theme: **rhythm**. Whether we approached it through the lens of neurobiology, quantum energetics, or lived experience, rhythm consistently emerged as the unseen thread weaving together regulation, connection, and wellbeing.

This is a crucial remembrance; children are born into rhythm. Yet modern life – filled with digital noise, hyper-scheduling, and fast-paced environments – often disrupts the natural flow, and instead shapes speed, structure, and stimulation. Our nervous systems are ancient. They thrive in stillness, nature, sensory experience, and attunement – not urgency.

So in essence, we don't need to 'teach' regulation – we need to **create conditions for it to re-emerge**.

Heart-Powered Self-Leadership

So how can we help children reinstate the humanness rhythm?

One of the most powerful ways to restore inner balance and self-regulation is through **rhythm anchored in the natural world**, supported by intentional rhythmic practices in everyday life.

Whether in a forest, a classroom, or a lounge room – rhythm is the body's way home.

Here are some suggestions:

Grounding with the Earth
Encourage barefoot walks on grass, sand, or soil to restore the body's electromagnetic balance and invite calm.

Lie under a tree, feel its steadiness, and invite children to simply 'breathe with the earth'.

Rhythmic Nature Movement
Tree climbing, log balancing, jumping between rocks, swinging – these repetitive, natural movements support sensory-motor regulation and balance.

Let children move at their own pace, following the rhythm their body craves.

Support emotional flow with elemental energy; teaching children that *water* helps move emotions, *earth* helps ground them, and *air* helps create space.

Sensory Nature Awareness
Pause outdoors to name what you hear, see, feel, and smell. This strengthens present-moment awareness and encourages emotional attunement.

Try: *Let's see how many sounds we can notice in one minute.*

Speak of Nature as Relationship
Help children see nature not as a destination, but a living presence:

The earth supports you.

The trees are breathing with you.

The ocean helps you feel.

These gentle affirmations plant seeds of belonging and reverence.

Music & Sound for Regulation

Use calm music, gentle drumming, or heartbeat rhythms to soothe the environment.

Children respond well to repetitive auditory patterns; especially when paired with movement or breath.

Sound frequency therapy is also incredibly powerful and scientifically supported; being incredibly valuable across health, holistically for the entire family.

Breath & Rhythm for Regulation

These can include:

- Match your breathing or gentle rocking to your child's body rhythm.
- Use phrases with rhythmic cadence when guiding transitions (e.g. 'In three … two … one … we go.')
- Sing or hum during moments of dysregulation to support nervous system synchrony.
- Sit or lie down together. Inhale for four, hold for four, exhale for six. Repeat five times. Let your own breath set the pace.

It is important for kids to learn and articulate what helps them regulate.

This plants the seeds for self-advocacy when needed in the long term within educational/workplace/professional contexts.

Lifelong Flourishing

Daily Rituals & Rhythms for Families, Educators & Therapists

Set the intention to bring rhythm into everyday life. You simply need presence and a willingness to slow down. When rhythm is felt, not forced, it restores connection to self, to others, and to the moment.

Micro-Moments of Reconnection

Creating micro-moments of reconnection through the day, which over time become anchors for regulation, wellbeing, and deeper self-awareness.

Some ways to do this include:

- Begin or end the day with an outdoor ritual: Watering a plant, sitting with the sunrise, or lying on the grass to stargaze.
- Cloud watching and stargazing: Let imagination flow with sky stories and shapes.
- Nature photo walks: Capture moments of beauty and make a gratitude collage or family photo journal.
- Barefoot beach time or bushwalks: Let feet touch earth. Let stillness meet the senses.
- Nature journalling: Invite the question, *'What did your heart feel in nature today?'*
- Share childhood stories: Reflect on your own nature memories to inspire connection across generations.
- Anchor the day with consistent sequences that are *experienced*, not rigid schedules:
    - Morning rhythm: Light stretching, soft music, same breakfast space.
    - Evening rhythm: Bath or shower, reading/drawing/journalling,

breath, sound frequency tracks, essential oil diffuser. These help the body anticipate and settle.

- Build in short, rhythmic movement breaks between daily activities/tasks:
  - Clapping patterns.
  - Walking in sync.
  - Dancing to a favourite beat.
  - Bouncing on a soft surface.

These can reset focus, support transitions, and reduce overwhelm.

Senses Communication in Nature

Let your senses guide your own communication and commentary:

- What you hear – e.g. *I love the **sound** of those birds.*
- What you see – e.g. ***Look** at the different types of blues you can see on the ocean.*
- What you smell – e.g. *I can **smell** the trees.*
- What you physically feel – e.g. *I love the **feeling** of salt on my skin.*
- What your heart and soul feel – e.g. ***My heart** feels so at peace here.*
- What you remember/story you can tell – e.g. *This brings up **a memory** of …*

Remember to *pause* after you make a comment – to allow space for your child to contribute their thoughts/feelings and questions.

Movement Rituals

Rhythmic rituals support transitions and restore flow. They can be quick, creative, and consistent. Try these before school, between tasks, or whenever energy feels scattered:

- Shake It Off: Shake each limb for 10 seconds. Make silly sounds. Let tension move out through the body.
- Roll Like a Log: On a soft surface, roll side to side with arms overhead. This helps reset the vestibular system.
- Animal Moves: Slither like a snake, crawl like a bear, hop like a frog. Let the body lead the way.
- Brain Balancer Cross-Crawls**:** March in place while tapping the opposite knee with your hand.
- Breath Meets Motion: Guide your child to pair movement with breath: *Inhale as you reach up to the sky. Exhale as you fold or curl down.* Repeat slowly, flowing with your breath like a wave.

The Language of Internal & External Rhythms

Help children become fluent in the language of **body wisdom**.

These phrases invite awareness:

Do you feel a wiggle or stillness inside?

Does your body want to move or rest?

Let's listen for your 'yes' and your 'no'; what do they feel like in your body?

Your breath is like a wave. Let's ride it together.

When a child trusts their body's signals, they build confidence, agency, and safety.

Legacy in Motion

Reflect. Integrate. Empower.

Rhythm isn't something we force; it's something we return to. It's felt in the quiet moments, in the body's gentle cues, and in nature's steady beat. This is where self-leadership begins, by remembering the natural flow we were born with.

When we offer children rhythm, we offer them a way to remember safety in their own body.

When we offer rhythm within connection, we offer them trust in the world.

When rhythm is restored, connection is restored.

What's both beautiful and powerful is that when we restore the natural rhythms of the body, we create the spaciousness for something deeper to emerge – our inner knowing.

As children learn to feel safe in their bodies and attune to their own energy, they become more open to the quiet whispers within.

From that grounded place … we begin to explore the sacred guidance of intuition.

Journal Prompts:

- *When do I feel most in sync with life; like I'm flowing, not forcing?*
- *How does nature help calm and reset me (and my child)?*
- *What rhythms feel missing in our home – and what's one gentle way I can bring them back?*
- *Where might my family and I need less structure and more spaciousness … more breath, more being?*

** When to Seek Therapeutic Support**

If your child experiences ongoing difficulty with regulation, motor coordination, or sensory overwhelm, consider seeking the guidance from a team of qualified allied health professionals who use rhythm therapeutically to support brain-body integration and nervous system healing in a trauma-informed and individualised way. (e.g. occupational therapist, music therapist, holistic health practitioner versed in regulation/energy healing/sound frequency therapy.)

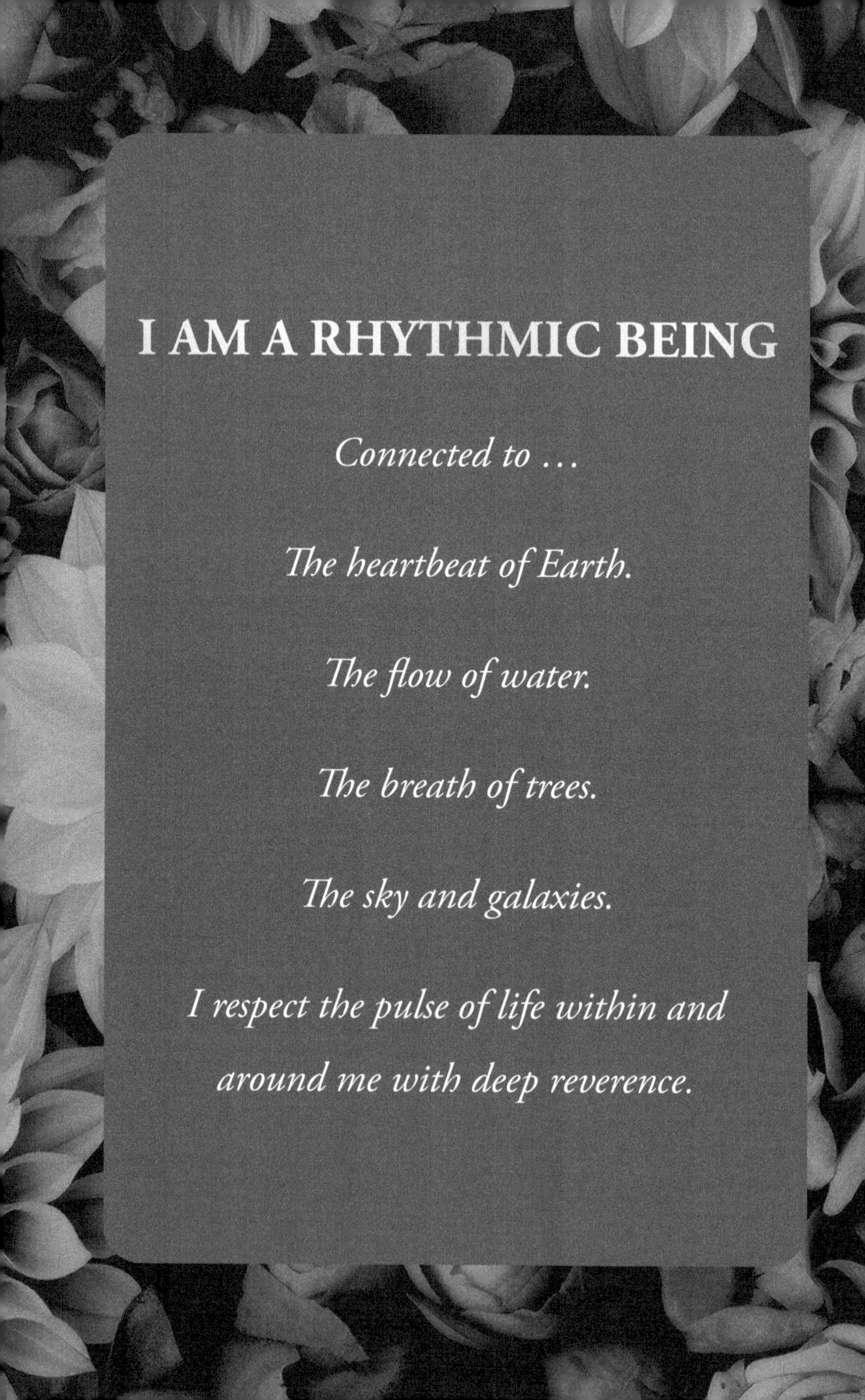

I AM A RHYTHMIC BEING

Connected to . . .

The heartbeat of Earth.

The flow of water.

The breath of trees.

The sky and galaxies.

I respect the pulse of life within and around me with deep reverence.

NOURISH INTUITION

Trusting the Inner Whispers of Your Sacred Guide

What if the most revolutionary act of parenting is liberating a child's ability to listen to themselves?

One morning, I was scheduled to host a live online masterclass. Afterwards, I needed to drive across Sydney for an important meeting. I'd prepped everything the night before: clothes laid out, bags packed, breakfast pre-made. I was ready.

Just minutes before the class began, I felt a subtle nudge: *get your car keys ready*. I reached into the handbag pocket where I usually kept them. Nothing. I searched quickly but couldn't find them. I had to let it go to begin my presentation.

As I prepared to go live, an image flashed into my mind: a cloth supermarket shopping bag; and I 'heard' the words *bottom of the bag*. I acknowledged this information quickly but had to get on with the masterclass.

Once the class finished, I headed for the door, then paused. *The car key!* I'd forgotten I never found it. Rather than trying to find the key amongst my collection of several identical supermarket bags, I thought it would be quicker to just get the spare key, so I went to retrieve that. But it was not where I thought I had left it! I paused, and in that moment, I felt a knowing. Then without hesitation, I walked over to my collection of identical shopping bags, reached towards one I felt drawn to, and there it was – my car key. No logic. No checklist. Just clear, guided direction.

Later that day, when my daughter returned from school we were sharing about our days, and I mentioned how I came to find my car key. Her eyes lit up.

'That happens to me too,' she said. 'Today at school I couldn't remember my locker passcode. Then, in maths class, a few numbers just "popped out" of the page I was working on. They were my passcode numbers!'

These might seem like small moments, but they point to something much deeper: *intuition is alive within us all.* It doesn't always shout. It doesn't always follow logic. But it *is* always available, especially when we learn how to listen. We don't have to teach kids how to be intuitive. We simply create space for it to stay alive, through conversation, validation, and example.

Intuition is your mind's way of understanding something quickly; without needing to think it through step by step. It's not just a guess or an emotion. Instead, it comes from your brain and body picking up patterns over time, often outside your awareness.

You might experience it as a calm sense of knowing, a gut feeling, or a quiet clarity. It often shows up before your logical mind can explain why something feels right or wrong.

Several scientific studies suggest that intuition draws on fast, subconscious processing, subtle bodily cues, and deep pattern recognition shaped by experience. It's your internal compass, quiet but powerful, guiding you from within.

It is fascinating to witness intuition in action. My daughter, when 12 months old, had her first tiny taste of peanut butter on toast. Within seconds of holding that toast to her mouth, bright red hives spread quickly from her fingers up her arms, neck, and face. Her body signalled, very clearly, this was not for her.

Following medical attention and specialised advice, some months later, we commenced a desensitisation program. A trace amount of peanut butter was mixed into the dough of one of her favourite foods: choc-chip muffins. She helped mix the batter, beamed as she watched the muffins baking in the oven, then she sat excitedly at the table when the oven timer *dinged*, awaiting to be served. As she raised a muffin to her mouth, it neared her nose of course, and then she paused. She gently placed it back down on her plate, shaking her head. Her body said *no*.

Similarly, several years later, at a gelato shop, my daughter was handed the 'special scoop of the day' gelato flavour. And as she neared her mouth to the gelato about to eat it, she stopped.

'There's peanut in this,' she said.

My reflex response was, 'I don't think there is peanut in it, the sign didn't say that.'

But my daughter didn't budge, 'I'm not eating it.'

And sure enough, on checking with staff, there was peanut in it. There were no signs stating it. No labels. No adult guidance. Just my daughter's pure embodied intuition, and her trust in it.

I was immediate in apologising to her and shared my gratitude that she listened to her intuition and encouraged her to keep doing that no matter who and what others have to say!

Intuition is like an invisible compass, already active in our children. It's more than just a feeling; it's a subtle interaction between:

The Body, which senses cues from the environment – like emotion, safety, or tension – often before conscious thought catches up.

The Mind, especially the subconscious, which rapidly recognises patterns and meanings we might not consciously register.

The Inner Self, which some describe as the soul or higher awareness, offering guidance through sudden insights, inner images, or a quiet sense of knowing.

When children are encouraged to honour this inner compass, they develop confidence, safety, and clarity. They learn that it's okay to pause. Okay to say no. Okay to trust what they feel. It's not something we need to install. It's something we need to *protect*.

Yes, our world may be shaped by rapid technological change, social upheaval, environmental uncertainty, and constant information flow; and for this reason, one of the most important things we can nurture in our children is a strong connection to their inner compass – by embracing curiosity, compassion, and authentic connection.

I had the privilege and joy of speaking with Sonia Choquette on my *Chatabout Children* podcast. Sonia is a *New York Times* bestselling author, globally recognised spiritual teacher, and intuitive guide known for empowering individuals to trust their inner voice and awaken their spiritual intelligence.

Sonia beautifully shared how the foundation for intuition was laid early in her life. Raised as one of seven children, with a profoundly intuitive and deaf mother, she was taught from the age of five that she had 'more than five senses'.

'I had an inner sense directly connected to the universe, to my highest self, to all that can guide and protect me,' she shared.

Her mother would always ask, 'What does your heart say? What does your inner sense say?' – teaching her to trust her own guidance before turning to others. This self-trust became her compass in life. Sonia raised her own daughters this way, and now a granddaughter continues the legacy.

'It's now three generations strong,' Sonia beamed.

She shared that this trust in intuition has preserved her integrity, shielded her from approval-seeking, and allowed her to live in deep self-connection.

One powerful story she recounted from her childhood was of a family trip, which was some hours away by car. On the way home from their trip, although everyone was weary and keen to get back, her mother asked her father to take an alternate route home from the highway – for no obvious reason.

Her father was not keen on this, but her mother gently insisted.

'Please, Paul, humour me,' she nudged.

Reluctantly, he did so. Soon after, they learnt that a truck had overturned on their original route, blocking the road for over six hours. Her father was stunned.

'We got home forty minutes later, not four hours,' Sonia shared.

These were the kinds of moments that shaped Sonia's upbringing; and they continued into her own parenting and, now, grandparenting.

'We have to stop treating kids as clay to be moulded, and instead honour them as sovereign souls,' she affirmed. 'Our job is to hold space and listen. Not instruct intuition – but invite it to speak.'

We empower children by reinforcing that their inner signals – gut feelings, inner pictures, and subtle knowings – are valid and valuable. In a world that rewards logic and performance, intuitive trust becomes a radical act of self-leadership.

Heart-Powered Self-Leadership

So how can we help children nourish their intuition?

Intuitive self-leadership is not about being perfect or always knowing.

It is about learning to *listen inwardly first*, and to move with coherence, not compliance. The more we centre this way of being, the more we raise humans who are anchored, discerning, and energetically aligned.

This also means parenting and educating with presence. Rather than rushing to solve, fix, or explain … we hold space. For when we validate a child's felt sense, we keep their intuitive channel open.

Here are some ways to do this:

Use Reflective Language

Regularly ask open-ended questions that help children explore their inner world. For example, *What did your inner voice say?* or *Did something feel off to you?* These questions encourage trust in their own sensing.

The 'Yes/No' Game

Ask playful questions like, *Would your intuition say 'yes' or 'no' to jumping in a puddle?* Then pause and have them *feel* the answer before saying it. It builds intuitive discernment through fun.

Model Your Own Intuitive Decision-Making Aloud

Share real-life examples of when you followed a gut feeling or inner knowing. Say things like, *I felt something was off, so I paused and chose another way*, or *I had a strong sense this was the right decision, even if I couldn't explain it.*

'What Did Your Body Say?' Check-Ins

Further to building somatic (body) communication, before making choices (what to wear, what to eat, how to respond), ask: *What does your body say?*

Normalise Pausing Before Choosing

Create intentional moments to pause when a decision arises. You might say, 'Let's just be still for a moment and see how this feels inside,' encouraging children to check in before responding or deciding.

Acknowledge When Intuition Helped or Protected You (and Invite Their Stories Too)

Share moments from your own life when inner knowing guided you and invite children to share theirs. Affirm their stories with curiosity: *That's powerful. What told you that inside?*

Celebrate Moments of Self-Trust, No Matter How Small

When a child says no to something that doesn't feel right, or changes direction based on a feeling, celebrate it. Say, 'You really listened to yourself there. That's something to be proud of.' This builds positive reinforcement for trusting themselves.

Lifelong Flourishing

Daily Rituals & Rhythms for Families, Educators & Therapists

Many activities shared in other chapters of this book (e.g. *Heart Sparkle Communication*; *Dreams as Divine Dialogue*) also implicitly help nourish intuition. Here's a few more powerful rhythms you may choose to incorporate in your day to day.

Stillness Time (5–10 Minutes Daily)

Create a calm, screen-free moment for the whole family to sit in silence, rest, or breathe deeply. Over time, this helps children notice subtle body cues and inner signals that are crucial for intuitive awareness.

Truth or Noticing?

Ask a basic question your child knows the answer to (e.g. *Do you like ice cream?*).

Ask them to notice how their body feels when the answer is true.

Then ask something silly and untrue (e.g. *Do you live on the moon?*) and notice the difference in the body. The core message here is: *Your body is more deeply aligned with truth. Trust it.* This builds somatic (body communication) trust and normalises inner listening.

Family Dream Journal

Keep a family dream book. In the morning, invite kids to draw or share any dreams they remember, without needing to explain them. This nurtures symbolic thinking and unconscious processing.

Honour Imagination as Valid (Symbolic Intuition)

Children naturally express their intuition through **symbols** – drawings, dreams, made-up stories, or role-play characters. These are not just 'pretend'; they are how the subconscious and intuitive mind process truth. So, encourage storytelling, role-play, and creative drawing. Say: *Imagination isn't just pretend; it's how your deeper self works through ideas and feelings in a safe, creative way.*

Intuition Walks ('Follow the Nudge')

Take walks where a different person leads based on 'what feels right' – no set plan. Let children practise decision-making based on feeling, curiosity, or interest.

Heart-Breath Ritual (Before Transitions)

Before school, bed, or challenging events, practise three deep breaths with hands on heart. Ask: *What does your heart know right now?*

Ask the Silence

Create moments where a child holds a question and simply breathes with it in silence for one minute. No pressure to answer – just letting the silence be a guide.

Symbol Spotting Walks

Go on walks where the focus is: *What symbol catches your eye? What does it remind you of?* Encourage meaning-making and inner interpretation; this is great for their 'intuitive' muscles.

The 'Tiny Truth' Share

At dinner or before bed, invite each person to share one small thing they *just knew* that day – no proof needed. This normalises intuition as valid and shared, not hidden or odd.

Legacy in Motion

Reflect. Integrate. Empower.

Our legacy isn't to *teach* children to be intuitive, it's to make sure they never forget they already are.

When we trust our own inner whispers, we model a way of being that transcends fear, doubt, and external noise. We show our children that truth doesn't need to be explained, it can be felt. That knowing doesn't have to be proven, it can be lived.

So, the invitation is for you to:

Pause before you answer.

Feel before you fix.

Remember the sacred intelligence already flowing through every child, and within yourself.

Because when we create space for children to trust their own timing, their own language of knowing, their own energetic yes and no … we are doing more than just raising intuitive humans – we're activating a ripple of wisdom that carries forward through generations.

And with that, let's now explore how children can give voice to their inner wisdom … through words, presence, and heart and soul-powered connection.

Journal Prompts:

- *How would life feel if I trusted more and questioned less; especially when the knowing is quiet but clear?*
- *What would it look like to raise a child who doesn't feel the need to second-guess themselves? Am I living that example?*
- *How do I speak about inner knowing with the children in my life?*
- *Where in my daily rhythm could I create more space to pause and listen within; before acting or advising?*

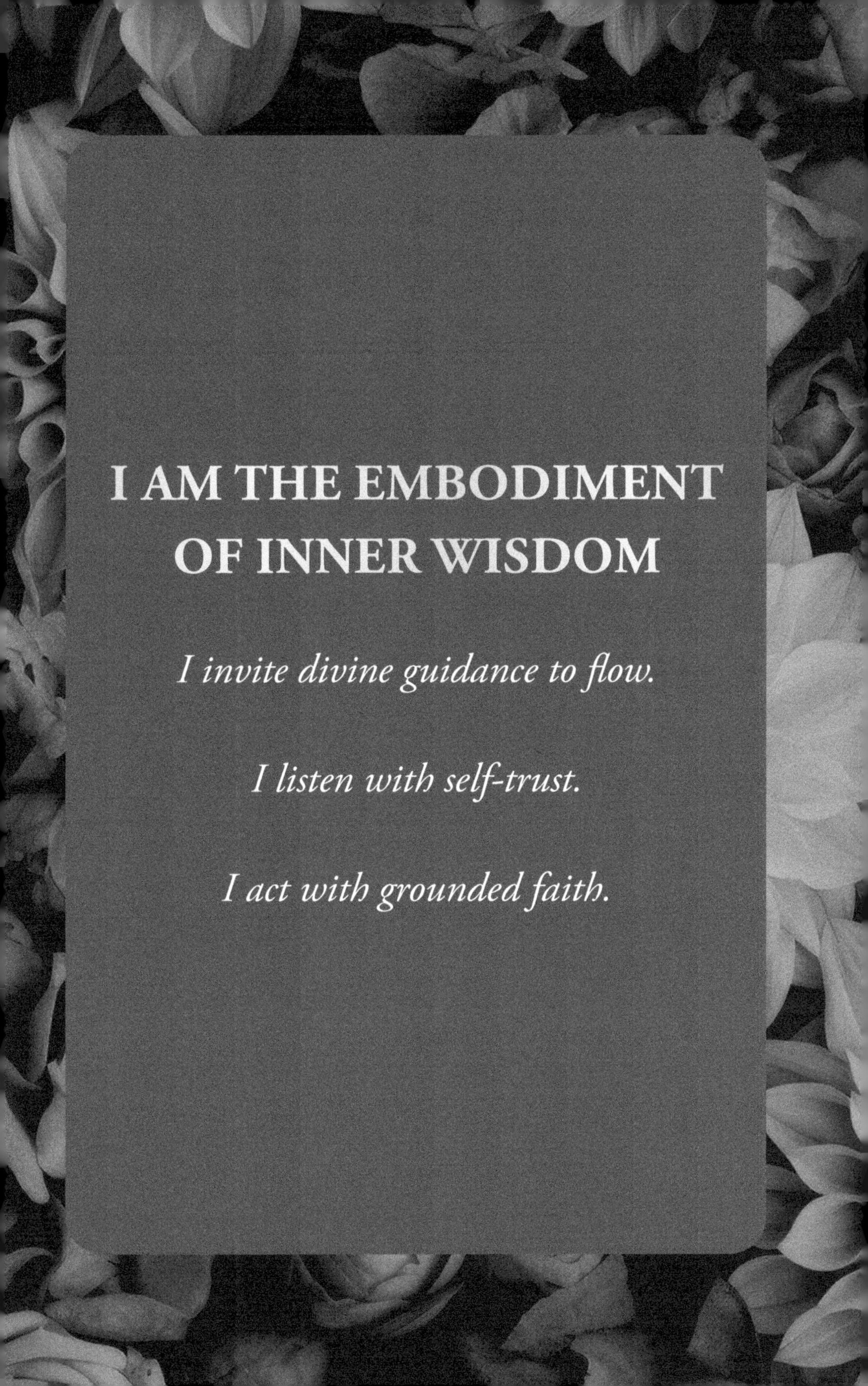

I AM THE EMBODIMENT OF INNER WISDOM

I invite divine guidance to flow.

I listen with self-trust.

I act with grounded faith.

HEART SPARKLE COMMUNICATION

Harmonising Connection, Compassion, and Truth

Beyond saying what matters - what if your greatest gift is BEING what matters?

The foundational truth is: your energy speaks before your words do. *Heart Sparkle Communication* is the term I use to reference tuning into the silent, felt frequency of your heart, where connection, compassion, and truth are not spoken but embodied.

There was a period in my life that I now call the 'intensive module' of the School of Life.

Within a very short space of time, my world reshaped completely:

A separation from my husband.

A move to the other side of the city; and two new households (for the kids).

A car accident that wrote off my vehicle (of which I was not at fault).

The passing of my mother (my children's beloved grandmother).

All three of my children starting at new schools – each in a different school.

As one of my beautiful friends observed after learning about it all: 'It's like someone picked up the snow globe of your life – and shook it. A lot!'

And yet, amidst the swirl, I was faced with a powerful choice. How do I show up?

For myself.

For my children.

For my friends.

For my colleagues.

For my work in the world.

There was so much I could not control, but I could embody the energy I wanted to hold. I could become a living example of leading from the heart – courageously, and vulnerably.

So, I chose to anchor in gratitude, humility, and truth.

I chose to lean in and receive the powerful pillars of unconditional love and support from close family and friends.

I chose to honour sacred silence more deeply; and just allow. Just be.

And with this … something extraordinary emerged from the rubble.

A powerful surge of creative life force moved through me. It was not just an idea, but a vivid, soul-anchored vision. It came with clarity, conviction, and the undeniable frequency of purpose … a mission in motion – to support children across the world in reconnecting with their inner wisdom; expressing themselves with joy; and remembering the radiant truth of who they already are. It felt like a global offering; one that would speak heart-to-heart, generation to generation, through imaginative wonder, emotional depth, and a resonance of real empowerment.

This creative vision has since grown the foundations as a heart- and soul-led movement and is something I continue to grow and nurture at the time of writing this book – a sacred project I look forward to birthing into the world in divine timing.

And … more quietly, more intimately, something else began in the sanctuary of my own home. The birth of what I called *Heart Sparkle Notes*.

These notes came to be, I believe, in response to one of the greatest challenges I was adjusting to in the marital separation … the shared care of my children. It felt extraordinarily unnatural not to have them present in my life every day. It activated a primal ache, but it also deepened my devotion to finding new ways of *feeling close*, even when physically apart.

So, I began writing them *Heart Sparkle Notes*.

Each week, I left small handwritten notes on their pillows, waiting and ready for them on the day they returned to our home. These were short, soulful messages, from my heart to theirs. Truths wrapped in love. Anchors of safety. Reminders of unshakable connection.

My kids couldn't always put into words how the notes made them feel, but I could see it in their eyes and could resonate with the felt sense of their heart 'sparkling' with deep love and acceptance.

It was a practice of heart frequency in action.

Here are a few examples (chosen by my kids to share with you).

Dearest Zara,

Enjoy some moments celebrating you. Life is to be lived, to be enjoyed, to be respected, to be cherished. Thank you for being such a wonderful light and love in my life, and in the world.

Love you always, Mum xo
PS Ensure you have a shower before bed!!

Dearest Maximus,
I trust you are proud of yourself for being so gracious, as you grow, learn and lead in life. Always remember, you create your reality … by the thoughts you think, the feelings you feel, and the actions you take.

Anything in life is possible … believe YOU ARE the magic in your life!

Love you always, Mum xo

Dearest Cleo,

What a year it has been and what a joy it has been to share it with you. It is an honour to be part of your journey, and have you be part of mine … I am always learning so much from you and inspired by your beautiful self.

Know that you are worthy of an abundance of love, an abundance of joy, an abundance of health, an abundance of happiness.

You don't need to earn anyone's love. You need to know you are worthy of unconditional love simply by being you.

You need to know that life is ever changing and that we are all here for a reason. You don't need to achieve anything, you simply need to practise nurturing a strong, healthy relationship with yourself, and keep trusting in your inner wisdom.

Love you always and unconditionally, Mum xx

And that is Heart Sparkle Communication.

Communication that holds the energy of heart and soul … harmonising trust, healing, and authentic connection. While it found form in a sacred family ritual for us, its essence extends beyond moments. It honours the soul's wisdom and guidance, and the heart's resonance, as a guiding force – for you, and for the children entrusted to your care.

To weave science into this heartfelt chapter (yes, pun intended): the heart isn't just a pump. It's a communication centre. Research from the HeartMath Institute shows that the heart produces an electromagnetic field that can be measured several feet away from the body. When we're stressed or angry, the heart rhythm becomes erratic. When we're calm, loving, or grateful, it becomes smooth and balanced.

We often hear that children thrive when they feel connected, but what does that really mean?

According to leading research, children who feel emotionally safe and connected with their caregivers develop stronger resilience, more confidence, and better emotional intelligence. In simple terms: *when kids feel truly seen and loved, they grow stronger on the inside.*

And here's the key: This rhythm doesn't just stay in our body – it influences those around us, especially children, whose systems are still forming.

The difference between head, heart, and soul communication is a felt experience. Simply put:

Head Communication sounds like: 'This is what you should do.' Its energy is logical, instructive, and sometimes distant.

Heart Communication sounds like: 'I'm here with you. We'll move through this together.' Its energy is warm, empathetic, grounded, and emotionally safe.

Soul Communication sounds like: 'You are loved just as you are.'

Its energy is deeply affirming and unconditionally accepting.

So, when we practise what's called *heart coherence* – slowing our breath, focusing on love or gratitude, and calming our emotions – we're not just helping ourselves. We're literally broadcasting safety and calm into the space our children live in.

Heart-Powered Self-Leadership

So how can we help children harmonise connection, compassion, and truth?

Children become powerful communicators not just through what they say, but through how they feel, listen, and attune. When we offer tools to help them sense their soul's wisdom and their heart's resonance, we activate their capacity for inner guidance, emotional awareness, and authentic expression.

The following activities are designed to help children explore the silent power of their heart field, cultivate compassion-based communication, and deepen their embodied understanding of connection and truth.

Heart Sparkle Practices

Heart Listening Time

Invite children to close their eyes, place a hand on their chest, and breathe into their heart space. After 3–5 slow breaths, ask: *What does your heart feel today?*

They can draw it, speak it, or write one word. This builds interoception and energetic awareness.

Feelings & Frequencies Chart

This is great for kids who may not have, or are developing, emotional literacy. Name some common feelings they experience. Together, assign each one a natural image or frequency metaphor. Keep it age-appropriate and personal, and importantly, let the child lead. For example:

Joy	Sunshine	Feels warm, light, bubbly inside.
Sadness	Raindrops	Feels heavy, cool, falling tears.
Anger	Thunderstorm	Feels loud, electric, fast heartbeat.
Calm	Still pond	Feels peaceful, quiet, slow breathing.
Worry	Windy Skies	Feels swirly, unsettled, hard to focus.
Excitement	Fireworks	Feels sparkly, fast, hard to sit still.
Love	Candle Flame	Feels warm, glowing, gentle.

This allows kids to tune into their body and describe their inner frequency.

Heart Sparkle Note-Making Station

Set up a small 'note-making' space with blank cards, pens, and stickers. Encourage children to write a loving message for someone else – sibling, parent, teacher, or friend.

This builds their 'heart and soul' muscle of compassionate communication.

Coherence Code Words

Create simple family or classroom 'code words' that invite a return to heart connection. For example: 'Pause + Heart Breathe' or 'Heart Reset'. This becomes a shared language for navigating tension, misunderstandings, or disconnection.

Heart Voice Role Plays

Practise scenarios with your child that let them explore their heart-led voice; for younger kids, finger puppets are great. Scenarios could include saying 'no' kindly/expressing hurt without blame/offering appreciation.

The most important thing to remember is to have fun!

Lifelong Flourishing

Daily Rituals & Rhythms for Families, Educators & Therapists

Heart Sparkle Communication begins as an energy and flourishes through repetition and rhythm. When homes and learning spaces anchor heart coherence into their rituals and routines, children receive consistent emotional nourishment, safety, and attuned connection.

The following practices make heart resonance a way of life.

The 'Heart Sparkle Note' Ritual

For kids who can read, place a handwritten note from you to your child once a week. On pillows, lunch boxes, backpacks, etc. Keep it short and true. Use affirmations, stories, gratitude, or reflections. For kids who can't read – draw them a picture. The mode of expression needs to come from your heart in a way your child can receive it.

Over time, these notes are internalised as a source of self-worth and soul support.

The Heart Sparkle Pause

Once a day, the whole family (or class) stops for three slow breaths, hand on heart. It's a collective pause to tune in to your heart before continuing with the day. When you attach this pause practice to a daily occurrence (e.g. after breakfast, after dinner, etc.) it not only makes it easier to remember initially, but it also becomes a grounding anchor of reconnection while elevating the vibe of energetic regulation.

Bedtime Heart Check-In

This is inspired by the bedtime routine I had with my kids when they were younger, where I would say good night and 'place kisses' on their heart, saying, 'You carry mum's love with you everywhere you go.' (This went on to be an award-nominated children's book called *Kisses in your Heart.*)

Heart-Centred Conflict Repair

When misunderstandings arise, invite a short 'Heart Sparkle Repair' moment. Basically, it is the 1:1:1 practice of sharing:

One thing they felt: One thing they wished had happened: One thing they love about the other person.

This helps soften the edges a little and restore emotional coherence without shame or shutdown.

Legacy in Motion

Reflect. Integrate. Empower.

Heart Sparkle Communication is felt in our tone, our timing, our intention.

It's shared in how we breathe with a child through a meltdown, how we hold presence during a bedtime story, how we soften our voice when guiding a tough truth. In essence, we could say it is more than just communication. It is communion.

A resonance that reminds us and our children: *You are safe. You are seen. You are loved.*

As we model this, children learn to trust their felt experience. They grow up not just speaking from the head, but expressing from the heart and soul, with courage, compassion and connection; with words that heal, silence that holds, and a frequency that uplifts every room entered.

We now take that connection further as we explore the multidimensional nature of what it means to be human – embracing all the intelligent layers that exist beyond what the eye can see.

Journal Prompts:

- *When do I feel most connected to my child without speaking?*
- *What does my heart want to say more often?*
- *How does it feel when I lead with love instead of control?*
- *What helps me return to calm when things feel chaotic?*

MY SOUL POWERS MY HEART

My heart powers my presence.

My presence powers my connection.

My connection powers my truth.

HOLISTIC HUMANNESS

Honouring the Multidimensional Self Beyond the Body

What if your child's true brilliance lives not in what they do, but in the wholeness of who they are?

We teach kids to brush their teeth, tie their shoes, and care for their bodies ... but how often do we help them to care for their energy, their soul – their unseen wholeness?

One of the quietest shifts we can make in how we raise, teach, and support children is this: to stop viewing them as a series of behaviours or diagnoses and begin to see them as layered masterpieces, full of energy, wisdom, and multidimensional wholeness.

I remember a call from a new client. Her voice was stretched thin, from years of advocating, trialling, adapting, and now re-evaluating everything. Her teenage daughter, neurodivergent with learning differences, had been pulled from school some years prior, and her mum had stepped away from allied health services that just 'weren't working'.

'She can't sit still at a desk for an hour,' the mother shared. 'And most approaches expect her to.'

She was tired, but she wasn't giving up. Her greatest concern was that her daughter's self-belief was eroding, as she said to me: 'My daughter told me, "Mum I just don't fit in! I don't feel like I belong anywhere!"'

And when a child begins to question their place in the world, it ripples through every part of them, body, mind, heart, energy, and soul. This mother's heart was quietly breaking, but deep down she knew there was a way to support herself and her daughter, honouring *all* her layers, in an integrated way. It was that fuel that spurred her to call me in the first place, seeking help.

It reminded me of the inner fuel that led me, early in my career, to question the systems around me. My work in speech pathology was never just about helping children speak. It was about listening deeply to what wasn't being said. It was about tending to the unseen; what's felt, what's feared, what's needed. It was about learning the whole ecosystem of the individual and the ecosystem of their family. And that's how I came to lead a speech pathology company built on whole human care.

Every new team member who joined the company heard this from me: 'Connect with the person; not their problems. Be curious about who they are outside the clinic room and what their 24/7 looks like. Know and understand their current story.'

Because when we approach children this way, something profound happens. They remember that they are whole.

Not broken. Not behind. Not too much or not enough. Whole.

This lens of wholeness is more than a philosophy. It is grounded in both ancient wisdom and contemporary science. Across Indigenous cultures, integrative medicine, neurobiology, and quantum fields, we see the same truth reflected: **human beings are multidimensional**. We are more than flesh and bone; we are fields of intelligence.

Raising a child today means more than meeting their physical needs; it means understanding them as whole, complex beings. While many cultures and healing traditions have always seen children this way, modern science is catching up. From brain development to emotional health to energy and intuition, research now supports what many parents instinctively know: **children are made of many layers**.

We begin with the **physical body** – the most visible part of a child. Their growing bodies, movement, hunger, sleep patterns, and energy levels all live here. It's also where we often first notice that something might be off, perhaps a stomach-ache, restlessness, or changes in sleep. But these physical cues are rarely isolated; they often point to something deeper.

Then there's the **emotional body**. Long before children can explain what's going on, they feel it. Emotions are often their first language. Joy, frustration, fear, sadness, etc. – these arise in powerful ways. When we create space for those feelings, instead of rushing to fix or quiet them, we help children feel seen, safe, and respected in their emotional truth.

Next is the **mental body**; a space of thoughts, self-talk, and beliefs. This is where their internal stories form: how they see themselves and how they interpret the world around them. And much of this is shaped by us – by our tone, our language, our mirroring. A harsh comment or a gentle affirmation can sculpt a child's self-worth more than we realise.

We then move into the **energetic body**. You've likely felt it – that moment when a child walks into a room and immediately senses the mood. Or how some kids need quiet space after being around lots of people. This is the subtle but powerful energetic layer. Children feel tone, presence, and intention more than we give them credit for. They flourish in environments that feel calm, attuned, and energetically safe.

Then we honour the **soul body**. The inner compass. It's the part of your child that knows, even when they don't yet have the words.

It shows up in imagination, gut feelings, dreams, and quiet wonder. When we choose to honour this subtle wisdom instead of overriding it, we protect their connection to truth – their own.

And finally, we acknowledge the **spirit body.** The eternal spark. The thread that connects each child (and us all) to the infinite ... to divine source. Not shaped by experience, but illuminated through presence, reverence, and love.

These layers aren't stacked like rungs on a ladder. They are alive in every child; moving in constant relationship, informing and flowing through one another. When one is out of rhythm, it impacts the others. So, when we meet children honouring these layers, something magical happens: a child feels seen and met, soul to soul, in their wholeness. And in doing so, we remember our own.

Heart-Powered Self-Leadership

So how can we help children embrace their multilayered self?

When we consistently reflect 'You are whole', children begin to live from that place. Not in parts. Not in performance. But in deep, steady self-recognition.

Self-leadership doesn't mean children need to have it all figured out. It means they're supported to notice, name, and nurture their inner world. And the more we model that ourselves, the more natural it becomes for them.

Here are powerful ways you can help your child stay connected to each layer of their being:

Listen to Your Body – Physical Layer

Support your child to check in each morning by asking: *What does your body need today? Rest, movement, water, or food?*

Use simple body maps or outlines they can colour in to show where they feel tired, calm, excited, or tense.

Repeat often: *My body speaks – I listen.*

Feel Your Feelings – Emotional Layer

Encourage daily emotional check-ins using a feelings chart or emotion wheel. Let them know it's okay to feel more than one thing at once.

Use emotion cards or a journal for them to draw or write what they're feeling.

Remind them: *All my feelings are okay – even the big ones.*

Notice Your Thoughts – Mental Layer

When your child is stuck, gently ask: *What story are you telling yourself right now? Is it kind? Is it true?*

Support them to explore thoughts with a 'thought detective' approach – separating helpful from unhelpful thinking.

Anchor with: *I can choose thoughts that help me grow.*

Tune Into Your Energy – Energetic Layer

After a busy outing or school day, ask: *What does your energy need right now – quiet, movement, or space?*

Create a 'recharge corner' at home with calming items like blankets, pillows, nature objects, or drawing supplies.

Affirm: *I take care of my energy so I can feel balanced.*

Trust Your Inner Voice – Soul Layer

Before making a decision, guide your child to place a hand on their heart and/or belly and ask: *What feels like a yes? What feels like a no?*

Offer space for an intuition journal where they can note dreams, drawings, ideas, or gut feelings.

Repeat together: *My inner wisdom matters – I can trust it.*

Remember Your Light – Spirit Layer

Create quiet moments together – in nature, under the stars, or at bedtime – to talk about the bigger questions: *What do you think your heart came here to share?*, or *What helps you feel connected to something greater?*

Invite practices like:

- breath prayers (e.g. inhale a phrase such as 'I am light'; exhale 'I am love')
- lighting a candle whilst holding an intention (aligning it with the highest good)
- giving thanks to the earth, sky, or spirit guides
- affirming together: *I am a spark of something greater – I shine with purpose and love.*

Lifelong Flourishing

Daily Rituals & Rhythms for Families, Educators & Therapists

To raise empowered humans, we must support them not only in parts, but as a living, breathing integration of body, heart, mind, energy, soul, and spirit. This doesn't mean adding pressure or perfection to our daily routines. It means weaving care into what we already do, with a little more presence, permission, and pause.

Here are everyday rhythms and rituals to complement your routine, drawing from the chapters shared in section one of this book:

Whole-Self Check In

Before the morning rush, take a quiet moment – together or individually – to ask: *How am I feeling in my body today? What emotions are present? What kind of energy do I need?* Let this shape your tone for the day ahead.

Create a Rhythm of Nourishment

Make mealtimes more than just refuelling. Invite children to notice what their body is asking for – warmth, crunch, colour, hydration – and honour that with simple, wholesome food. Involve them in preparation as a way of tuning in.

Keep Movement Intuitive & Joyful

Instead of rigid schedules, allow space for movement, whether it be dancing before dinner, stretching after homework, or barefoot time in the yard. Let their body lead. These pockets of flow support regulation and vitality.

Hold Space for Emotional Weather

Just as we dress for rain or sunshine, create space for the emotional 'weather' your child is experiencing. Whether they feel stormy or sunny, offer them a calm, safe presence; through breathwork, a quiet walk, or a few minutes lying under a weighted blanket.

Build in Story Moments

Share empowering stories – real or imagined – that remind your child of who they are beyond struggle or labels. Invite them to co-author their own stories with affirmations, drawings, or simple reframes of the day's events.

Weave in Grounding Practices
After transitions (like returning home from school), help your child come back to themselves; through a grounding drink (a warm, nourishing, calming drink), a body shake out, or a few minutes lying on the grass. This helps restore balance in their energetic field.

Honour Inner Knowing
In decision-making, even small ones, pause and ask: *What does your gut say?*, or *Which one feels like a yes?* This builds trust in their intuitive voice and gives it permission to guide.

End the Day in Soul Presence
At bedtime, invite soft reflection.

As mentioned previously, in my family, each night before we retire to bed, we do a 'Gratitude Candle' ritual, where we light the candle and take turns holding the 'gratitude candle' whilst sharing what we feel gratitude for. We also use it as a time to intend prayers of support for anyone or anything that we feel called to.

Ultimately, flourishing in life is not a destination; it's a felt rhythm. One that emerges when we honour our children as layered, luminous beings. In doing so, we offer them not only strategies for today, but a sacred relationship with themselves that will serve them for life.

Legacy in Motion

Reflect. Integrate. Empower.

To honour a child's full self, we must first be willing to see it.

Beyond behaviours to be managed.

Beyond diagnoses or labels to live by.

Beyond expectations to achieve.

When we meet them at every layer – body, emotion, mind, energy, soul, and spirit – we create a legacy of deep recognition. A felt sense of *I am seen. I am safe. I am whole.*

This is how we raise empowered humans … by honouring and celebrating them in their fullness.

Wholeness isn't something we give children. It's something we protect, mirror, and trust them to carry forward.

Journal Prompts:

- *In what ways am I already holding space for my child's wholeness, even if I didn't realise it?*
- *What layer of my child needs the most support right now? Am I responding to the symptom or the source?*
- *How often do I pause to honour my own energy, emotions, or inner knowing – without judging, or needing to fix or rush?*
- *Where am I invited to reclaim my own layered self?*

And with that, we close Section One.

You have now received the first golden key – *The Frequency of Foundations.*

From here, we journey into what it really means to live in the resonance of abundance.

Because empowered humans don't sit back and wait for the future to unfold …

They shape it.

Word by word.

Belief by belief.

Moment by moment.

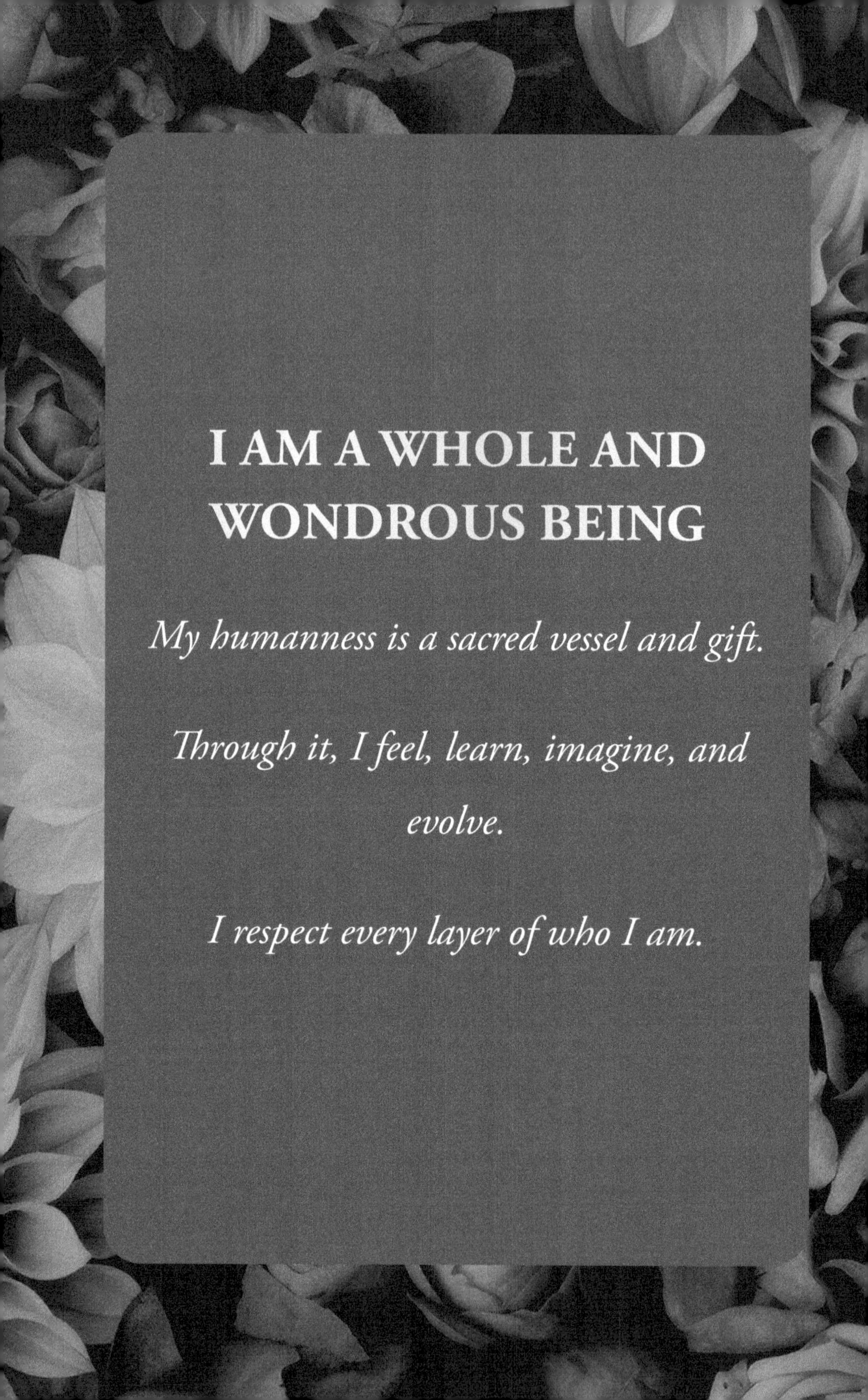

I AM A WHOLE AND WONDROUS BEING
My humanness is a sacred vessel and gift.
Through it, I feel, learn, imagine, and evolve.
I respect every layer of who I am.

GOLDEN KEY TWO

THE FREQUENCY OF FREEDOM

The Resonance of Abundance

Freedom: noun

/ˈfriː.dəm/

An expansive state, unbound by fear and doubt, free from societal or self-imposed barriers; liberating one's full potential with pure and peaceful power.

LIBERATE BELIEF SYSTEMS

Rewrite Stories that Limit Self-Leadership

What if the limits we perceive in ourselves, and our children are echoes of stories we've unknowingly absorbed as facts?

As a child I had a lot of questions for the world. Ultimately, at the core of all my questions was: *Why doesn't everyone in the world just get along?* Yes, I held the universal yearning for *peace*. With a focus on the world around me, I set myself a hefty mission and belief that I needed to 'fix it' … and 'fixing energy' is always the fuel of disempowerment. Everything changed when I understood the true path for change in *the* world began with changing *my* world … from the inside out.

From the moment we're born, we begin receiving messages, about who we are, what's possible, and how the world works. These messages often become belief systems, etched into the subconscious, like background programs quietly guiding our choices, emotions, and self-image.

I (like many of you) came to learn my beliefs weren't just tucked away in my mind. They showed up in everything I did (and didn't do) every single day. They created my reality.

There was a time when I found myself getting 'bored' with things that felt *too easy*. Deep down, it was a belief saying *you have to work hard (or struggle) to deserve it.*

I also had a pattern of quietly undervaluing my work; overdelivering, undercharging, not asking for the support I needed. That belief whispered, 'You're only worthy if you give more than you receive.'

Then there was the 'over-efforting' … pushing myself to standards of perceived perfection 'to feel good enough'. And when abundance or joy began flowing in, a quieter part of me would question it … *Can I really have this much?* That's what I call shaming the overflow – feeling unworthy of more than just the basics.

No doubt you can relate to some of these patterns. These patterns didn't make me 'less than'. They were loving messengers, revealing belief systems I'd absorbed over time. Many of which weren't even mine to begin with.

In childhood, our brains operate predominantly in theta waves, a state ideal for learning but also for absorbing beliefs without conscious filtering. As Dr Bruce Lipton's research highlights, this makes early childhood a critical window where our subconscious programming is most easily shaped by our environment, especially our caregivers, culture, and emotional experiences.

I have followed the work and research of Dr Lipton for some time. A cell biologist and author of *The Biology of Belief*, he explains that our subconscious mind runs about 95% of our daily behaviours, and that these patterns are not fixed. Through awareness and repetition, we can rewire them. In other words, we can rewrite the stories we've inherited or internalised – and support our children to do the same.

I've witnessed thousands of school-aged children over the years experiencing communication and/or learning difficulties with beliefs of 'I'm dumb', or 'there is something wrong with me because I need extra help', and quite often, they would express non-verbal responses or 'behaviours' that were essentially communications of their inner world; of their feeling of being 'less than' and not knowing what to do about it.

I recall working with a young adult client, supporting his social-emotional communication and broader life skills. He had experienced a lifetime of support services and 'fixing', so learning within a traditional school context had been very difficult for him. He now mostly stayed home, slept, and watched YouTube. His mother was concerned with his lack of motivation to work, to complete any courses, to participate fully in life.

Together with the client, we explored his inner world, starting simply with what he believed to be true about himself and his current circumstances. Some of these beliefs included, 'I can't learn things', 'My memory is not good', 'I'm not smart', 'I'm not fit enough', and 'Finding a job is hard'. We set about challenging and 'playing' with these beliefs. I was keen for him to imagine how his life would feel different if he felt he *could learn* things, if he had *a good memory*, *was smart*, *was fit*, and *had a job*?

Very quickly his lens widened ... widened to a whole new world of possibilities and an energy of hope. On that day, he said *yes* to honouring his renewed vision, which ultimately was a *yes* to honouring himself. Within months of us working together, he had a paid part-time job, was completing a certification, doing volunteer work, having sessions with a personal trainer, regularly consuming personal development audiobooks, and was ready to start a 'side hustle' business.

This is the power of challenging the ingredients that make up your current reality. Limiting beliefs are often quiet and disguised as 'truths' we've accepted. But the truth is: **beliefs are not facts – they are choices**. And you can choose again.

In my decades of mentoring allied health professionals, one key pattern I've helped unravel is the projection of *unconscious bias*. These biases are often formed from the professional's own belief systems, and unless examined, they can distort how we interpret the behaviours or experiences of the children and families we support.

I recall a conversation with a thoughtful and well-meaning practitioner who was feeling a little unsettled regarding one of her teenage clients.

'She didn't seem to react appropriately to her new diagnosis,' she said.

'What do you mean?' I asked.

'Well … if I'd just been told I was Autistic, I'd be really upset. But she didn't seem that fazed!'

I explored with her the full picture of the client's medical, developmental, and educational history and current life functioning. What emerged was a thriving young person with strong friendships, academic success, highly supportive parents, a sense of purpose, and a passionate interest in becoming a doctor. Her lack of distress wasn't denial – it was alignment. The practitioner had unknowingly projected her own fear-based narrative about what the label *should* mean.

This highlights an important core truth: **labels never define identity**. They may hold value to inform understanding, but they do not hold the power to shape a person's wholeness – unless we give them that power.

Our beliefs create energetic signatures in the body. When we hold limiting beliefs, we often feel constricted, small, or fearful. When we hold empowering beliefs, our frequency rises, and we feel expanded, open, and capable.

Heart-Powered Self-Leadership

So how can we help children rewrite stories of limitation?

This is done by helping children become aware of their inner dialogue and the stories they're telling themselves and equipping them with the power to lead themselves – not from old programming, but from presence, purpose, and possibility.

Beliefs either bind or liberate. The choice begins with the gift of awareness with things like:

Co-Create Empowering Inner Narratives

- Help children identify a repeating belief with curiosity, not shame: e.g. *What's a story you've been telling yourself when things get hard?*
- Model reframing: e.g. *I used to believe I had to do everything alone. Now I know I can ask for support.*
- Explore identity language: e.g. Instead of *I can't draw*, guide them to try: *I'm learning how to express myself through drawing.*

Use Mirror Phrases

I periodically write phrases on the mirror of my kids' bathroom with my large purple Posca pen. Simple messages can range from 'Smile! It's contagious!' to other affirmations such as:

- 'I am growing every day.'
- 'Mistakes help me learn.'
- 'I trust myself to try again.'
- 'I am kind and brave.'

This build's identity rooted in truth, not comparison.

Flip the Thought

When a child says something limiting ('I can't do it.'), pause and gently ask: 'What would it sound like if we flipped that thought?' (e.g. *I'm learning to do it, one step at a time.)*

We go a lot deeper on this in the chapter: *Wisdom of Wordology.*

'What's the Story?' Journalling (or Drawing)

Create a simple prompt like: *What do you believe about yourself today?* or *What's something you used to believe, but now you know differently?*

Invite reflection through drawing, speaking, or writing.

Lifelong Flourishing

Daily Rituals & Rhythms for Families, Educators & Therapists

'Inner Radio' Conversations

Tune in to what's playing in the mind.

Ask your child: *If your thoughts were a radio station today, what would they be saying?*

Help them name the 'playlist' of beliefs: e.g. 'Worry FM', 'I Can't Rock Radio', or 'Courage Channel'.

Then ask: *Do you want to change the station?*

This builds playful self-awareness and normalises belief-shifting.

Possibility Mapping

Draw a map with your child where each pathway leads to something they *might* try, dream, or do; even if it seems far away. Let them lead the vision. Label the roads with words like 'courage', 'belief', 'asking for help', and 'practice'.

'You're More Than That' Check-Ins

This is gentle redirection when children say something limiting about themselves.

When your child says something like 'I'm not good at this', respond with: 'That's something you're learning; not who you are.'

Then offer a truth-based reflection: What I see is someone who keeps trying and shows up with heart.

Feel It in the Body

Explore what empowering vs. limiting beliefs *feel* like.

Ask: *What happens in your body when you say 'I can't'?*

Then, *What happens when you say 'I'm getting better at this'?*

Let them notice their own energetic truth.

'I Am Becoming …' Dinner Table Ritual

Build in daily affirmations and awareness at mealtime.

Go around the table and each person completes the sentence: *Today, I am becoming someone who …*

Encourage affirming statements like:

… trusts themselves.

… knows it's okay to make mistakes.

… asks for help with confidence.

This keeps evolving beliefs visible, vocal, and valued.

Family 'Reframe & Rejoice' Jar

Keep a decorated jar or box in a shared space.

Invite everyone in the family to write (or draw) something that felt hard or discouraging, along with a 'reframe', a more empowering belief or insight.

For example: *I thought I couldn't speak up in class. But I did. I now believe I'm brave enough to try.*

Read them aloud together once a week. Notice patterns and celebrate small mindset wins.

And just as we support our children, we also get to listen inwardly with compassion when our own beliefs surface. That's part of self-leadership too; learning to meet those parts of us with grace, rewrite the stories, and model what it looks like to grow *with* love, not fear.

When children witness that, we're not just teaching self-leadership. We're living it.

Legacy in Motion

Reflect. Integrate. Empower.

Here's what you now know to be true:

Our children don't need to inherit our outdated patterns. They can inherit our *liberation*.

So let's live it with them.

Let's walk beside them as they explore who they are and what they believe to be true – not just about themselves, but about life, love, and what's possible.

When we meet limiting beliefs with compassion and curiosity, we unlock a whole new kind of freedom. And from that freedom, the empowered human emerges; not defined by what they've been told but led by who they choose to become.

So, from here, we go deeper into that world … into the power and energy of our words; and how language can either limit or liberate our minds, bodies, and spirits.

Journal Prompts

- *What belief about myself or the world am I ready to question?*
- *How different would my life look, sound, and feel if I liberated that belief?*
- *Where in my life am I still operating from an old story that no longer feels true?*
- *What is a current limiting belief I have witnessed in my child (or a child I work with).*

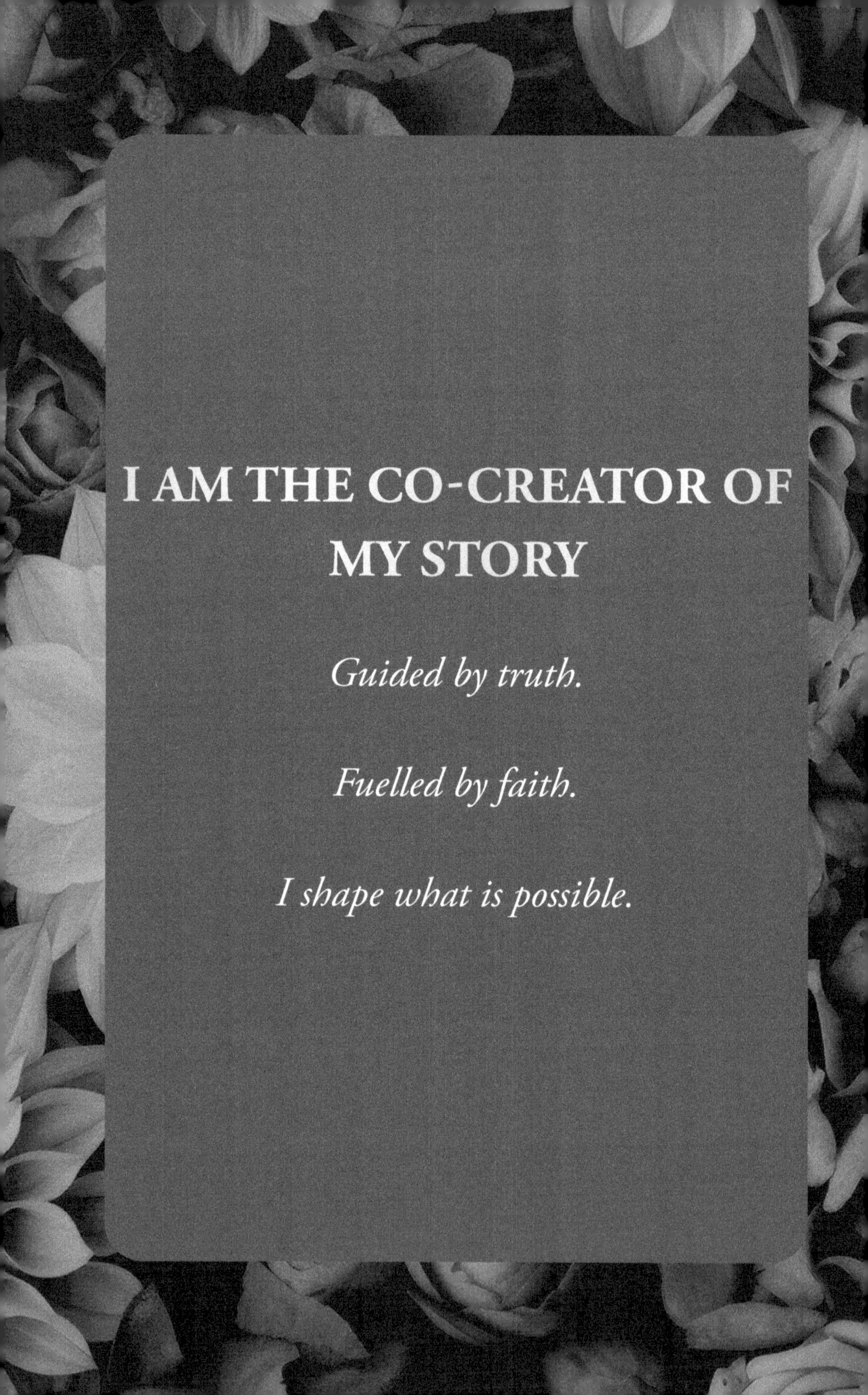

I AM THE CO-CREATOR OF MY STORY

Guided by truth.

Fuelled by faith.

I shape what is possible.

WISDOM OF WORDOLOGY

Let Language Liberate the Mind, Body, and Spirit

What if our words hold the power to shift energy, shape reality, and tune our children – and ourselves – into aligned truth?

One of my neurodivergent young adult clients entered her session flustered.

'I feel anxious,' she said as she stepped into the room.

'Okay … about?' I asked gently.

'About everything!' She threw her arms in the air before placing her hands on her head.

'That's a lot,' I replied, offering a pause. 'What if I gave you a magic wand; what would you change right now?'

'I'd feel less anxious about an outing I have coming up,' she announced.

'Okay … and what would you like to be feeling?' I responded.

She paused, in thought. 'Less anxious. I just don't want to feel anxious.'

Her body language was tight, and I could almost hear her thoughts looping those words. To help her connect the dots, I gestured towards the small Coca-Cola bottle she'd brought in.

'You chose that Coca-Cola drink today, right?' I asked.

She nodded.

'Okay, imagine me going into a café wanting cola, and they ask me, "What can I get you?", and in response I say, "Hi, I don't want orange juice …!"

'They wouldn't know what to get me!' I continued.

'They may ask again, "Sorry, what can I get for you today?" And I respond, "I don't want lemonade …!"'

She smiled before saying, 'They'll just stare at you.'

'Exactly,' I said. 'Until I say "I want Coca-Cola", I'll keep getting nowhere.'

She let out a laugh, and then softened, as the 'dots connected'.

'Okay,' she said, **'I want to feel calm. I want to feel safe.'**

As a final check-in, I asked, 'So are you feeling calm and safe?'

'Yes, I am feeling calm and safe,' she said as her body relaxed and her presence in the now felt palpable.

That moment was both a beautiful and powerful reminder: that our words are not just expressions; they are declarations of energy. They are how we align with what we truly desire … or stay stuck in what we fear.

Whether it's a parent, a therapist, a teacher, or a child; when we become aware of our word choices, we unlock a powerful pathway of liberation for the mind, body, and soul.

And here's the thing … it actually starts *before* the words even leave our mouth.

Our thoughts carry energy. They're electric in nature, literally. Brain science shows us that thoughts generate electrical signals in the body. They create ripple effects that shape how we feel, how we show up, and what we believe is possible.

Every thought sends a signal. When we repeat the same thought again and again, especially one charged with strong emotion, we're wiring it into our system. That means we're not just thinking a thought … we're building a belief. We're shaping our experience of life from the inside out.

So when we speak, we're not just saying words, we're sending out frequencies. Which is why becoming intentional with our words is such a powerful practice. When we choose words aligned with truth, compassion, and possibility, we begin to raise the energetic tone of our world … one sentence at a time.

Often what many don't realise is the incredible amount of information the words that we share actually mirror. They reflect our beliefs, our values, our nervous system state, and our inner world.

The *Wisdom of Wordology* has been one of my favourite masterclasses to teach; and powerful way to help people within my 1:1 intuitive life coaching format.

Why?

Because no matter what area of life is being navigated as a challenge; learning how to shift the energy of your communication and 'uplevel' its frequency is an absolute essential ingredient. It's also a key contributor to lifelong flourishing and nourishing your relationship with self and others.

It's important for me to emphasise, the words we speak aren't just sounds; they are *felt frequencies*. Every word carries vibration with an immediate effect. When children become attuned to this, they realise that words are not just how we describe the world around or within us … they're *how we create it*.

Wordology isn't about having a big vocabulary (although it does help immensely) – it's about becoming aware of the energy our words hold; honouring them as tools of transformation, as well as a fundamental support in our emotional mastery (we will get to that later).

At its core, Wordology is about helping children build a healthy, strong relationship with themselves, through the words they think, speak, and embody.

I remember the day my son came home from school; he was around seven years old.

'Mum,' he said, 'Jack told me today I was his best friend.'

'That's lovely,' I replied.

'But I told him that wasn't good,' he continued.

'Oh? Okay … why's that?' I asked, curious.

'Well,' he said, 'he told me *you're* my best friend, and so is Luca, and Billy, and Nate, and Sam …'

I nodded, waiting.

He added, 'When I asked if he had any other best friends, he said no.'

And then, with utter conviction, he declared:

'So I told him – "Jack, that's not good! You have to be your own best friend first!"'

I love this example for many reasons – one of them being how clearly it shows that children know truth when they're connected to it. When that connection is alive, they can access it and express it with clarity, confidence, and heart.

Whether in coaching, energy healing, or speech therapy, I've witnessed this truth time and again: The energy behind our words shifts everything, and when we become aware of our word choices, and how we speak to ourselves, to others, and through our intentions, we unlock a liberating pathway for the mind, body, and soul.

Heart-Powered Self-Leadership

So how can we help children embrace the Wisdom of Wordology?

The truth is kids don't need lectures about 'speaking nicely' or long lessons in grammar to master communication.

What they really need … is embodiment.

When we model conscious communication, rooted in self-awareness and energy integrity, children naturally rise into it with us. It's not about sounding smart. It's about being attuned to how words feel in the body and recognising their power to create or constrict.

The tools and rituals to follow are invitations to live, to play with, and to explore together. And when practised with consistency and love, they become anchors for clarity, connection, and expression that is both conscious and liberating.

Ground in Word Awareness

Invite children to notice not just *what* a word means, but *how* it feels.

- *Does that word feel heavy or light in your body?*
- *Does that word sound warm or cold to your heart?*
- *Let's swap the word and see which one feels best.*

This helps kids grow their emotional vocabulary while developing a subtle, powerful skill: energetic discernment.

Flip It Fun – From What's Always & Never … to What's Really True

This one is a classic, in homes and in many of the therapy and coaching sessions I've facilitated over the years.

Children often speak in absolutes when they're emotionally charged.

'He always sits in the front seat!'

'I never get a turn!'

'I always spell things wrong!'

'No one ever listens to me!'

Sound familiar?

In these moments, *Flip It Fun* becomes a gentle, playful way to return to truth.

When a child says, 'He *always* gets to sit in the front', you might respond with a sequence such as:

'Always, huh? Has there ever been a time you've sat there?'

(They pause … think … then nod slowly.)

'Ah, so it's happened before?'

'Sounds like what's true is … you really want a turn today.'

This isn't about 'correcting' language; it's about guiding children to feel the difference between a *reaction* and a *real need.* Between a *default narrative* and an *empowered truth.*

I often ask my own kids: 'What's really true?'

It's not about dismissing how they feel; it's about helping them find the power that lives beneath the big words.

This simple reframe cultivates:

- Self-awareness (*What am I really trying to say?*)
- Emotional honesty (*What am I feeling and needing?*)
- Respectful communication (*How can I express myself without blame?*)

And most importantly, it brings them back into relationship with their inner voice … one that doesn't need to shout or exaggerate to be heard.

Discover the Roots of Power Words

Discovering the roots of words is so incredibly fascinating, and helping children see that words are *alive*, that they have origin, story, and energy, is also a lot of fun. This not only builds vocabulary; it builds reverence.

Here's some to start with:

- Did you know the word *courage* comes from the Latin word *cor*? It means 'heart'. So, when you're being courageous, you're doing something brave … with an open heart.
- The word *respect* comes from Latin too: *respiciō*, which means 'to look again'. It's like saying: I'm willing to see you more clearly; to look again with kindness.
- *Health* is connected to the word *whole*. When we say we want to be healthy, we're really saying: I want to feel whole – in my body, in my heart, and in my energy.
- *Decision* comes from the Latin *decidere*, meaning 'to cut off'. So when you make a decision, you're choosing one path and cutting off the others. That's powerful. And it's okay to take your time to choose with clarity.
- *Kindness* comes from the word *kin* – which means family or connection. So being kind is like saying: I see you as part of me.

Model Your Self-Talk Out Loud

Kids absorb more from how we speak to *ourselves* than how we speak to them.

So let them hear how you coach your inner world.

For example:

- *I felt nervous, so I told myself: 'It's okay to be scared and brave at the same time.'*
- *I chose the word gentle today. It helps me speak to myself with softness when I get things wrong.*
- *This is tricky, but I'm telling myself: 'I'll give it a go and ask for help if I need it.'*

This is how children learn to become the compassionate leaders of their own minds.

Use Words to Honour, Not Override

It's easy to fall into 'positive talk' traps … but when we ask kids to rush past their feelings with 'positive sunshine talk', our loving intention to divert them from discomfort, reinforces a bypassing of their truth.

That's called **spiritual bypassing**; it creates disconnection, not growth.

It's okay to feel sad. Sadness has something to say, Let's listen together.

Honouring the *real* by guiding children to **name**, **process**, and **shift** without suppressing, nurtures wholeness; then we can reach for the *reframe.* This helps children build emotional integrity and trust their inner world.

When we support children to choose words that honour how they feel, what they need, and who they are becoming, we offer them one of the most empowering gifts of all: the ability to lead themselves with loving clarity.

And that is the *Wisdom of Wordology* in motion.

Lifelong Flourishing

Daily Rituals & Rhythms for Families, Educators & Therapists

A powerful place to start for caregivers and professionals is by becoming aware of whether your communication is rooted in a place of fear or a place of faith and possibility.

I have popped some common phrases together with conscious ways to reframe them. Even saying them aloud yourself and tuning in to how it feels differently in your body is quite powerful.

Reframing Everyday Language: From Fear-Based to Conscious Communication

Fear-Based Phrase	Conscious Reframe	Energetic Shift
Don't mess it up.	Take your time and focus.	Anxiety › Trust
I hope I don't forget.	I am remembering more and more each day.	Doubt › Self-belief
Just don't get sick.	We're choosing health and wellness.	Fear › Empowered wellbeing
I don't want to be late.	Let's be on time together.	Stress › Presence
Try not to cry.	It's okay to feel. I'm here.	Suppression › Safety
I can't afford that.	We're prioritising money differently right now.	Scarcity › Possibility & Choice
Don't embarrass yourself.	Let's show up as our best selves.	Shame › Self-respect
This always goes wrong.	We're learning how to make this work.	Defeat › Growth mindset
I just want them to behave.	I value calm and cooperation.	Control › Collaboration
I'm so tired of this.	Let's reset and move forward.	Resistance › Renewal
Don't talk back.	Use your voice with kindness.	Suppression › Respectful expression
I don't have time.	Let's make space for what matters.	Lack › Spaciousness & Choice
I'm worried they'll fail.	I believe in your success.	Projection › Empowerment
Please don't make a scene.	Let's stay grounded and graceful.	Fear of judgment › Dignity

Some additional ways include:

Word of the Day: Choose one high-frequency word to explore, draw, and use in conversation.

Flip-It Journal: Help children write out tough words and then choose one empowering alternative.

Emotion Jar: Create a jar of feeling words; pull one out and act it, draw it, or match it with music.

Word Collage: Collect empowering words from books, printouts, or magazines to build a collage of 'words I want to live by'.

Affirmation Art: Let children create posters with affirming phrases they choose for themselves.

These tools and rituals are for us to practise, have a little fun with, *and* to consciously use words in service of clarity, connection, and aligned expression.

Legacy in Motion

Reflect. Integrate. Empower.

Our words are energetic invitations, which can uplift, soothe, liberate, or limit.

As you reflect on this chapter, remember that the Wisdom of Wordology begins within (as per *Heart Sparkle Communication*). It begins with you tuning into your inner dialogue and choosing to speak life over yourself and those in your care.

Whether you're guiding a child through emotional regulation, rewriting a limiting belief of your own, or simply wanting to deepen connection, this chapter calls you to become more intimate with the language you choose.

Speak from the soul. Listen with your heart. Shape your words like seeds … and watch what grows.

In choosing language that liberates, we shape how empowered humans learn to relate; to themselves, to others, and to the world around them.

And yes, that includes their relationship with money.

So now, we open into a new conversation – one where money becomes less about stress or status ... and more about self-leadership, soul-aligned service, and energetic flow.

Journal Prompts

- *What words or phrases do I use that might carry old or limiting energy?*
- *Where could we bring more intention into our home's everyday vocabulary?*
- *How might I speak more intentionally to myself; especially during moments of self-doubt or challenge?*
- *What is one word I want to infuse more consciously into my daily life? How can I embody its frequency?*

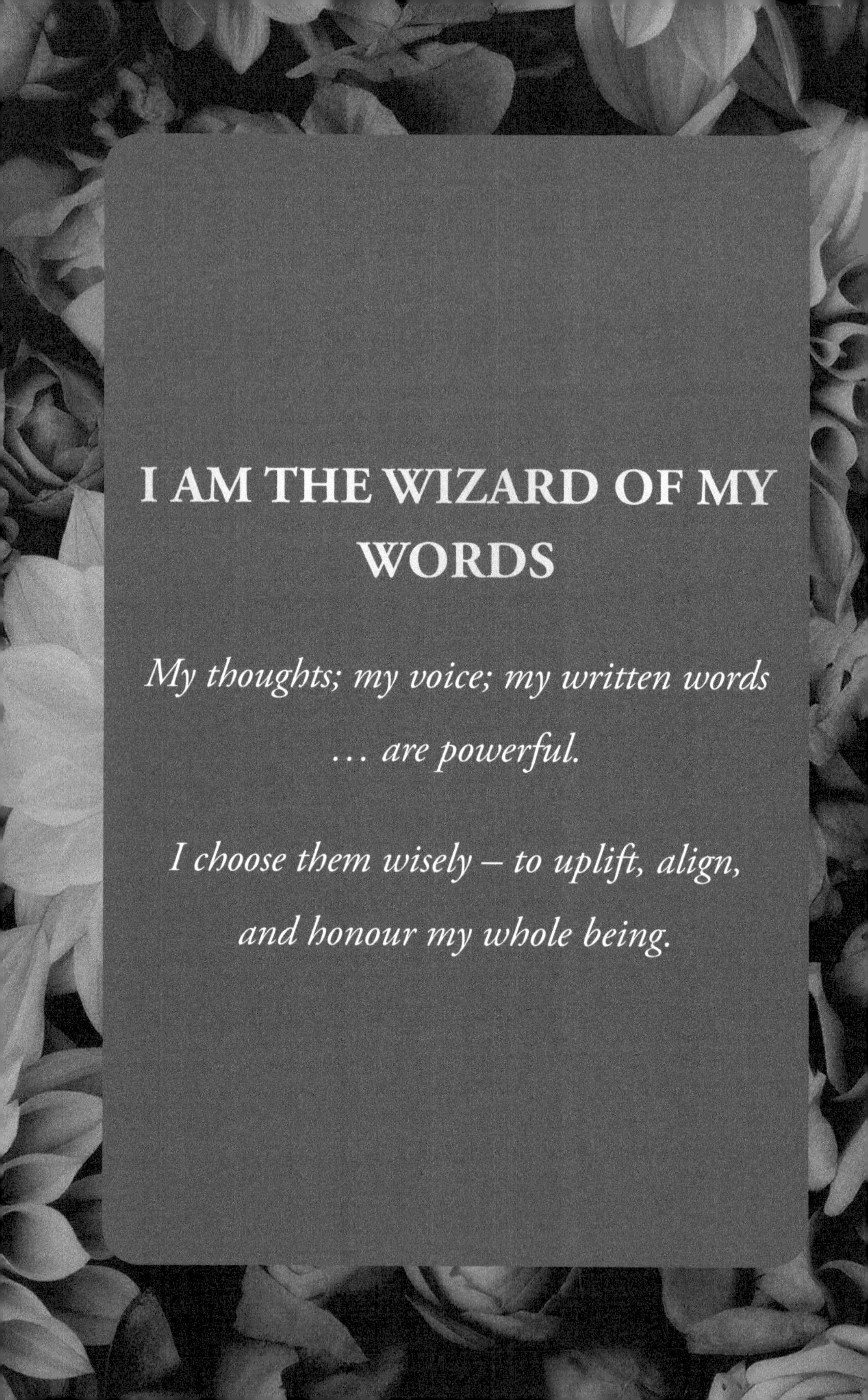
I AM THE WIZARD OF MY WORDS
My thoughts; my voice; my written words
… are powerful.
I choose them wisely – to uplift, align,
and honour my whole being.

THE MAGNIFICENCE OF MONEY

Foster a Purified Partnership

What if you embraced money as sacred circulation, not a cycle of survival.

Money.

Is one chapter really enough? For the purposes of this book, my answer is yes … although, maybe one day I will write it as a book on its own. For now, with reverence and honesty, it's time to adopt a willingness to reflect deeply on how you relate to money as an energy, a teacher, and a partner in your life.

There's been a gradual (but growing) collective shift around money; how we understand it, how we speak about it, how we manage and circulate it, and most importantly, how we relate to it. This chapter is an invitation to ask yourself …

What kind of relationship with money am I modelling, for myself and my children?

Because whether we realise it or not, we are shaping our children's financial frequency with every word, every action, and every belief absorbed through the atmosphere of our homes.

I grew up in a home of hardworking parents, both of whom had migrated to Australia with no English when they arrived. They gave their all to create a life of opportunity for their four children; a life they could only dream of when they were young.

When I began working at 14, I loved the freedom that came with earning money. It gave me choice: travel, connection, independence, and adventure.

But money took on a different form when I married. Roles shifted, responsibilities morphed. And when that chapter (of marriage) ended, and I stepped into a new season – solo, with three children – my relationship with money needed to be completely reimagined.

I vividly remember saying to a money coach in our first session, 'My money muscles have undergone financial dystrophy. I was operating at "manual wheelchair status", feeling dependent and disempowered. I need to relearn how to "stand" and how to "walk".'

It was raw and real. But the deeper truth was, I wasn't just learning how to *manage* money. I was being invited to *rebuild a sacred partnership* with it. To move from fear to flourishing; to alchemise old stories into new pathways of trust.

So, I did the work. I read. I took courses. I sought out mentors.

Most importantly, I surrounded myself with people – online and offline – who *embodied* abundance, not just financially, but energetically, spiritually, and emotionally.

Here are some of the most powerful recalibrations I came to know:

Money is energy. It is neutral. It is not inherently good or bad; it simply mirrors the meaning and frequency we assign to it. When we unknowingly put money on a pedestal and attach our worth to it, we disempower ourselves. The invitation is to reclaim that power, to remember that *we are the source.*

I love the analogy shared by the great Ken Honda …

Celebrate money as you would a dear friend. When it arrives, greet it with joy and gratitude. And when it's time to release it, when you circulate it, let it go with love and appreciation.

Say goodbye to it like you would to a friend who's welcome back anytime … preferably with more friends!

Where your attention goes, energy flows. If you focus on lack, you will feel more lack. But when you choose to notice abundance – in the leaves on the trees, the blades of grass, the synchronicities in your day – you attune your awareness to the natural state of plenty.

And here's the most beautiful truth:

You are abundance. You are living in a physical body of abundance, sustained by an infinite life force. You are not separate from abundance; you are one with it.

Faithful action is a practice. Money moves where trust lives. We are invited to act not from fear or pressure, but from faith. To give with presence. To receive with grace. And to trust the dynamic dance between the two.

The moments in life that split us wide open often contain the golden lessons. I interviewed the inspirational Julia Scott, Money Mentor and founder of Love Luck Wealth, who lived one of those moments through the unravelling of a life she once considered secure. She described herself as someone who had done everything by the book.

'I was the kind of person who just followed the rules. I was a good girl … and then divorce came, and my whole world just fell apart.'

Suddenly navigating single motherhood, financial devastation, and the collapse of her former identity, Julia found herself in unknown territory.

'I couldn't even afford to put petrol in the car. People were like, "Why don't you just go back to work?" But I had two young children, no support, no childcare; and my mindset was just totally dishevelled.'

What shifted everything wasn't a bank loan or a business plan. It was a beam of light.

'It was like divine intervention. A ray of sunshine came through the window of a bookshop and landed on a book about Feng Shui. That started it all.'

That single moment sparked an awakening: everything is energy.

'Your surroundings, your language, your beliefs – they all influence the reality you're experiencing.'

From that awakening, she built something powerful. Not just a business, but a philosophy, a movement, a recalibration of what it means to relate to money from the inside out. Love Luck Wealth was born not just to teach financial strategy, but to support women in transforming *their energetic relationship* with money.

'Anyone can read a finance book. They all say the same thing – spend less than you earn. But that's not the issue. It's the energy and emotion around money that matters.'

She spoke of frequency and field – the unseen forces shaping our lived experiences.

'Everything is energy. We are electrical beings. Your beliefs; they're frequencies. Your thoughts; they're programming your field.'

Our internal signals – our beliefs, our fears, our self-worth – broadcast constantly.

'It's like a Wi-Fi signal. You're either attracting or repelling based on the narrative you're carrying.'

And our children? They're tuned in more than we realise.

'You can't fake it with kids. You can say everything's fine, but if you're vibrating fear – they'll feel that. They have an energetic cord to your thoughts and feelings.'

Julia offered a reframe on one of society's most entrenched money myths; that money must be earned through hard effort.

'We don't want to teach kids they only receive money through effort. Wealthy people don't earn through effort; they earn through ideas, value creation, connection. Let's reward children for creativity and service, not just chores.'

She encouraged parents to dig deep into their own history.

'What were the stories you heard about money growing up? What phrases? What feelings? Because that's what's unconsciously running your show.'

And when it comes to healing those old money patterns, she offered a simple but profound truth:

'Letting go isn't for them. It's for you. You can't create a new financial future while clinging to resentment.'

Julia's personal reinvention became a pathway of wisdom for others. She now supports women in rebuilding not only their finances, but their entire energetic field; so they can model that same empowered frequency for the next generation.

'Money is just a tool. It's not good or bad. It amplifies who you already are.'

Her words remind us that what we model – energetically, emotionally, practically – is what shapes our children's financial blueprint. And that the first step towards raising abundant humans … is choosing to become one ourselves.

It is in the everyday conversations, the small decisions, and the intentional modelling of values where the architecture of an empowered human is quietly constructed.

In this spirit, I spoke with Robyn Saranah; an accomplished leader in finance, innovation, and social impact who's seen how money can either limit or liberate entire generations. She offered a grounded and grace-filled lens through which to view money as a conscious tool for empowerment.

From her earliest memories, Robyn's understanding of money was shaped not by secrecy or scarcity, but by attentiveness and dialogue. Her migrant parents ran a small business, and around their dinner table, financial matters were never off limits. In fact, they were part of everyday life.

'It wasn't just about how smart you were,' her father told her, 'but about what you did with what you earned.'

This became what Robyn now calls a 'dinner table education'. Her mother played an active role in financial decisions. And as children, they absorbed not just facts or tactics, but values, discernment, and a sense of agency.

'Children are always watching,' Robyn said. 'They learn not just from what we say about money, but how we behave with it.'

Yet in wider society, money remains a taboo topic. While we've grown more comfortable discussing mental and physical wellbeing, financial wellbeing is often left behind. Robyn believes this needs to change because money is deeply intertwined with health, stability, and family life.

She invites us to reframe money through two powerful lenses: **empowerment** and **wellness**.

Empowerment is about self-assurance and readiness. *Wellness* is about literacy, behaviour, and accountability.

She shared the story of a woman navigating divorce, raising three children with minimal financial resources. Her transformation didn't begin with a windfall, but with a single choice: to plan intentionally for both the present and the future.

'Empowerment,' Robyn said, 'is a daily practice of reclaiming agency, even in the midst of challenge.'

She also addressed the gendered patterns around money. Women, she observed, often associate money with security and autonomy. Men may bring an identity-driven assertiveness to their financial decisions. These patterns aren't wrong, but they're worth understanding, so we can move beyond them when needed.

Robyn has raised her own daughters through open, practical conversations. Topics like borrowing, debt, savings, and investing were always on the table, starting with part-time jobs and evolving through university and into adulthood. She introduced them early to concepts like superannuation, compound interest, and values-based investing.

She remembers a teacher once advising to allocate 30% to savings, 30% to investing, and 30% to living. While this ratio may need adjusting in today's economic climate, the principle remains:

'Allocate consciously. Start small. Build from there.'

To Robyn, the magnificence of money is not about accumulation, it's about **contribution**. Through giving, sustainability, and community care, she's seen how money becomes a force for **generational healing**.

'The magnificence of money is like a little red car – you don't always notice it until you choose to see it.'

And when asked what she would bring into school curriculums, her answer was clear:

- The psychology of money.
- The basics of budgeting.
- The foundations of savings and investing.

Not just as theory, but as living tools that evolve as we grow. Her parting guidance is simple and powerful: Be honest with yourself. Stay curious and seek guidance. Start early and start small.

Because as Robyn beautifully put it:

'A healthy community is also a financially empowered community.'

And that kind of health begins not with policies, spreadsheets, or systems, but in homes, hearts, and conversations brave enough to reimagine what money could truly mean.

To raise empowered humans is to raise stewards of value, children who grow into adults with confidence, clarity, and a peaceful sense of self-worth. In that light, money becomes not the goal, but the **magnificent instrument**.

Heart-Powered Self-Leadership

How can we help children foster a purified partnership with money?

Connect Spending to Values

Invite children to ask: *Does this reflect what I care about?* Help them match their spending with their values, whether that's saving for something meaningful or donating to a cause they love.

Name Money as a Form of Energy

Teach them to see money not as 'good or bad', but as energy that moves. Ask: *What kind of energy are you sharing when you spend?* This builds conscious intention.

Practise Conscious Giving

Whether it's a coin to a charity box, a small gift to a friend, or kindness in action, let giving be something they choose and feel proud of. Link it back to their inner compass: *Does this feel aligned?*

Use Money Affirmations (with feeling)

Offer child-friendly affirmations like:

Money flows to me when I share my light.
I can grow, give, and receive with balance.

Encourage 'Earning with Meaning'
Rather than reward-for-chore models, create projects where they offer value in exchange (like making bookmarks, baking, or tutoring a sibling). Help them experience the joy of contribution.

Create a 'Gratitude Ledger'
Alongside tracking savings/spending, add a space to note what they're grateful for. This associates money with presence and appreciation, and the energy of abundance and *all needs being met* rather than a focus on what they perceive is missing.

Lifelong Flourishing

Daily Rituals & Rhythms for Families, Educators & Therapists

Get Honest About Your Own Money Story
Children absorb our beliefs more than our words. Take time to reflect: *What messages did I receive about money growing up? Do I feel safe, stressed, or ashamed when money is discussed?* By becoming aware of your own emotional landscape around money, you model transparency and healing. This clears the way for your child to form a more empowered, neutral relationship with money; free from inherited fear or limitation.

Normalise Money Conversations Early
Create a home culture where talking about money is not taboo, but natural. Use age-appropriate language and curiosity-based questions like: *What do you think money is for?* or *How do you feel when you receive or spend money?* When kids can talk about money without fear or

shame, they're more likely to grow into self-aware stewards.

Teach That Money Can Work for You

Help kids understand that money isn't just something you work for, it's something that can be grown, managed, and aligned to serve your vision. Simple metaphors like planting seeds (savings/investments) or building bridges (spending aligned with purpose) make these concepts relatable. Share examples of how wise money choices created freedom/ opportunity in your own life.

Use Everyday Purchases as Teachable Moments

At the store or online, talk out loud: *I'm choosing this because it's lasting and kind to the earth.* Kids learn what you value by what you voice.

Celebrate Non-Material Joy

Regularly ask: *What made you feel rich in love, fun, or peace today?* Reinforce that wealth is multidimensional, not just financial.

Demystify Bills & Budgeting

In age-appropriate ways, show how budgeting works. Invite them into 'family money mindfulness' without stress: *We're saving for something beautiful.*

Encourage Saving & Sharing

Set up three jars: Save, Spend, Share. Use real coins to build tactile understanding and let them choose how to divide birthday or allowance money. From a young age, my kids had money jars, which when filled, they helped count out. Then allocate for *saving*, for *spending* and for *sharing* (community contributions/gifts).

Limit Language of Scarcity
Shift from *We can't afford that* to *That's not our focus right now.* This preserves openness while modelling discernment.

Integrate Conscious Money Themes
Share stories that link money to generosity, problem-solving, or creativity; not greed. Reflect afterward: *What did you notice about how they used money?*

Reflect on Joyful Earning
Let children see adults engaging with purposeful work. Share what you love about your work; not just the stress or obligation. It frames earning as empowering, not exhausting.

Model Aligned Generosity
Show how you give; not to impress, but to uplift. Let them see you pause, feel into a choice, and give with presence. That energy imprints.

Legacy in Motion

Reflect. Integrate. Empower.

Money doesn't just shape bank accounts; it shapes identities, opportunities, and inherited beliefs. When we purify our partnership with money, we don't just heal our own stories, we shift the energetic blueprint passed on to our children.

This isn't about getting it perfect. It's about being intentional.

Every honest conversation …

Every choice to invest in values over fear …

Every moment of receiving with gratitude and giving with love …

It becomes part of the legacy.

May we raise children who see money not as power over, but as power within.

A tool of freedom, and a companion of purpose.

In reimagining our relationship with money, we open a gateway to deeper energetic integrity – where abundance meets intention.

And with that, in the next chapter, we arrive at one of the greatest gifts we can offer our children …

The ability to choose.

Consciously. Courageously.

And to rejoice in their power to decide, direct, and consciously design a life with aligned intention.

Journal Prompts

- *What stories about money did I inherit, and which ones am I ready to rewrite?*
- *How do I want my children to feel when they think about money?*
- *Where in my life can I recirculate money with more trust, joy, or purpose?*
- *What does an empowered, heart-led relationship with money look like for me now?*

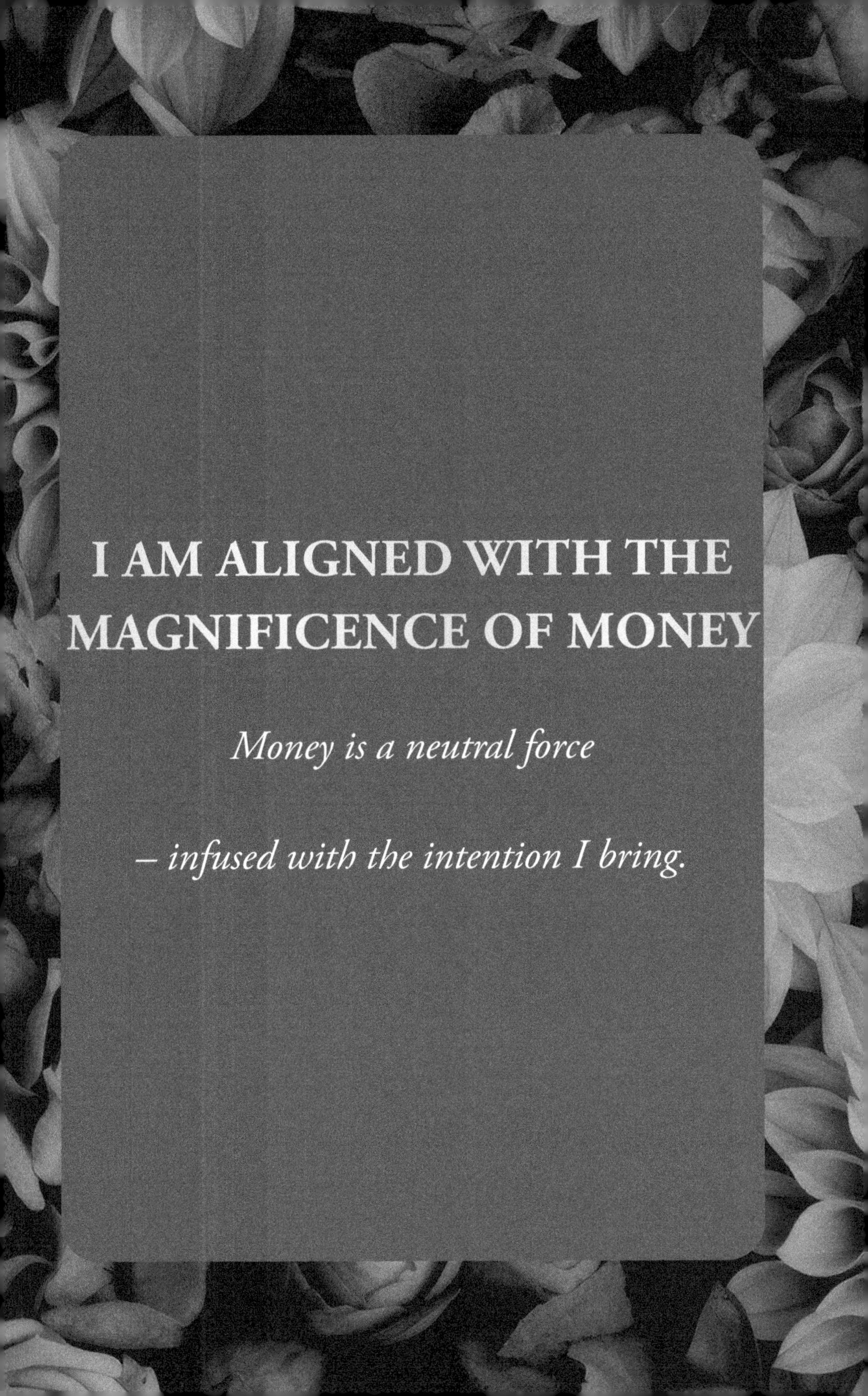
I AM ALIGNED WITH THE MAGNIFICENCE OF MONEY
Money is a neutral force
– infused with the intention I bring.

REJOICE IN CHOICE

The Practice of Intentional Decision-Making

What if how one chooses is more important than what one chooses?

As I finished my lunch and readied to start my afternoon of clinical sessions, I heard the raised voices of my next client (an Autistic young adult) and her mother entering the clinic and sitting in the waiting area.

'But why, Mum? I don't understand?' she exclaimed, her voice sharp and intense towards her mother.

'You can't take that supplement,' her mother replied firmly. 'It has too many side effects that are not good for you.'

'But I want to take it. I'm an adult – I can choose!'

Her mother responded softly, yet with conviction, 'You can, but not when you're making a choice that can harm you.'

The disagreement continued, with frustration and anger building. By the time I walked to the waiting room, my client had 'shut down' when invited into session with me. All she could focus on was the injustice of not having what she wanted. For ten minutes, we remained in the waiting room – she in a mild storm of frustrated distress, me in quiet yet acknowledging presence.

Eventually, she followed me into the clinic room. Unhappy. Still confused. Still angry. Still clinging to her sense of self through the lens of independence.

On entering the room, my response was not to convince, correct, or command. It was to meet her with a frequency of acceptance and love. I offered basic choices: sit on a chair, the floor, stand, lie down … the decision was hers. She chose to sit on the floor. I followed her lead. Then, silently, I began building a tower of wooden blocks; no pressure, no spoken invitation, just presence and rhythm.

There was a gradual and subtle shift from her. A softening.

She slowly joined me, placing blocks one by one while continuing to loop through her confusion, repeating her feelings of injustice, and challenging the authority that was denying her what she believed was her right.

I didn't try to fix her frustration. I acknowledged it. When she told me she was 'pissed off', I mirrored genuine agreement in how she felt … without sugarcoating, without judgment. I offered her choices along the way: what to build next, what other activities we could engage with. Her hands and mind continued to engage rhythmically in the block tower, while her heart began to unwind.

Eventually, she reached a point of clarity; where the emotional charge eased, and her words slowed. Together, we could reflect. She came to an understanding: love and care were the motivations behind the limits set for her. Her agency wasn't being denied; it was being safeguarded.

This story shares something we all feel deeply, at any age: the innate human desire for agency. We want to feel free. We want to feel like we have choices and have meaningful influence over our world. When that sense is threatened, it's no surprise our nervous system pushes back ... sometimes with resistance, sometimes confusion, sometimes anger ... often all three at once!

Take children's meltdowns, for example. I don't view them as acts of defiance. I see them as flare signals, a child's way of expressing 'I feel out of control'. In those moments, it's not misbehaviour we're witnessing, but a dysregulated nervous system overwhelmed by unpredictability. What we're really seeing is a human being trying to reclaim their footing.

Our role in these moments is to stay steady and to reframe. To offer what I call *anchors of agency*. Even the smallest choice – *'Would you like to sit on the floor or the couch?'* – can be enough to shift the energetic landscape.

And it's not just something I've observed and practised through experience; there's research to back this up too. The way we communicate with children *really* matters. Studies have shown that when teachers use directive, one-way language instead of offering choices, it doesn't just affect compliance, it actually shifts how children feel about their own power and sense of autonomy. Their sense of being seen and valued.

So now that we understand the importance of empowered agency, let's dive into the energetics of choice, and how *intention* shifts the frequency of our everyday decisions.

Over the years, I've discovered that weaving intention into the fabric of everyday life transforms even the most ordinary moments into sacred ones. It's less about what we're doing and more about who we are being while we do it.

As I shared earlier; each morning before getting out of bed, I set my intention for *What do I intend to be today?*, letting that one word or few words drop in ... *patient, grateful, joyful, gentle*. That word becomes my frequency anchor, gently guiding my choices and how I show up.

Then, when I step into the shower, I consciously invite in light. I might say something like: *May divine light and love move through me. May I step into this day with clarity and calm.*

Even breakfast holds intention. Before that first bite, I pause and say to myself: *May this food nourish me with high-frequency energy and goodness for the day ahead.*

And every evening, that same shower becomes a space for energetic release. I'll set an intention like: *I lovingly let go of anything that isn't mine. I wash away what no longer serves and reclaim my sovereign energy with grace and gratitude.*

These aren't rituals for the sake of being 'spiritual' … they're grounded, embodied practices that remind me I am a co-creator in my life. They anchor me in presence.

Intention doesn't require grand gestures. It's found in those quiet, everyday moments where presence meets purpose, and where choice becomes an act of love.

And just like with my own rhythm, I do my best to hold space for my children's daily rhythm too. Every morning, as each of them heads off to school – at a time that aligns with their own pace – I offer them a simple ritual: a heartfelt 'I love you', a wish for a great day, with one final reminder … 'Have fun!'

Now, this doesn't mean 'don't take things seriously' or 'mess around'. It's more about inviting in an intention of openness and curiosity. The kind of energy that welcomes surprise, growth, and wonder.

And of course, there are the classic moments in caregiving, you might know the ones ...

'I don't want to watch that movie – it's going to be boring.'

'I don't like Geography – it's boring.'

By now, my kids already know what I'm going to say in response to anything being declared 'boring', I smile and ask, 'What do you think

I'm going to say?'

With a half-smile, they'll beat me to it, articulating my unspoken response: 'Well, if you've decided that … then yes, it probably will be boring!'

We usually share a laugh, but the deeper reminder is there too: **We choose.**

And the energy of intention we bring into a moment shapes how we experience it.

When I reflect on the role of intentional decision-making, in the context of my work helping people with conscious, assertive communication, I always guide them to begin with intention. Before picking up the phone, initiating a conversation, sending an email, or responding to something emotionally charged, I encourage a moment of stillness to ask: *What is my intention?*

Maybe it's to ask for clarification. Maybe it's to have a productive conversation with calm centredness. Maybe it's to hold compassion in a hard conversation. That microsecond of awareness and intentional choice can shift everything because it doesn't position intention as an afterthought, it positions it as the starting point.

And, I would have to say that when I work with life coaching clients, one of the most powerful shifts they make is choosing to live *at cause*, rather than *at effect*. This circles back to the opening chapter of owning our creatorship; as it deeply matters when raising empowered humans.

Living *at cause* means we recognise ourselves as creators of our experience. We own our energy, and model intentionality, in everyday moments. Living *at effect* feels like life is happening *to* us, showing up as blame, reactivity, and powerlessness.

Yes, I have, and you have, moments of slipping into 'effect', but catching yourself and *choosing* to shift back to 'cause' is the frequency reset kids need to witness too. It's more than just a mindset shift, it's energetic in nature. And it's a truth that's been backed not only by lived experience, but by science too.

A while back, I came across the work of Lynne McTaggart, author of *The Intention Experiment* and *The Power of Eight*. I loved learning about her research as it put scientific words to what I'd always *felt* deep in my bones: intention isn't just a nice idea or a hopeful wish. It's a real, measurable force. A kind of living energy that shapes the way we experience reality.

Her experiments, done with teams of scientists across disciplines, showed that when groups of people focused on a shared intention, actual change happened. Plants grew faster. People's bodies healed quicker. Conflict softened. Even water molecules, when photographed, shifted into more coherent patterns.

This is exciting! It's what so many ancient traditions have been saying for centuries: our focused intention carries power. Real, ripple-creating, life-shaping power.

But the part that really spoke volumes to me?

Was that intention is most impactful when it's *shared*. When it's not about controlling the outcome, but about aligning our energy, with clarity, love, and the intention for the highest good.

So … what's this got to do with raising empowered humans?

Everything.

Because when kids grow up in a space where intention is named, felt, and lived out loud, they start to understand that they're not just here to go through the motions. They're here to co-create. To rejoice with choice … and to contribute their energy with purpose.

That really is the essence of true empowerment … the practice of choosing with love and living it forward with intention.

Heart-Powered Self-Leadership

So, how can we help children practise intentional decision-making?

Micro-Intentions for the Moment

Before starting a task (e.g. homework, playing, eating), invite your child to pause and say: *What energy do I want to bring into this?* (e.g. 'Calm', 'Creative', 'Focused', 'Kind', etc.)

Let them choose a word and breathe it in. This activates conscious presence before action.

Feel – Choose – Flow Practice

Help children build emotional fluency and decision-making awareness by using three steps:

1. **Feel:** *What's happening in my body and heart right now?*
2. **Choose:** *What choice can I make that honours how I feel?*
3. **Flow:** *What's one small thing I can do to shift or support myself?*

This is helpful for moments of frustration, disappointment, or hesitation.

The Empowered Language Shift

We've touched on this previously, but it's an important one, so worth reinforcing: Choose language that reflects living 'at cause'.

For example:

- 'I choose to …' instead of 'I have to …'
- 'I can respond with …' instead of 'They made me …'

Invite children to try saying both versions and notice how it feels. Even younger kids enjoy the sense of power this brings!

The Pause Power

Practise building a 'pause habit' before big or small choices.

You might say: *Take a pause before deciding,* or *Check in with your heart first.*

This encourages an intentional check in with their inner compass.

Draw the Decision Map

Invite your child to draw out 2–3 choices visually, including imagined outcomes. Ask:

- *What would this choice feel like tomorrow?*
- *What might happen next?*

This is super helpful in externalising thoughts and seeing them in form; to help with reflective awareness.

Empowerment Mirror

Each day (or week), invite children to complete this sentence while looking in the mirror:

'Today, I choose to show up as __________.'

They can decorate their mirrors with words or drawings. This builds self-image and anchors intention to identity.

Lifelong Flourishing

Daily Rituals & Rhythms for Families, Educators & Therapists

The power of choice and the practice of intentional decision-making is never one-dimensional. It's energetic, emotional, developmental, and deeply spiritual. The way we make choices (and support children in making theirs) reflects our values, our presence, and the frequency we hold.

Here's some ritual and rhythm ideas for you …

Growth Pebbles – Every Choice Teaches Me Something

Use a small bowl or jar where your child places a pebble, shell, or bead each time they reflect on what they *learnt* from a choice (especially those choices they wish they'd made differently).

This proactively guides a growth mindset, rather than being stuck in cycles of regret and shame. Over time, the bowl becomes a visual symbol of self-awareness and growth that honours learning, not perfection.

Energy Check-In – Where Is My Decision Coming From?

It is important to help children tune into the energy behind a choice; so they can lead from clarity. Before or after deciding, invite this simple inner question:

Am I choosing this from love … or from fear, guilt, pressure, or habit? What energy is behind this choice?

You might model this yourself when applicable; for example: *I noticed I was about to say yes … but then realised I was coming from guilt, not love. So, I'm choosing again.*

This process is so important in nurturing inner confidence to lead from truth.

Morning Intention Planting

Begin the day by sharing your intention for the day … your 'to be'. And invite your child to pick one word (e.g. 'kind', 'focused', 'fun'). You can return to it later in the day and reflect on how your intention unfolded … (or not) throughout the day.

'This or That' Empowerment Games

Remember to offer micro choices in the day; to reinforce agency. Narrow choices down to two (binary choice) if your child is in a state of overwhelm (or might become overwhelmed with too much choice).

The Three Doors – Inner Compass Visualisation

You can use simple guided imagery to help children feel into the energy of different choices. You do this by inviting your child to close their eyes and take a few calming breaths, then guide them to imagine they're standing in front of three doors. Behind each one is a different choice they're thinking about. As you guide them to open each door one by one, you can check in about: how their body feels, any emotions that show up, and what feels aligned or off.

Legacy in Motion

Reflect. Integrate. Empower.

Every choice a child makes – what to wear, how to speak, who to trust – is a chance to build their inner compass.

As carers and educators, our role isn't to control every decision, but to model and mirror intentionality: how we pause, reflect, and choose with alignment. This practice strengthens a child's sense of autonomy, discernment, and responsibility … the cornerstones of lifelong confidence and resilience.

When we create environments where choice is honoured, children learn that their voice matters, their feelings are valid, and that their decisions shape their reality. This helps them stand tall in their own sovereignty – honouring the energy behind every choice.

And with that sense of inner authority comes the magic of vision, and the freedom to imagine new paths entirely. So, let's now explore how to help children visualise and manifest futures that feel aligned, expansive, and joyfully theirs.

Journal Prompts

- *What does intentional decision-making mean to me right now?*
- *How does it feel in my body when I make a choice that's truly aligned?*
- *Where in my life am I living 'at effect', and what would shift if I chose to live 'at cause'?*
- *How can I help my child feel safe to learn from their choices?*

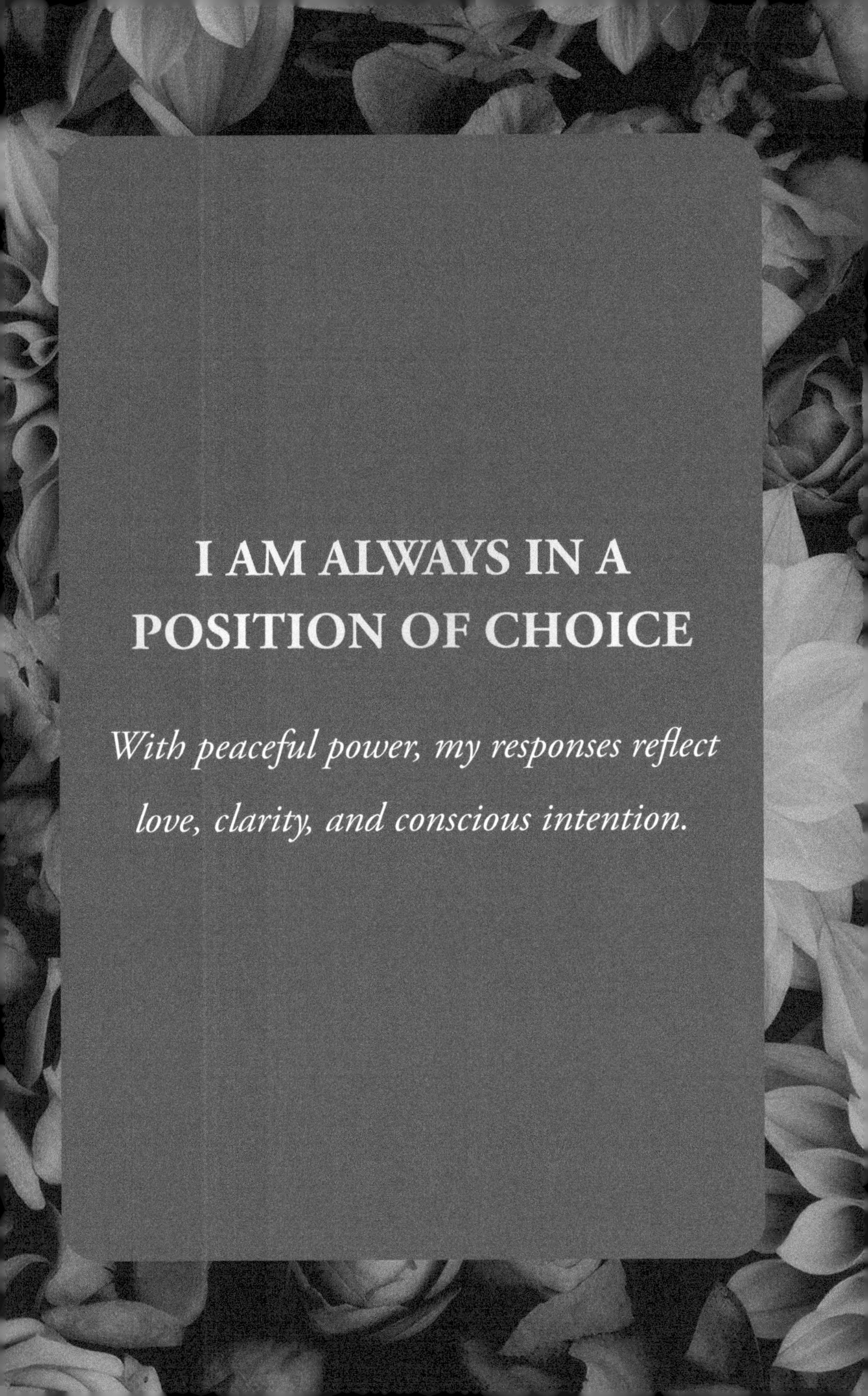
I AM ALWAYS IN A POSITION OF CHOICE
With peaceful power, my responses reflect love, clarity, and conscious intention.

EMPOWER THE PRESENT ... AND FUTURE

Visualise. Imagine. Manifest.

What if our true role isn't to push children ahead … but to meet what's already flourishing within?

I've always known imagination to be a sacred bridge. And when held with intention, it becomes a mirror, a compass, and a quiet revolution.

I began journalling from seven years of age. Every day. Pencil to page, heart to hand. It was never something I was told to do; it just felt like a natural rhythm for me.

Well into adulthood, I stumbled across one of those early journals while unpacking and sorting clothes after returning from overseas work and six months of travel … mostly in Italy.

Curious, I flipped through the pages and paused in disbelief. There, in my small, childhood printed handwriting, I'd written: *One day I see myself living and working overseas … and travelling for six months in Italy.*

I was stunned. Not because it didn't sound like me; but because I had no memory of writing it. Yet here I was, years later, having brought that exact vision into form without even consciously realising it. I hadn't obsessed over it or clung to it. I had simply written it with quiet certainty … and let life unfold.

That's the magic of visioning. We plant seeds, sometimes long before we see the garden grow. And when we're not forcing the outcome – just trusting, imagining, being – it's often then that the most aligned realities take shape.

I've long used guided imagery and visualisation as both a healing tool and a channel for creativity. In stillness, in nature, and in the automaticity of everyday routines (driving, showering, washing dishes, etc.), I often receive my most potent downloads; not as a list of instructions, but as vivid imagery.

That's how my children's books came to life. I *saw* the stories unfold like a film in my mind's eye, then 'heard' the rhythm of the rhyming words accompanying the stories … Within hours, my manuscripts would be refined.

Similarly, while working on an animation script, I witnessed the storyline emerge like a moving narrative; I didn't force it, I followed it. It is a reverent process; reinforcing that when we quiet the chatter of our mind enough, we don't just *think* new things, we *receive* and *experience* them.

Visualisation isn't just a tool to manifest a holiday or a dream job. It's a powerful evidence-based technique I've used with people of all ages: from helping children strengthen their reading comprehension to guiding Autistic adults in breaking through anxiety and fear around everyday activities – things many of us take for granted.

I remember working with a young Autistic woman in her late twenties. Her anxiety around interacting with people in the community was so challenging that she couldn't enter a store alone, let alone make a purchase. Her mother had done all her shopping for her for almost thirty years. When she began working with me, one of her goals was to go into a shop to buy her own clothes and to use spoken words to respond to any sales assistants who approached her. And so, guided visualisation became our tool each session; simulating the experience using all of her senses, we recreated the scene …

She began by imagining herself walking towards the store of her choice in the shopping centre she might realistically visit. She pictured the logo above the entrance, the specific colours, the familiar font. She tuned into the ambient sounds: the murmur of other shoppers, the shuffle of footsteps on tiled floors, the distant hum of music from neighbouring shops. She visualised herself stepping inside the store, seeing the racks of clothing, noticing the retail assistants. She imagined one of them smiling and greeting her and heard herself respond. She felt the touch of garments brushing her fingers as she browsed before selecting an item and entering the change room to try it on.

It wasn't easy at first. The imagery brought up doubt. Discomfort. But with each session, she stayed with it; anchoring into her breath, into her body, into the possibility of a different outcome. Her nervous system began to slowly shift; its baseline of calm expanding. What once felt impossible began to feel ... available.

And one day, during a session, she came in glowing. 'Guess what?' she beamed. 'On the weekend … I went into a clothes store. By myself. For the first time ever. And I bought something. For me!!!'

I almost cried; my heart was bursting with so much emotion.

That moment wasn't just about buying clothes. It was a reclamation. A quiet revolution of self-leadership and possibility. The practice of visioning helped her step into a world she had previously imagined only from the outside; and choosing to bring it into form – one thought, one step, one sacred breath at a time – was an incredible and momentous breakthrough.

These stories remind me that visualisation, imagination, and manifestation are not about chasing what we lack. Too often, manifesting gets tangled in the idea of getting more, achieving faster, or ticking boxes on vision boards. But in truth, manifesting isn't about lack. It's not about fixing or filling in gaps. It's about alignment and tuning into what's already encoded within us, just waiting to be remembered and expressed.

Children are born with imagination already activated. Watch any child play, and you'll see visioning in motion. They're not manifesting Ferraris or designer shoes; they're becoming astronauts, lion tamers, superheroes, healers, inventors. In those moments, they *are* the vision. They aren't visualising their future, they're inhabiting it.

So how do we keep that frequency alive as they grow?

We start by reimagining what manifesting really means. So let's redefine the myth of manifestation from *attainment* … to that of *alignment.*

When children hear the word 'manifest', they shouldn't feel pressure to prove or perform. Instead, it can become a sacred invitation:

What wants to move through you?

What feeling, what contribution, what joy is already in your field, waiting to be brought into form?

In short, there is no projecting far ahead or obsessing over outcomes. It's about aligning with your soul's current frequency … so ultimately, it's about embodied presence.

To be clear … manifesting isn't about getting what we want. It's about becoming what we already are.

This shifts the energy completely from chasing to co-creating, and this liberates children (and us!) from the trap of conditional happiness. It anchors in the knowing that they aren't incomplete. They're unfolding.

So, visualisation … imagination is not just child's play; it's soul tech – for all of us!

When a child closes their eyes and sees and feels a future, they're not escaping. They're remembering. Neuroscience backs this, confirming visualisation activates many of the same regions in the brain as actual doing.

But even more powerful than what's happening *neurologically* is what's occurring energetically. Children who imagine with emotion, who see and *feel* their visions, are entraining their field to those frequencies. And they do this naturally when we don't over-script it.

Let's not teach children to visualise a perfect house, a big job title, or someone else's dream. Let's teach them to feel what joy feels like in their chest. To imagine helping someone and feeling the ripple. To trust that vision lives inside them, not outside.

So, what's the most powerful energy field for manifesting? The frequency field of *now*.

We create from deep, rooted presence. We don't create from frantic future-jumping.

When a child learns to ground themselves – to breathe, to observe their senses, to pause before wishing – they begin to understand that their power doesn't come from what they want. It comes from who they *are*, right here.

Every time we help a child return to breath before setting a goal, or pause to reflect on what really matters, we're training their inner compass to seek coherence, rather than chaos. And this creates a natural essence of manifesting … from a place of both alignment and peace.

Heart-Powered Self Leadership

So how can we help children empower their present and their future?

Here are some ways we can support soul aligned manifestation:

'I Remember' Boards

Move beyond the typical vision board focused on material desires. These boards can be a collage of soul memories; what your child *loves*, what lights them up, what they're curious about, and who they feel they're becoming. Include images, symbols, colours, and textures that feel meaningful to *them*. The goal isn't to manifest from lack, but to *remember* what already lives within.

Guided Imagery

Use gentle meditations or storytelling to guide children inward, into their heart's desires and felt sense of purpose. For example, instead of asking *What do you want to be when you grow up?*, you might ask: *What kind of world do you dream of living in?*, or *What does your heart feel excited to share?* Let their inner landscapes shape the story.

Intention Stones or Jars

Invite your child to write, draw, or dictate intentions onto small pieces of paper. These can be stored in a decorated jar or tucked beneath intention stones; each one symbolising something meaningful to them. Revisit the jar weekly or monthly to reflect, update, or simply *hold presence* with what's unfolding, free from pressure or performance.

Affirmation Anchors

Affirmations are like internal tuning forks. Choose statements that reflect their essence, not just their goals. For example, *I am curious,*

I listen to my heart, or *I bring kindness wherever I go*. Energetically, to empower the intent of an affirmation, being in the 'feeling tone' is also important. So you might speak and *feel* them during morning routines, write them on mirrors, or create affirmation cards together.

Inspired Action Lists

Rather than to-do lists, co-create 'Inspired Action' lists based on what lights them up. These can include things they *feel* ready to try, like 'bake something new', 'learn about space', or 'help someone smile today'. It shifts the focus from achievement to *alignment with joy*.

'Future Letters' to Self

This activity I have also recommended in another chapter, as it resonates on so many levels. This is when you invite your child to write a letter to their future self, dated one or five years from now. They can describe what they hope life *feels* like, what they're learning, and what makes them feel proud.

Seal it and store it somewhere special. It plants seeds gently, without rushing their growth. I do this together with my kids on New Year's Eve, with our letters to be opened in the period between Christmas and the following New Year.

Lifelong Flourishing

Daily Rituals & Rhythms for Families, Educators & Therapists

Vision Pebbles

Invite children to choose a small pebble or crystal and hold it while speaking a dream or wish aloud. They can carry it in their pocket as a physical reminder of what they're calling in. This grounds manifestation in tangible presence.

'One Day ...' Dinner Conversations

During family meals, take turns finishing the sentence: 'One day, I imagine ...' Let imaginations soar without interruption or correction. And if you want to take it a step further, you can write these down on a 'Family Dream Scroll' that you revisit and add to as you feel called.

Dream Drawing Time

Set aside quiet time where children draw something they'd love to experience. This might be a place, an invention, a book they want to write, or how they want to help others. You might choose to display these as reminders of their inner vision.

Manifestation Walks

Take walks together and speak dreams into the air. Have children speak in the present tense: *I love being a marine biologist!* or *It feels amazing writing my own comic series.* Help kids know that expressing out aloud is an energetic commitment.

Scripting the Day Ahead

Before sleep or at breakfast, co-create a 'script' for the day. What kind of energy do they plan to bring? What feeling do they intend to have at the end of the day? This helps foster more conscious intentionality.

Imagining with the Senses

Encourage children to describe their visions/dreams using all five senses. This deepens embodiment and connection with their envisaged desire. For example, *What does your dream house smell like? What sounds do you hear when you're living that dream?*

Voice of the Future

Have children create a short voice recording of their future self, talking about the life they're living. Replay it every few months. This can be humorous, sincere, or a mix; what matters is resonance and joy.

Legacy in Motion

Reflect. Integrate. Empower.

We model what we manifest.

When we speak from trust rather than control …

When we delight in the now rather than fixate on the next thing …

When we show children that soul joy isn't something earned; it's something remembered …

We invite them into a deeper way of creating.

You don't need to teach your child the law of attraction. You do need to facilitate within them the law of awareness.

Invite conversations that tune in, rather than tune out. Ask them:

- *What does your heart love to imagine?*
- *What would it feel like to bring that alive in your own way?*
- *Who would benefit from what you dream?*

Let them feel the truth of this. For when children know how to tune into their inner world, feel their dreams in their body, and take even the tiniest step towards them with trust and love, they become creators of futures that serve not only themselves, but the world.

Journal Prompts

- *When have I experienced the power of imagining something before it came to life?*
- *How can I make space for stillness, so new ideas and images can emerge through me?*
- *What does it feel like in my body when I trust in the unseen becoming real?*
- *In what ways can I support a child to visualise their own dreams and trust their timing?*

We now bring Section Two to a close.

You've just received your second golden key – *The Frequency of Freedom.*

A powerful resonance that invites living with intention, clarity, and multilayered abundance.

So now, we pause to integrate … as I invite you to enter the heart of it all

– the *Five Golden Frequencies of Self-Leadership*.

A special space in this book, offering timeless truths to carry forward … because empowered humans aren't built by chance.

They're tuned.

Refined.

Energised.

And remembered.

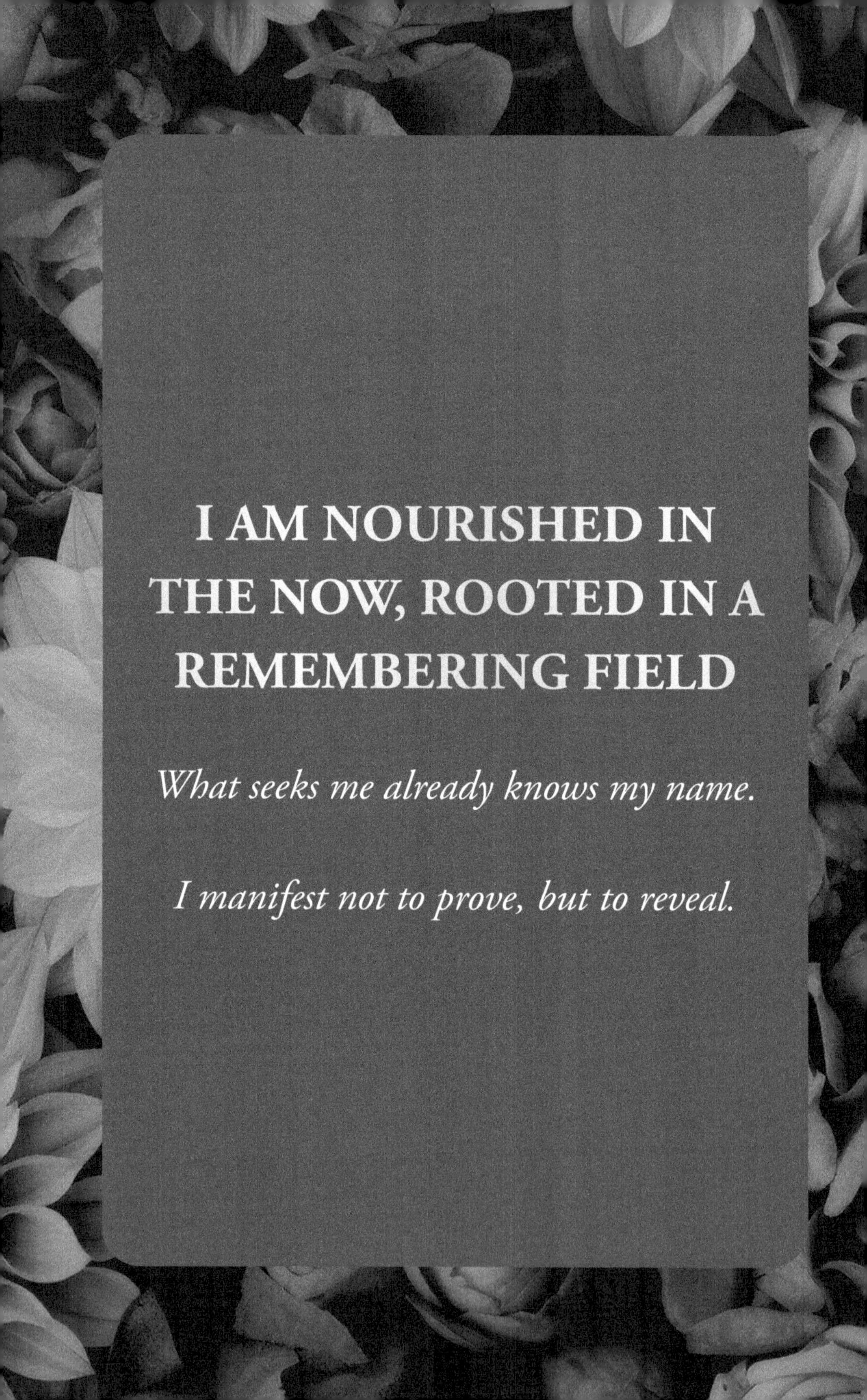
I AM NOURISHED IN THE NOW, ROOTED IN A REMEMBERING FIELD
What seeks me already knows my name.
I manifest not to prove, but to reveal.

THE 5 GOLDEN
FREQUENCIES
OF SELF-
LEADERSHIP

#1
GOLDEN FREQUENCY OF SELF-LEADERSHIP

Radical Love... unlocks Lifelong Flourishing

Let's talk about love – real love.

Not the kind that's been packaged, twisted, or watered down over time. I'm talking about the kind of love that liberates. That heals. That remembers. That roots us in something deeper than approval or praise.

For many of us, love was first experienced in ways wrapped in expectation.

I know I grew up believing that unconditional love meant tolerating everything … even what didn't feel right. I confused love with sacrifice, silence, and shapeshifting. I thought to be good was to please. To belong was to mould myself.

And I know I'm not alone in that.

Because here's the quiet truth: Many of us were raised on *conditional* love. Not because our parents didn't love us, but because they were shaped by the same inherited patterns. Patterns born of survival, not wholeness.

As children, we learn fast. We feel out what earns affection, what invites praise, what keeps us safe.

So we adapt. We perform. We please. And we carry those habits into adulthood, wearing masks and wondering why we still feel unseen.

But **Radical Love**?

It doesn't ask us to become. It invites us to *remember.*

And that changes everything.

Radical love begins with safety; not the kind created by control or correction, but the deep, energetic safety of being met without condition.

And no, fear isn't the opposite of love. Judgment is.

Judgment of self. Of others. Of all the ways we think we're not enough yet. Every time we shrink, compare, or strive from shame, we dilute love's frequency.

But something beautiful happens when we stop striving and start softening.

When we stop fixing and start listening. When we accept what is, even before it's 'healed'. That's when true transformation begins because we don't demand change, we allow it to be organic, gentle, and true.

I've seen this truth come alive again and again, especially in my work with children who had no or limited spoken language, whose systems were surviving in an environment that couldn't fully hear or feel them.

And over time, I realised something vital …

The most sacred work I'd ever done, and was doing, wasn't necessarily about the specifics of what I was teaching, but more about being **a safe, steady, loving field of non-judgmental presence.**

When we become that field – when our *being* says, 'You're loved exactly as you are' – children respond. *Everyone* responds.

They soften. They open. They communicate (in their own unique way).

Because at its essence, **love is the current**. Not a prize, nor a transaction; a *presence* that flows where it's welcomed.

When we parent from this space, we raise children who no longer hustle for their worth.

They begin to trust themselves.

Their nervous systems relax.

Their capacity to connect, lead, and grow is no longer tied to performance, but to the felt knowing that they are already whole.

Love is their home, not their finish line.

The Golden Invitation

Radical Love invites us to:

Stop outsourcing our worth.

Stop waiting to be 'ready'.

Begin loving from *now*.

When children feel loved from this deep, unwavering place, they flourish.

They don't just grow. They expand. Their hearts stay open. Their presence deepens. And their ability to lead from within becomes unshakable.

Radical love is not soft.

It's *fierce*. It's *faithful*. It's *cleansing*. And it is the most powerful force we can gift our children – and ourselves.

#2
GOLDEN FREQUENCY OF SELF-LEADERSHIP

Emotional Mastery… unlocks Inner Harmony

Let's talk about emotions – those waves that rise, fall, crash, and calm.

Not to be controlled. Not to be avoided. But to be understood and to be honoured.

Emotional mastery means learning to listen deeply. To feel what we feel without being ruled by it.

It's the sacred art of recognising emotions as energy in motion, and leading them with presence, rather than reacting from pressure.

I didn't learn this overnight. And I'm still learning. But what I know now is this:

Our relationship with emotions is at the heart of our relationship with life.

When children learn that emotions are not 'good' or 'bad', but simply information, they begin to move with life, rather than against it. They soften instead of shutting down. They feel safe in their bodies and trust themselves.

During the time when great changes were stirring in my family, I would make it a regular routine to go walking with my kids by the ocean. Long, open walks, where the only agenda was to be in the presence and energy of expansive space. No questions. No fixing. Just breath, movement, and the rhythm of the sea. Some days, when my kids had some worries surface, they learnt to voice them out aloud, not just to me, but also to the waves, offering them for release, and for recalibration; in a continuum of motion.

Those moments were organic, and essentially, they were about remembering … that emotions move. And we are allowed to move with them.

I recall one morning when my son woke before anyone else was out of bed. I noticed his quiet footsteps walk further than the bathroom (where I expected he might be going) before quietly returning to his bedroom … from which there was stillness.

Some minutes later, I got up to start my day, and as I quietly walked past his room I saw his bed quilt pulled over his head, and a light coming from underneath it.

The iPad, I thought to myself. I continued to the kitchen and, yes, the charger was still plugged into the wall with no iPad charging. I decided to leave my son to continue playing 'in secret'.

Later that morning, when his sisters were busy playing outside, I gently invited him into a conversation.

'Hey buddy, I noticed you woke up early this morning …'

He froze. His eyes wide. His body tight.

So I crouched to his level and said, 'Hey, you're okay. What's happening?'

He continued to look at me with widened eyes.

'Are the words feeling a bit stuck?' I asked.

He nodded.

I paused for a moment before calmy saying, 'You got the iPad this morning, yeah? And you were playing it under the covers?'

Another nod from him.

'What you're feeling right now in your body,' I said, 'it doesn't feel so comfortable, does it?'

He shook his head.

I continued … 'It's a bit of a yuck feeling … it is something called guilt … and maybe some shame too because you were hiding away … keeping it a secret. Shame and guilt can feel a bit heavy in your body.'

The rigidity in his body softened a little, but he still didn't speak.

'Show me … where do you feel it in your body?'

One of his hands went to his chest and the other hand to his throat.

'All is okay – just breathe into there,' I reassured him. 'And then breathe out from there, through your legs and feet, deep into the ground underneath your feet.'

We breathed together.

Slow. Safe. Connected.

Within less than a minute, he softened.

'How are you feeling now?'

He finally spoke … 'Much better …'

From there we had a very brief chat about how emotions can feel a bit stuck sometimes, and that the word emotion actually means *energy in motion*. The key is to just be with them without judging and keep breathing with them – because they want to, and will, keep moving along.

Then we circled back to the original conversation about the iPad …

'It's okay to want to play the iPad. Let's work out the best times together, and for how long; so, it feels like the right balance for you and everyone.'

That moment wasn't about discipline. It was about emotional leadership – unconditional acceptance – and … a cue for honest accountability.

Many of us received subtle messages of:

'Smile to be liked.'

Or not so subtle messages of:

'Stop crying.'

'Be brave and get on with it.'

Even when we were hurting.

Children have been praised for suppressing, punished for expressing, and left without the tools to understand what they were feeling and how to be in relationship with that.

No more.

To be raised as empowered humans, who practise emotional mastery, they need the opportunity to apply emotional fluency as best they can. And yes, we are dynamically doing the same by:

- naming what is felt (without shame)
- staying present in the body
- choosing responses, not reactions.

And from this place, inner stability and strength compounds in the felt knowing that emotions don't make you weak … they make you wise.

The Golden Invitation

Emotional Mastery invites us to:

Normalise all feelings as valid.

Help children witness their emotions without becoming them.

Speak in a way that supports self-leadership (e.g. 'I'm feeling anxious in this moment' vs. 'I am anxious').

Model grounded presence, especially when big feelings arise.

Make space for movement, breath, and regulation (especially outdoors).

When children learn to honour their emotions without fear or resistance, they unlock the pathway and frequency of inner harmony. This means that they don't try to 'run' from themselves or bypass. They learn to lean into themselves with compassion and reclaim the power to choose peace, whilst embracing the sacred art of listening and meeting emotions with loving presence.

***** See EMOTIONAL MASTERY PARENT-CHILD COMPANION in the Resources Section *****

#3
GOLDEN FREQUENCY OF SELF-LEADERSHIP

Radiant Self-Belief… unlocks Our Gifts to the World

Let's talk about radiant self-belief: That quiet trust in your inner light, even when the world feels dim. It doesn't shout or strive; it simply glows. I would say radiant self-belief is the sacred certainty that who you are, at your core, is worthy, wise, and whole. It's the luminous knowing that you are here on purpose, as purpose.

I feel like there's a beautiful dance between self-belief and inner knowing. They often intertwine, but they are actually quite distinct in essence.

Inner knowing, I'd define as the seed of soul truth … that deep resonance of: *This. Is. Who. I. Am.* It lives in the body, beneath words, and doesn't require evidence. It's innate.

Self-belief, on the other hand, is the muscle of inner confidence. It is built over time, through doing and trying and rising. It is cultivated, encouraged, and practised.

Inner knowing shows the way. Self-belief helps us walk it. And together, they become the wings of empowered humans.

For children, this union of knowing and belief is foundational to their empowerment. When a child says 'I just know I want to do this' and they are met with 'I believe you can', something powerful happens. They become anchored in both their truth and their capacity.

In my own life, radiant self-belief has been a practice, not a passive experience. I remember walking into my first ever meeting with the Society of Children's Book Writers and Illustrators. I had no idea what to expect.

A warm-hearted lady greeted me and asked, 'What brings you here?'

I told her I had two picture book manuscripts commissioned, and I was simply curious to learn more about the industry.

She lit up. 'Amazing! Tell me how you came to have your manuscripts commissioned.'

I blinked. 'Ah … I just submitted them to the publisher.'

She paused, sensing my innocence, and her face drew closer to mine as she gently said, 'Do you know *how hard* it is to have your manuscripts selected from a publisher's *slush pile*?'

'Ah … no,' I replied honestly.

What I did know was this: I had an unshakeable certainty for many years that I would have children's books published. I had never thought I wouldn't.

Several months later, at the celebratory launch of my second published picture book, friends reminded me that I'd spoken of becoming a children's author all the way back in high school; something I couldn't even remember consciously. But that certainty had continued to 'reside' within me.

Now it would be lovely to just feel certainty and have everything land in your lap, but certainty alone isn't enough. It is like the soil with the planted seed. And then self-belief is like the water and the sunlight. It's the nurtured action of inner knowing, the muscle that strengthens each time we honour our truth, regardless of any 'rejection' or external opinion from others.

So, just for a moment ... imagine your child, expressing themselves without fear of rejection. Navigating feedback without collapse. And moving through life with courage, clarity, and compassion.

That is the powerful essence of heart-led self-leadership.

It's not ego.

It's not performance.

It's alignment.

Quiet. Consistent. Devotional.

This same message echoed in my conversation with global entrepreneur and founder of Powerful Steps, Tory Archbold. She shared how self-belief isn't something we wait for; it's something we choose and embody daily. Her boldness and voice, once misunderstood, became her superpowers, inspiring the writing of her own book, *Self-Belief is your Superpower*. By trusting her inner guidance, even without external approval, she built a life aligned with joy and truth.

'When you honour who you are,' she said, 'the right people and paths find you.'

This kind of belief isn't manufactured. It's remembered. It's the trust that your essence matters, that your voice belongs, and that your presence is enough.

Radiant self-belief is a frequency, a sacred vibration of self, and it whispers ...

You don't need to bend to be accepted. You don't need to dim to be loved. SHINE.

It is humble; not because it hides, but because it doesn't need to prove. It allows you to stand tall in your light, while holding space for others to rise in theirs. What I'm describing is the energy of wholeness. The courage to be seen and the grace to know that not everyone will understand, and that's okay.

Belonging doesn't begin when others accept us. It begins when *we* accept ourselves.

And as parents, caregivers, and educators, this is one of the most powerful gifts we can offer our children.

The invitation to remember their worth – not to earn it.

When we can name what we love about ourselves – not to compare, but to *celebrate our signature frequency* – we model this too. Not only when we feel confident, but especially when we're unsure and choose to keep showing up anyway.

When children are rooted in radiant self-belief, their confidence becomes expansive without any superiority –rather with a radiance of illuminating what is *true*. And with this, their humility connects, and their presence begins a quiet revolution

Golden Invitation

Radiant self-belief invites you to …

Return to the truth that was never lost; only buried beneath expectation.

Stop seeking proof of your worth and start standing in the knowing that you are already whole.

Release being perfect, polished, or praised.

Reclaim being real. Being rooted. Being you.

Model courage by being authentic, not invincible.

Ask yourself … *What if my child saw me love myself – 'flaws' and all*

– and learnt to do the same?

Praise essence over achievement.

Honour voice over volume.

Embody the notion that confidence is the frequency of connection to self.

Rise in embodied certainty.

Become a living invitation for your child to remember:

'I am not here to be the same as anyone else. I am here to be me … And that is the greatest gift to the world …'

#4
GOLDEN FREQUENCY OF SELF-LEADERSHIP

Graceful Reflection… unlocks the Wisdom Within

True self-leadership isn't about control or dominance.

It's about presence.

Deep listening.

Inner attunement …

… and acting from the quiet clarity of the heart.

At the core of heartfelt self-leadership lies **Graceful Reflection**; the practice of pausing, tuning in, and aligning with one's higher self, or what I call the **Sparkle Self**. This radiant aspect of who we are holds infinite wisdom, guiding us towards truth, peace, and soulful decision-making.

When children learn the art of graceful reflection, they develop the capacity to lead themselves from within, rather than being pulled by external pressures or fleeting emotions. They learn to honour their own rhythms, receive inner guidance, and move through life with grounded integrity.

This practice isn't reserved for adults or advanced seekers; it begins early, through small, sacred moments of pause.

And for me, it began at seven years old.

I didn't know it then, but the journal I began keeping at that age became a sacred portal – my quiet companion in times of change, celebration, or confusion. It was a place where I learnt to befriend my thoughts, feel my emotions, and track the whispers of wisdom that didn't yet have a name. That practice of writing became a life anchor, a way of communing with my *Sparkle Self* before I ever knew the term. It was an early form of soul-listening, and it continues to this day.

Decades later, and especially in my work as an intuitive life coach, I've witnessed how journalling remains one of the most powerful tools for graceful reflection. I often invite clients to keep a dedicated journal throughout our work together; not to perform or report, but to **listen**.

What unfolds is always beautiful. Subtle shifts begin to surface – tiny yet profound moments of awareness … whether it be a recurring emotion that is understood, or a pattern discovered and embraced with compassion, or a decision arising from stillness, and absolute clarity.

These micro-breakthroughs, captured on the page, begin to **compound**. They reveal a timeline of becoming. A track record of courage. A mirror of how far they've come.

And here's what happens: They (my clients) start to normalise their own progress, almost forgetting how much has truly transformed. Until they look back … and suddenly, they remember.

This is the power of graceful reflection.

When we slow down long enough to **listen deeply**, we reconnect to the quiet wisdom within. We become attuned to the subtle shifts that are often missed in the rush of life. And we realise we were never lost … just moving too fast to hear the guidance.

Modern life often makes this difficult.

Children are constantly stimulated, measured, and scheduled. Silence can feel unfamiliar – even uncomfortable. They may equate stillness with boredom, rather than seeing it as a space where something sacred can be heard.

Without gentle support and modelling, many grow up over-relying on external validation, avoiding inner stillness, and disconnecting from their heart's guidance.

Graceful reflection changes this.

It teaches children to slow down, not as a retreat, but as a return. It reminds them that their truth doesn't live outside of them, it lives within them.

Over time, this becomes one of their greatest gifts: the ability to navigate with clarity, make empowered choices, and honour their *Sparkle Self*, even amidst chaos.

The Golden Invitation

Graceful Reflection invites us to:

Pause.

Breathe.

Listen.

Not just to the chatter of our thoughts, but to the subtle, sacred wisdom that lives beneath them, in the heart and soul.

Children who grow up anchored in reflection become tuned instruments of their own truth.

They act with calm clarity. They speak from felt knowing. They honour their journey, one moment at a time.

And slowly, powerfully, their lives become a mirror of the inner wisdom they've learnt to trust.

An Important Note

How handwriting slows us into wisdom

Writing by hand gently slows the mind, grounds the nervous system, and invites presence.

It helps children move from reaction to reflection; where true self-leadership begins.

Neuroscience shows it activates brain regions tied to memory, emotion, and language, supporting emotional clarity and deeper self-awareness.

I know handwriting isn't easy or accessible for every child

And that's okay … I've shared a range of beautiful alternative practices in the Resources section of this book. There's always a way to meet children where they are and support them in gently connecting with their *Sparkle Self*.

#5
GOLDEN FREQUENCY OF SELF-LEADERSHIP

Energetic Integrity…

unlocks Forgiveness and Compassion

Let's talk about forgiveness and compassion.

These aren't just moral ideals; they are two of the most profound forces for personal and collective healing, and at their core, both require one thing:

Energetic integrity.

This means your 'inner' and 'outer' worlds are congruent. You're not saying one thing but feeling another. You're not overproviding to earn worth or holding anger beneath a smile. You're real. And from that congruence flows clarity, healing, and love.

When our energy is clear and coherent, we naturally become more forgiving … more compassionate.

Why?

Because we're no longer tangled in old stories, grudges, or emotional debris.

There's space. Breath. A softness that returns.

We stop leaking life force into past pain and begin reclaiming it for peace.

Forgiveness, from this place, is no longer an obligation, it's a liberation. This is not about saying what happened was okay. It's about saying: *This no longer gets to shape me*. Energetically, it's the release of cords that keep us bound to hurt. It's a powerful act of sovereignty, not softness.

And compassion?

It blossoms right there in the space forgiveness creates. Compassion isn't about tolerating bad behaviour or being endlessly available. It's about seeing with the heart. Holding humanity without judgement. Meeting someone where they're at, while staying anchored in where you are.

This becomes especially important as parents, for our kids are tuned into our field. When we carry resentment, emotional suppression, or inner chaos, they feel it. We may not say a thing, but our energy does. Practising energetic integrity as a parent is one of the most loving gifts we can offer, not just for our own wellbeing, but for our children's emotional safety and development.

Personally, I experienced this most profoundly when our family dynamic transitioned to two households. It was a season of deep adjustment, new rhythms, and unfamiliar terrain. And in that chapter of life, energetic integrity became my non-negotiable number one. I had to choose, again and again, to honour what was true in my field.

To let go of what didn't serve. To stay anchored in clarity, even in the face of discomfort or grief.

There are chapters in life that demand a higher intensity of learning; that was one of them. And in those times, having practices of energetic hygiene – and embracing the support of close, trusted friends to help uphold that – wasn't optional. It was essential.

We matter. And when I say that, I say it from a place of powerful love and radical self-reverence; for our worth, and for our wholeness so we can give and serve … from overflow.

Within professional life, it has been quite humbling to bear witness to the immediate shift in energy that occurs when the process of forgiveness is practised. The resulting 'lightness' and 'liberation' is palpable.

So, when it comes to raising children with strong self-leadership, energetic integrity is key. It teaches them to notice when something feels 'off' in their body, emotions, or space, and instead of pushing it down, they pause, breathe, and choose again. This skill becomes their internal compass. They start asking questions like: 'Is this mine, or someone else's?' or 'Does this feel true for me?' These are the early seeds of sovereignty.

Children don't need to be perfect at managing their energy, but they do benefit from knowing they have energy, and that how they tend to it shapes how they move through life.

Practising simple, sacred acts that help you come back into coherence daily – whether that's grounding, journalling, breathwork, or simply pausing to ask *Is my heart clear right now?* – is an important fundamental of self-sovereignty.

On a final note, and just to be clear, energetic integrity doesn't mean being in a constant state of calm. It means being honest. And it means being willing to feel what's true, even when it's messy; clean it up and choose again. From that place, forgiveness is more organic, and compassion becomes less effort and more essence.

Golden Invitation

Energetic Integrity invites you to …

Let this be your permission slip to stop carrying what isn't yours.

Let go of the energy that's keeping your heart heavy.

Be bold enough to forgive … let it clear and liberate from a place of deep self-respect and wholeness.

Be brave enough to offer compassion; both outward to others and inward to self.

And most of all, be in the right relationship with your energy.

Because from that integrity … love flows.

Peace returns.

And your children?

They'll feel it. They'll learn it. They'll live it.

And now, we emerge from the golden centre of this book …

Having explored the five core, golden frequencies that awaken empowered self-leadership, we're ready to play in a whole new way.

Because when self-leadership is alive, so is curiosity.

So is imagination.

So is the joy of what *else* is possible.

And with this, we next step into our third golden key – *The Frequency of Fun* – a portal of playful pathways, where creativity, learning, and soul spark lead the way.

GOLDEN KEY THREE

THE FREQUENCY OF FUN

The Pathways of Possibility

fun: noun
/fʌn/

The connecting bridge between our roots (foundation) and growth (expansion), where curiosity, creativity, joy, and exploration flow; activating ideas and dreams within an infinite field of possibility.

PRIORITISE THE POWER OF PLAY

Discover Ways to 'Fun-ify' Life

What if play is the original language of the soul – the essential frequency of self-leadership and lifelong flourishing?

'What is the ONE GREATEST superpower that readies children for the school of life?' I asked the group of parents and educators attending my masterclass on Holistic School Readiness. Various answers were voiced:

'Resilience!'

'Emotional Intelligence!'

'Perseverance!'

'Communication!'

'Yes,' I responded – they are all valid responses.

'However – what is *the* superpower that *powers* the resilience, the emotional intelligence, the perseverance, the communication?' I asked them.

They looked at me in thoughtful wonder, awaiting … as I then revealed the answer on my slide …

'PLAY!'

Words cannot even begin to share the depth and importance of play as a sacred, multidimensional frequency, that naturally awakens energy, insight, and intuitive power within children. Basically, it becomes a profound portal for cultivating self-leadership.

Rather than something 'extra' to fit into a busy schedule, play becomes the very structure through which children learn to self-direct, regulate, create, relate, and flourish.

It's often said that it takes around 400 repetitions to learn something through rote memorisation, but only 10 to 20 repetitions when it's learnt through play. This insight, often linked to child development expert Dr Karyn Purvis, might be anecdotal, but the message is powerful.

Play is not just fruitless fun!

I know that for many allied health practitioners, when it comes to play, there can be an internal tension to navigate – the fear of being seen as 'just playing' rather than 'doing real work' when supporting children and families. But here's the truth we come back to time and time again: play *is* the work. It taps into the whole child, activating their brain, body, emotions, and energy. It sparks curiosity, creates a sense of safety, and gently lowers stress. When we remember the *why*, the power of play speaks for itself.

Play is incredibly far reaching … I've trained health practitioners on the energetic science of play to optimise their own wellbeing; helped caregivers learn how to bond with their children through the dynamics of play; and worked with countless non-speaking children – where play *is* our communication medium and channel of connection.

If we broaden our lens, play becomes so much more than just fun and games; it's a language, a healer, and a sacred space for becoming.

When we understand play in this way, we begin to see its role in supporting children's emotional, spiritual, and energetic wellbeing.

So let's take a look at play in a few different powerful ways.

Play as the Soul's First Language

Long before children speak in words, they speak through play. It's their native tongue; a natural way of expressing feelings, thoughts, and imagination. Through pretend games, storytelling, movement, and creativity, children explore realms beyond the physical. Play becomes a bridge between their inner world and the world around them, helping them process experiences and connect with something greater – what some may call soul, spirit, or source.

Play as a Pathway to Nervous System Regulation

Beyond expression, play restores. When a child feels safe and free to play, their nervous system responds with calm and balance. Stress hormones settle, breathing deepens, and the body shifts into a state of healing and flow. Especially after emotional or physical challenges, play gently regulates from the inside out – offering the body and mind a natural reset. This helps us remember: play is not an extracurricular, it's energetic recalibration.

Play is a Lens – Not a Luxury

It's easy to confuse play with toys, games, or busy activities, but at its core, play is a *mode of being*. It's a way of seeing the world through colour, curiosity, and zest. It lives in imagination, not material things. A stick becomes a spaceship. A laundry basket becomes a dragon's cave. Play finds magic in the mundane – it transforms the everyday into possibility. When we honour play as a perspective, we empower children (and ourselves) to move through life with wonder, flexibility, and joy.

The Sacredness of Play can be Influenced
The spaces where children play – both indoors and outdoors – hold energetic influence. Inside, thoughtfully designed environments filled with natural light, soft textures, gentle colours, and an intentional sense of beauty can soothe the nervous system and invite calm focus. These spaces aren't just visually pleasing – they carry a frequency of care and safety. They become sanctuaries.

Equally, the outdoors offers a wild and wondrous canvas for play. Nature doesn't need to be arranged; it invites play through its textures, sounds, unpredictability, and open space. Climbing a tree, jumping in puddles, creating fairy homes in the garden; they all awaken sensory integration, resilience, creativity, and freedom. **The elements – sunlight, breeze, earth, water – naturally co-regulate the body and spirit in ways that no indoor setting can replicate.**

Whether it's a softly lit room or an open field, what matters most is the intention behind the space. When we honour the environments where play unfolds, we create the conditions for children to feel safe, expansive, and fully themselves, ready to imagine, express, and flourish.

Play is the purest, most powerful way children learn who they are and how they relate to the world, and … *is not just reserved for children; it is just as important across ALL AGES and stages of life.*

Heart-Powered Self-Leadership

So how can we help children lead themselves through the power of play?

When children are empowered to infuse their everyday moments with the energy of curiosity, fun, and imagination, they begin to self-direct their emotional regulation, creativity, and confidence.

The key lies in **prompting their ownership** of the play frequency, even in life's most routine rhythms.

Here are some playful question prompts to help children *lead the way* with the energy of play:

'What Could We Turn This Into?'

This can be asked during routine tasks like cleaning, packing, or even brushing teeth.

Ask your child something like:

If this was a game, how would we play it?

What could we turn this into if you were a character right now?

This invites them to transform the mundane into magic.

'You're the Play Director!'

Offer leadership in planning a 10-minute play break.

This could sound like:

What kind of fun are you leading today?

Want to invent a new game or remix an old one?

Let them decide the rules, themes, and props, building agency through playful planning.

'Let's Play With Sound.'

Turn car rides, dinner prep, or dressing into a sound adventure.

So, question prompts could be:

Can you make a sound or a song for this moment?

What's your theme song right now?

These tap into energetic expression and self-awareness through vibration and rhythm.

'What's Next ...?'

When reading or storytelling, pause and hand it over.

Ask them:

What do you think happens next?

Can you invent a new character or magical object?

This encourages imaginative authorship and flexible thinking.

'How Would Play Help Right Now?'

This question prompt can be helpful in moments of low energy or transition.

You could say:

If we sprinkled some fun into this moment, what would happen?

Let's pause and press play on a new scene ... what's next?

This invites children to lead their own energy shift, with creativity and emotional intelligence.

Lifelong Flourishing

Daily Rituals & Rhythms for Families, Educators & Therapists

There are heaps of ways to infuse a bit of magic into the mundane; it makes life more enjoyable and interesting for everyone! Rather than getting bogged down in resistance, you can redirect and reframe it.

Home Tasks Fun (Gamify the Mundane)

Change the vibe of household tasks in whatever way works for your family dynamic; whether it is catching their own item of clean laundry as you empty the laundry basket or helping with the dishes with energising dance music or a comedy show in the background, it's up to you to choose the mood you want to create.

Speed Clean Showdowns

Set a 5-minute timer. Add music, rotate roles (DJ, timer master, inspector). Many kids love a timer or clock countdown to activate some energy. It is also a powerful visual for them to see (and feel) the start and end of the task too.

Spot-It Quests

Assign missions whilst on the go (e.g. spot three yellow cars or a triangle-shaped sign). And take turns assigning what needs to be spotted. Yes, it's super simple, and it helps to encourage presence, observation, and active awareness.

Bathtime Mix Lab

Offer safe sensory ingredients like lavender drops or bath fizzies. Children create their own 'bathfun-formulas'. (You can also adapt this for the shower.) This opportunity can be used to have kids set an intention for their bath; once they've tuned into how they are feeling and what they feel they need. For example, *I'm having a bath to relax my legs after playing soccer.*

Invent-a-Game Nights

Let your child create a simple game (board game, movement game, or card-based). You can create one too! It doesn't have to be sophisticated or perfect, keep it simple and fun. Play it as a family and acknowledge their creativity and leadership.

Dinnertime Dice

Use a dice where numbers correspond to an action, for example:

1 = Tell a joke
2 = Share a wish
3 = Act out a scene
4 = Give a compliment
5 = Share something new you learnt

6 = Give a review of your meal in a funny voice

This helps with confident communication and emotional literacy.

Family Play Jar

Have everyone write down fun, quick-play ideas on slips of paper. Draw one daily or weekly to surprise and spark joy (e.g. '5-minute dance-off', 'Backyard picnic', 'Make up a handshake').

'Play it Out' Problem-Solving

When a challenge arises, you can invite kids to role-play different solutions with toys, puppets, or even silly voices. It helps them externalise emotions and explore options in a safe, creative space.

Role Reversal Day (or Hour!)

Let the kids be 'the grown-up' for an hour. They plan a (safe!) activity, explain the rules, and guide the family. It empowers voice, decision-making, and empathy.

Legacy in Motion

Reflect. Integrate. Empower.

Honouring play as a sacred frequency activates a natural code of connection and co-creation, which helps children experience themselves as leaders of their own joy, wisdom, and expression.

They (and you) become empowered not just to participate in life, but to actively shape it, and with this we unlock much more than just fun and laughter; we open children to presence, possibility, and empowered expression.

And what often follows?

Curiosity.

Because play naturally sparks questions and often invites dynamic dialogue.

So next, we'll explore how to nurture *curious conversations*; the kind that helps kids think for themselves, speak from the heart, and tune into the wisdom within.

Journal prompts

- *How often does play lead the way in my daily life?*
- *Where can seriousness soften into spontaneity?*
- *What would shift if I was 'being more playful' in my day to day?*
- *How can I invite more play into daily moments?*

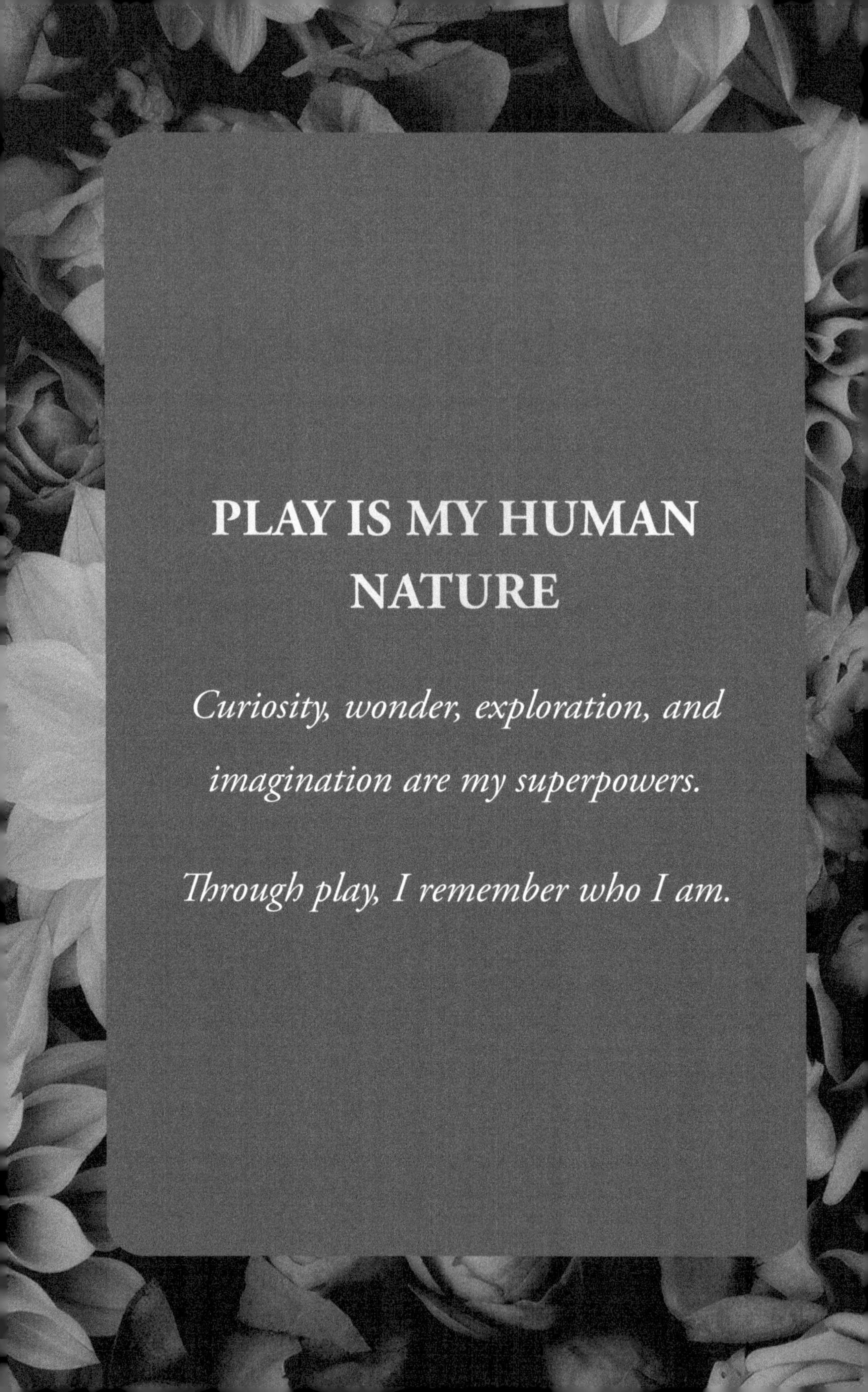

PLAY IS MY HUMAN NATURE

Curiosity, wonder, exploration, and imagination are my superpowers.

Through play, I remember who I am.

CURIOUS CONVERSATIONS

The Doorways to Connection, Learning, and Discerning

What if our everyday dialogues are sacred invitations into awareness, truth, and trust?

Okay, this is a topic I could completely 'nerd out' on. Just like many other chapters in this book, this one could easily be a book of its own. So, let's begin (and stay) at the heart and soul of it ...

Have you ever paused to notice the *shape* of your everyday conversations with children?

Not just the words you say, but how you guide the flow?

The tone, the space, the rhythm, the *why* beneath it all?

Years ago, I was having my legs waxed, and the beauty consultant, on learning about my work, declared:

'My daughter hardly talks to me! It's so hard to have a conversation with her!'

'Okay, tell me more,' I prompted.

'Well, she's 11 years old, and when I pick her up from school and ask her about her day, she just gives me one- or two-word answers! I'll ask things like, "Did you have a good day? Did you have all your lunch today? What happened in your day?" But she hardly says anything!'

'Okay …' I responded, 'I'm just curious … do you share about your day? Let her know what you did, and your reflections of your day and how you felt about it?'

She paused. I allowed silence to honour her some time to reflect.

'No, I don't … I never really thought about that …' she said in quiet realisation before asking, 'but is that called *reverse psychology*?'

'Not at all.' I smiled respectfully. 'It is called having a *natural* conversation – rather than staging an interrogation.'

The penny dropped. 'Oh my goodness! Yes that is exactly what I have been doing – interrogating!'

'Unknowingly,' I reassured her. 'Your intention was (and is) to connect with your daughter, but asking lots of questions, especially *closed questions* – that only need a *yes/no* answer – is common cycle many of us can get caught in.'

We often autopilot our way of communicating; so why not set the autopilot mode to conscious and curious? Because the art of dialogue is one of the most powerful yet underestimated tools in raising empowered humans.

And at the core of it lies something beautifully simple: **curiosity**.

Within my years of work within communication sciences and human potential, I've observed that when we nurture and refine our communication to meet everyday moments with conscious language, presence, and curiosity, we build more than communication skills. Our daily dialogues (both internally and with others) have a direct relationship to the quality of our self-leadership, connection, and discernment, especially in a rapidly changing world.

In a world that so often prizes having the answers, my intention is for you to reawaken the magic of questions too; whilst also leaning into the subtle power of comments and *felt* listening not only as tools for exchanging information, but as **energetic bridges**:

Between one another.

Between our 'inner and outer world'.

Between the self and the society we're shaping together.

So, let's talk about the magic of questions and questioning …

Our questioning plays such a crucial part in shaping the pathways of possibility in our lives, yet the natural impulse to question doesn't always survive the schooling years. Years ago, whilst researching for my School of Life Readiness masterclass, I came across a study by Dr Michelle Chouinard that was both startling and eye opening. She found that *preschoolers ask an average of 76 questions per hour* when engaged with an adult … and that in more verbally active sessions, this number exceeded 100 questions per hour.

And yet, by the time children are aged around 8–10 years, the number of questions they ask declines significantly to near zero in the classroom. This isn't because they've grown out of wonder. It's often because they've received subtle (and not-so-subtle) messages that their curiosity is inconvenient, naïve, or off-topic. They begin to prioritise *being right* over being *curious.*

This is a critical loss.

And … this isn't just philosophical; it's neurobiological. When we do engage with and encourage our children to ask reflective questions, it is more than a pathway to expand knowledge and intelligence; it's the **engine of critical thinking**, **emotional literacy**, and **personal agency** – engaging parts of the brain responsible for *metacognition* (thinking about thinking) and *empathic attunement.*

Curiosity, after all, is how children learn to:

- challenge limiting beliefs
- identify emotional needs

- notice social patterns
- make wise, soul-aligned decisions.

Without it, they become more passive. More externally driven. More likely to silence their own inner knowing.

And super importantly – curiosity is the antidote to passive consumption.

It awakens discernment, which is especially essential in this time of misinformation, deepfakes, and AI-generated influence. By encouraging questions like *Where did this come from?* or *Why might someone want me to believe this?*, we nurture a generation of truth-seekers; children who are grounded, reflective, and connected to their own wisdom.

This isn't about making kids suspicious, but it is about helping them become conscious, intentional thinkers that become adults who don't just absorb ideas. They evaluate, feel, and choose what aligns. Emotional literacy and media discernment are no longer optional; they're foundational to empowered living.

A powerful way to embody this is for us, as parents/carers and professionals working with children, to **adopt the role of a 'guide', not a guard**.

A **guide** creates space for children to think and feel for themselves, asking questions that build trust in their inner voice. A **guard**, often acting from love or fear, may jump in to protect or direct too soon. Guiding nurtures self-trust. Guarding can interrupt it. The difference is small, but it shapes how children learn to face the unknown and trust their own wisdom.

In today's digital world, **guiding children to ask good questions is more important than ever**. Whether they're talking to a parent, a friend, or using technology, the answers they get depend on the questions they ask. When kids learn to ask thoughtful questions, they're not just finding facts; they're learning how to understand and discern the world and their place in it.

So how can we learn to ask the right questions?

By listening.

To ask the right questions, we must first step into the role of listener. Listening is a core superpower of self-leadership; it is the vessel through which curiosity travels. When we listen to truly understand and attune, we create space for reflection and meaningful insight, rather than reaction or external persuasion.

This kind of listening we call **active listening**. It involves more than just hearing words; it's about signalling to another (or to ourself) that what is being shared matters.

Active listening includes:

Reflecting: *It sounds like you felt hurt.*

Paraphrasing: *You're saying you needed more space.*

Inviting continuation: *Would you like to tell me more?*

These are simple yet powerful, especially when helping children navigate their inner world or engage thoughtfully with others.

In the context of media discernment, it requires listening to the undercurrents of intent from the source of who created or shared the content.

So … what is another feature of conversational 'art' that is often overlooked?

The art of commenting. And pausing.

The practice of commenting is lesson '101' when supporting individuals in developing social and emotional intelligence. As is the practice of pausing after you offer a comment; to allow 'space' or airtime for your conversational partner to respond.

While questions open the door to connection, **comments build the bridge**. They offer validation, demonstrate presence, and reflect understanding without the pressure of a response. In essence, comments are relational glue; they say 'I see you.' without needing to fix, interrogate, or direct.

Comments can:

Reflect shared experience – e.g. *That must've been so exciting!*

Acknowledge emotions – e.g. *That sounds really frustrating.*

Celebrate or affirm – e.g. *You worked so hard on that – amazing!*

Connect gently – e.g. *I noticed you really love being outdoors …*

For children (and adults), being met with a thoughtful comment rather than a rapid-fire question often feels more spacious and emotionally safe. It models how to tune in and encourages internal dialogue, allowing the child to notice their own reactions, rather than being nudged towards someone else's agenda.

In parenting, modelling the balance between **asking and commenting** equips children not only with expressive tools, but also with the ability to build emotionally rich and reciprocal relationships.

Heart-Powered Self-Leadership

How do we help children use curious communication to connect, learn, and discern?

Make Questions a Shared Adventure

Instead of asking all the questions yourself, invite your child to be the question-asker too. You might say: *Let's each think of one question we're curious about today, it could be about each other or the world.* This models mutual respect, gives children permission to wonder out loud, and reminds them that questioning is a shared gift, not a test.

Practise the Power of the Pause

When a child speaks, give them space to finish. When you comment, leave room afterward. Silence is not a gap to be filled; it's a bridge for reflection. You can even name the pause gently: *I'm going to give this a quiet moment before I respond because it feels important.*

This encourages children to attune to energy, not just words.

Active Listening as a Superpower Practice

Invite your child to step into the role of a 'Heart Listener' for someone else in the family or class. Let them know their only job is to *really listen*, with their whole body, without interrupting, fixing, or jumping in. You can say: *When we listen with our heart, we're not just hearing words, we're letting the other person feel seen and safe.*

When the speaker finishes, the listener reflects one thing they heard, e.g. *It sounds like you felt left out when that happened.*

The more this is practised, the more naturally it is embodied.

Lifelong Flourishing

Daily Rituals & Rhythms for Families, Educators & Therapists

Model Micro-Moments of Inquiry

Vocalise your own process of discernment so kids experience the power of questioning.

For example:

I wonder who made this video. What do you think their goal was?

That headline seems a bit dramatic – do you think it's fully true?

This made me feel a little off. Do you feel anything like that?

Two Truths & a Wonder

Each day, invite children to share two things they learnt and one thing they're curious about. This can be easily incorporated into dinnertime or car ride routines. Remember, you do not want to interrogate your child. You can start by sharing about your day first, then pause to create space for them to contribute.

Inner Voice Mirror

Children are constantly shaping their inner voice, that quiet narrator of their day, their doubts, and their dreams. Supporting kids to gently reflect on and reshape this voice builds self-trust, emotional resilience, and metacognitive awareness. And at its core, critical thinking begins with one powerful inner question: *What's really true for me?*

This simple end-of-day ritual invites children to become conscious authors of their inner dialogue:

1. Ask, *What did your inner voice say during that moment today?*
2. Reflect together: *Was it kind or helpful?*
3. Rephrase it with compassion and encouragement (as relevant).
4. Invite your child to speak the new version aloud, as their self-chosen truth.

Over time, this practice nurtures cognitive sovereignty and helps children stay connected to their inner compass in a world of external noise.

BONUS EMPOWERMENT

Children who ask questions as they scroll, pause before they believe, and speak up when something feels off, are doing more than simply thinking; they are leading from within. In the age of AI and overstimulation, the question *What's true for me?* becomes a sacred act of sovereignty. It is the soul's refusal to be automated.

To bridge between emotional literacy and cognitive sovereignty, I created the QLEAR Framework. This supports children in both self-communication (inner dialogue) and interpersonal discernment (navigating information, interactions, and relationships).

You can use it as a visual (on wall or fridge); but of course, it is more powerful when modelled by you in daily life.

The QLEAR Framework for Curious Questioning

Q – Question the Source: *Where did this come from? Who created this, and why?*

L – Listen to Your Body: *How does this make me feel? Is there a signal of discomfort or alignment?*

E – Evaluate the Emotion: *Am I reacting or reflecting? What emotion is shaping my perception?*

A – Ask What's Missing: *Is there another side to this? What might I not be seeing yet?*

R – Reflect Before Reacting: *Do I want to agree with this? What's my own truth or next question?*

Legacy in Motion

Reflect. Integrate. Empower.

Curious conversations create space for children to listen, question, and reflect … powerful ingredients for inner confidence and clarity.

And the way we speak with children today shapes how they speak within themselves and with others tomorrow. It's how we cultivate future leaders grounded in heart-led truth.

Ultimately, our children's inner compasses must be stronger than the algorithms they scroll.

And from there?

They're far more equipped to take the next step: to problem-solve with purpose and trust their own thinking. And that's exactly where we're heading next … into the power of proactive problem-solving that helps kids stay in a momentum of flowing forward in life.

Journal Prompts

- *Am I guiding or guarding in the way I speak with children?*
- *What's one way I can easily apply the QLEAR framework at home/in the classroom?*
- *When do I feel most present in conversation?*
- *How can I make space for more active listening in my day?*

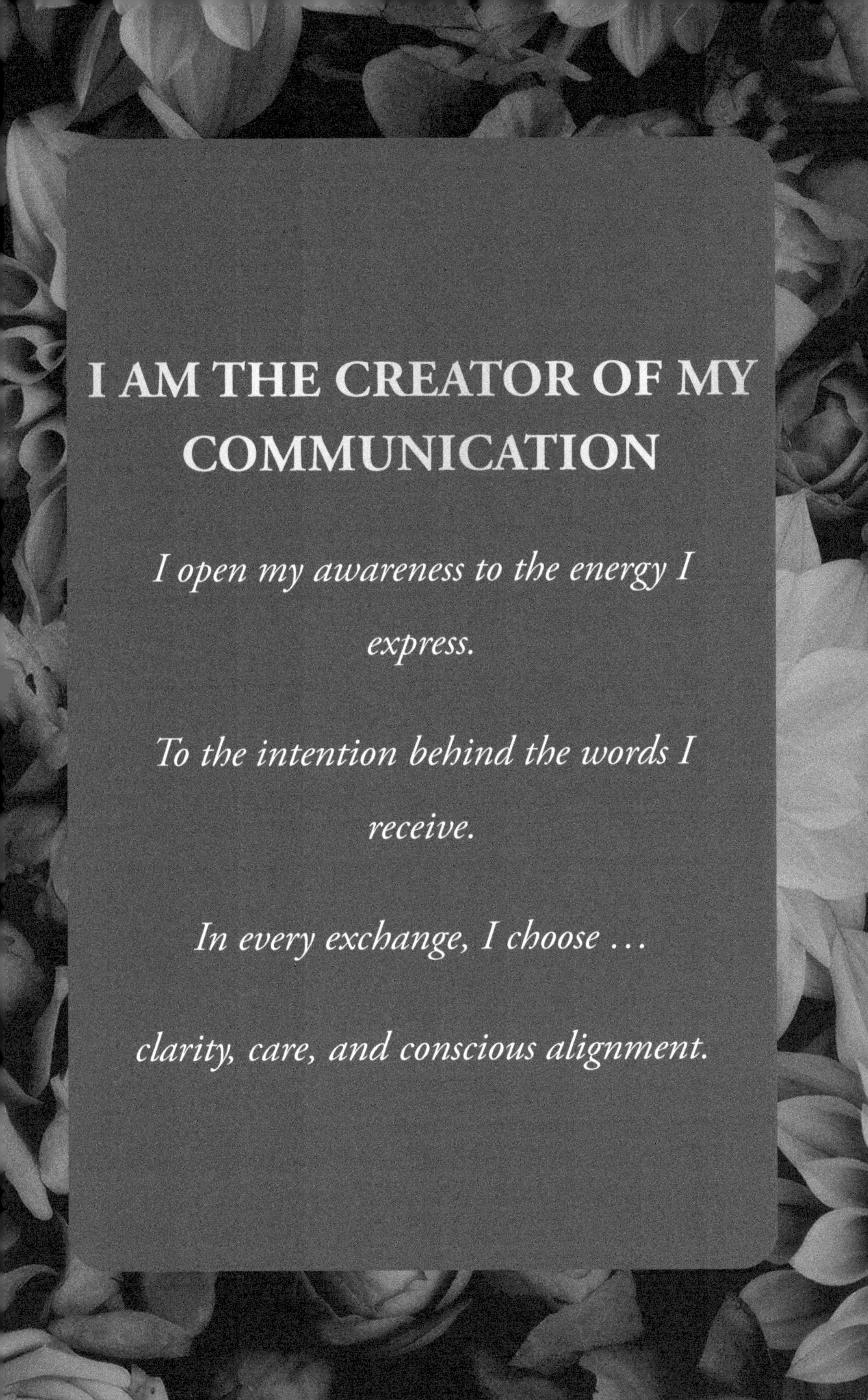
I AM THE CREATOR OF MY COMMUNICATION
I open my awareness to the energy I express.
To the intention behind the words I receive.
In every exchange, I choose …
clarity, care, and conscious alignment.

PROACTIVE PROBLEM-SOLVING

Flow Forward

What if every 'problem' was a portal, inviting flexible trust and grounded presence to lead the way?

As I sit here reflecting on what story to share to start off this chapter … there's nothing instantly landing that feels *interesting enough*.

Do I share something from a child I've supported in therapy? Or a moment when one of my own kids worked through a friendship challenge?

Do I talk about founding a company in response to a gap – a 'problem' I observed in the system?

Do I draw from the countless so-called problems I've moved through in my own decades of life?

Or maybe I mention my son and his rap music dilemma – where the 'problem' wasn't his love of rap, but the fact that I'd set a condition: he could only listen to tracks without swearing and with messages that were meaningful and respectful? And that when he first hit a wall trying to find songs that fit, my response was simple: 'If it doesn't exist, create it … maybe write your own.' So he did. And along the way, he also discovered some incredible global artists with good things to say.

Hmm … how about the 'problem' of my daughter being an ambidextrous tennis player, which all started from her dislike of hitting backhands. She decided instead to switch hands mid-game so she could play forehands from both sides. Problem? Or pure coordination and creativity merging in real time?

And then I smiled at the irony of it all – *Is it a problem not knowing which problem to share?*

The truth is, I don't often use the word *problem* in my own inner world. I'll reach for *challenge* or *obstacle* – words that reflect a pause, a moment to reassess and re-navigate. But professionally? The word *problem* comes up a lot. Because it's part of the explicit work I do.

As a speech pathologist, I've supported thousands of children in developing practical and creative problem-solving skills. As a coach, I help people gently peel back the layers of what's really going on – the stuck points, the fog, the overwhelm.

I get paid to solve problems. Most of us do.

And the moment you become a parent? You basically sign up for elite-level problem-solving; no manual, no map – just intuition, trial, error … and love.

So where am I going with all this?

Let's be honest: 'problems' pop up all the time … some small, some stretching; and how we respond to them shapes more than just the moment.

It shapes how we see ourselves. What we believe we're capable of. And whether we expect life to move *with* us or *against* us.

That's why this chapter matters.

Because empowered problem-solving isn't about always having the right answer. It's about building the *inner readiness* – the mindset, the emotional agility, and the energetic trust – to meet challenges as opportunities for growth, through a process of pausing, breathing, reflecting, asking, and *moving forward.*

Even if it's just one small step at a time.

As parents, educators, and therapists, we often want to protect our children from discomfort. That's natural. But real empowerment doesn't come from removing all the bumps in the road; it comes from helping our children learn how to move through them. With curiosity, creativity … and heart.

Paul Sullivan, founder of *The Company of Dads*, lives this truth daily; not only in his role as a writer, entrepreneur, and community-builder, but most significantly in his role as a parent. A former *New York Times* columnist, Paul stepped into a new paradigm of fatherhood when he became what he calls a 'lead dad'; deeply involved in raising his three daughters while continuing to work full-time.

I interviewed Paul on my podcast to dive deeper.

He shared how at a time when he and his wife had two young daughters, she was let go from her organisation. She wanted to start her own business but was worried about what this would mean for the kids. He recounted their exchange …

'I'll become the lead dad. And she said, "What does that mean?" And I said, I have no idea, but is this really a time to panic?'

Fast forward some years, they now had three daughters. He shared that like many parents, the pandemic brought his balancing act to a halt.

'I mean, let's be honest here. I was a lead dad who worked full-time, and it didn't work in COVID,' Paul reflects. 'I thought, shit, this is not good. What am I gonna do?'

That moment – raw and real – didn't lead him into collapse. It led him into inquiry. Instead of fighting the stuckness, Paul leaned in. He listened. He noticed the gaps. And from that space of uncertainty, *The Company of Dads* was born: a community and media platform redefining the conversation around modern fatherhood, care, and leadership.

'All the stuff for parents is really for moms, and all the stuff for dads is very niche … And that started me along this journey.'

This was problem-solving not as a quick fix, but as contribution. Rather than lament what didn't exist, Paul built what he wished had been there. Not just for himself, but for every parent navigating invisible labour, evolving identities, and unmet cultural narratives.

But the road wasn't smooth.

'There was a moment where I was like, "God, are you dumb, Sullivan? What did you do?"' he shared, laughing. 'This is like the summer of my discontent … What in the world have I done? What kind of dumbass leaves *New York Times* to start this?'

His honesty is disarming. And it's exactly what makes his story so powerful.

Paul's success didn't come from certainty. It came from trust. From riding the wave even when the outcome was unclear. From staying in motion, emotionally and practically, and holding the larger intention at the centre.

Eventually, the vision landed, beyond business transformation to cultural modelling. Paul began organising his work hours around his family's rhythms, leading with what he calls 'the care shift':

'It's about 9 to 3 every day … that's the time when I'm available for synchronous conversations. And I send emails, I work on presentations early in the morning before my kids are up, and at night when everyone's going to bed.'

He didn't just create flexibility; he demonstrated how empowered choices ripple out to challenge old systems and became a living case study for the kind of structural change he was advocating for.

'I started doing things in my own business I wanted other businesses to adopt.'

And this is what flow-forward leadership looks like: moving beyond reimagining policies to embodying them. Living them and letting your life become the practice ground for the world you want to build.

And while his way of working inspires, it's the small moments at home where Paul's grounded leadership shines.

'Whoever cooks the dinner in our house is not cleaning up. Whoever's cooking the dinner is also not setting the table ... Somebody else is gonna wash the dishes ... It's little things like that,' he shared.

Meaningful responsibility. Real-life learning. Shared contribution. His daughters, he says, help walk the dogs, put their clothes away, and are also cooking meals for the family. Not out of obligation, but agency.

'Could we put their clothes away for them? Of course we could. But what is that gonna teach them?' he says.

This very much speaks to the essence of flow-forward parenting. Not perfect or prescriptive. Just intentional, responsive, and alive.

'Hard now, easy later. Easy now, hard later.'

This has become a guiding principle in Paul's home, and it captures the spirit of this chapter beautifully. Empowered problem-solving isn't about removing friction. It's about embracing what challenges can teach us; about ourselves, each other, and the world we're shaping together.

Heart-Powered Self Leadership

So how can we help children flow forward with empowered problem-solving?

'Try–Tweak–Trust' Mindset

Introduce the concept of solving as a loop, not a line. The loop goes like this ...

- Try an approach with presence.
- Tweak it if it doesn't feel right or gets stuck.
- Trust the process (and ask for help if needed).

You can then use this language in everyday challenges: *'Hmm, sounds like you're in the tweak part of solving!'*

'What Else Could Be True?' Exploration

When a child feels stuck, invite a curious shift.

This could sound like …

What else could be true about this?

What would your future self say right now?

What would [favourite character/animal] try?

This kind of exploration trains flexible, lateral thinking and also helps kids see beyond the perceived obstacle.

Flow Vocabulary Chart

Yes, we are tapping into the Wisdom of Wordology here, as I encourage your use of a few high-frequency 'flow words'. So here are some word flip suggestions …

Use the words:

- 'Explore' instead of 'fix'
- 'Navigate' instead of 'solve'
- 'Experiment' instead of 'get it right'
- 'Progress' instead of 'perfect'.

Stick these on the fridge, class wall, or therapy room door.

Sleep-Time Solving – Ask the Subconscious

Before sleep, invite children to gently ask their inner wisdom:

What do I need to know about this problem?

Show me a helpful step while I sleep.

They can place the question in their heart or under their pillow. This calms the nervous system, builds trust in inner guidance, and opens the door for insight. Research shows that sleep supports creative problem-solving and fresh perspectives by allowing the subconscious to process and reframe challenges overnight.

In the morning, invite a moment of quiet reflection: *Did anything come to you in a dream or feeling?* This is a beautiful way to model trusting the flow rather than forcing a fix.

Next-Step Staircase

Turn overwhelm into a focus on moving forward one step at a time. A simple way to help kids break down big problems into small, doable actions is by using a staircase metaphor. You can draw or imagine a staircase and label the top step with the 'big thing' they're facing.

Pause and ask: *What's one small step you* can *take right now?* Naming and claiming this helps to recentre. There is also the optional mantra or reminder that, *One small step is still moving forward.*

Lifelong Flourishing

Daily Rituals & Rhythms for Families, Educators & Therapists

'Mini-Moments of Solving'

Build a family or classroom rhythm where everyone shares one mini challenge and how they approached it that day. You can then reflect on: *What did you actively work through today? What worked? What didn't? What might you try next time?*

This helps to model **reflection > resilience > re-trying** rather than being overly solution-focused.

'Brainstorm Buddy' Stations

Have a weekly family or class routine where a 'problem' is explored together and **wondered about**.

For example, *What would ten silly solutions be?* or *Who else might know more about this?*

This models collaboration and creativity as a key to problem-solving.

Flow Forward Walks

Being out in nature can be an amazing space in which problems can lessen in intensity. Use a nature walk to pick one 'stuck' thing to reflect on. As you walk, invite your child to **notice metaphors**: leaves falling (letting go), rocks in the path (obstacles), changing direction (pivoting).

Kids can then learn to **use environment for inner movement** and healthy rhythm of flowing through rather than avoiding or bypassing.

Unfinished Stories

Share a story (real or imagined) that stops right before the resolution. Invite children to co-create **how the character might flow forward**, and why. This helps to expand imaginative flexibility and self-identification with solutions.

Legacy in Motion

Reflect. Integrate. Empower.

Empowered problem-solving grows our capacity to flow forward, even when the path isn't clear. The beauty is that when we raise kids in spaces where mistakes are safe, effort is valued, and thinking differently is welcomed, kids start to see challenges as invitations, which can often energise them with determination.

It's time to co-create solutions with our kids.

Get curious.

Tap into courage.

Take a step forward – one intentional choice at a time.

With trust.

So what's one of the most powerful tools we can offer children to strengthen that trust?

Story.

Next, we'll tap into storytelling as a superpower; one that fuels emotional growth, creative thinking, lifelong learning … and most importantly, a deep sense of belonging and connection.

Journal Prompts

- *What helps me shift from feeling stuck to feeling curious?*
- *When have I found a way forward through something that felt too big at first? What did I learn?*
- *How do I model empowered problem-solving in my daily life, even in the small moments?*
- *What does 'flowing forward' mean to me – and how can I support children in doing the same?*

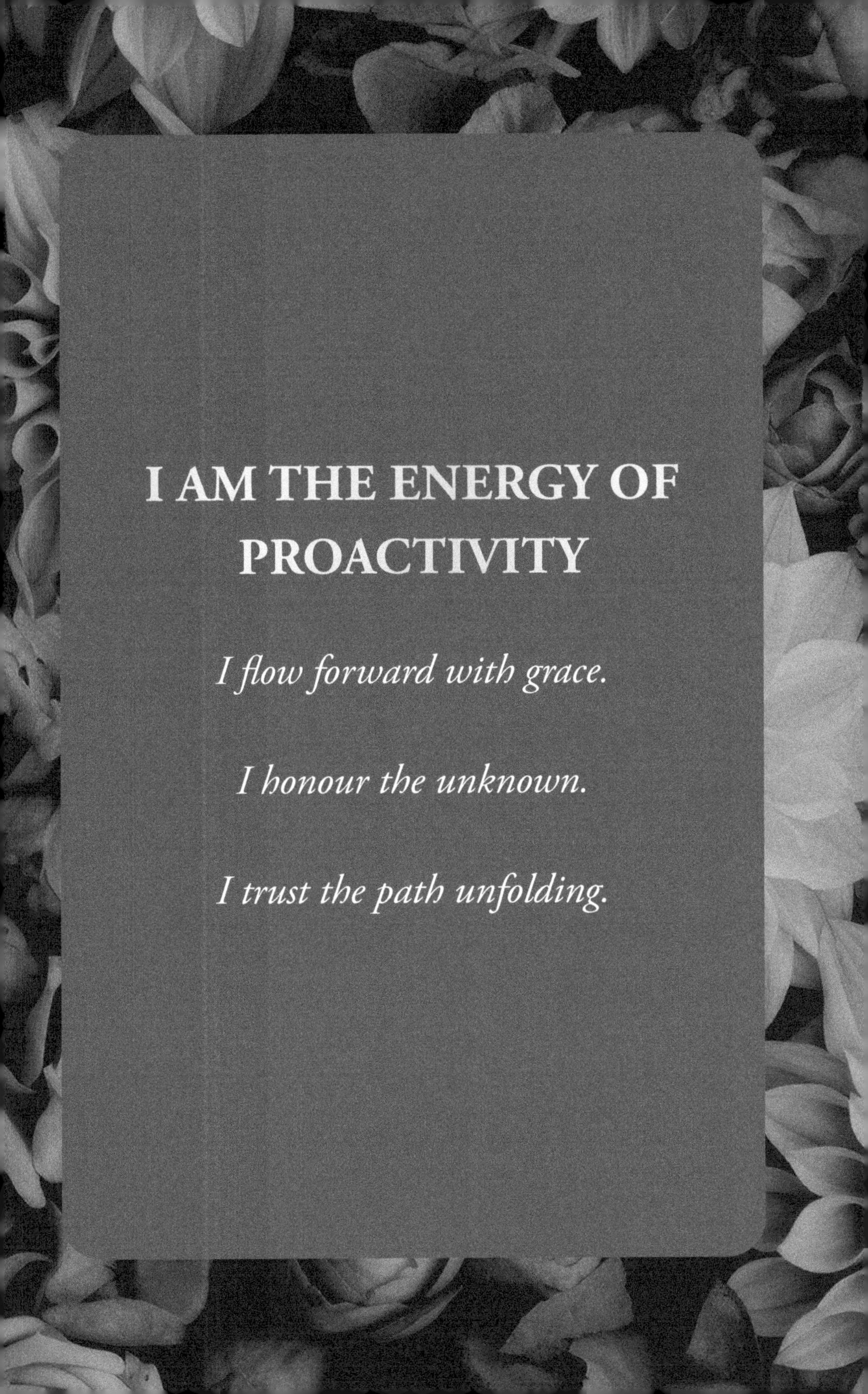

I AM THE ENERGY OF PROACTIVITY

I flow forward with grace.

I honour the unknown.

I trust the path unfolding.

SUPERPOWER STORYTELLING

Fuel Imagination, Growth, and Lifelong Learning

What if the stories we tell, and the stories we receive, hold the power to transform not just the mind, but the soul?

We all know a storyteller. Because essentially, we all are wired to be.

And we all know a story lover. Because essentially, we are all wired to be.

Truth is: storytelling is etched into our human nature. It's how we make sense of the world, how we pass on wisdom, and how we stay connected across generations.

That's why this chapter is called *Superpower Storytelling: Fuel Imagination, Growth, and Lifelong Learning.* Because the ability to share and receive story is more than a communication skill; it's a foundational pillar for raising heart-led self-leaders. It nurtures a child's ability to think creatively, feel deeply, connect meaningfully, and lead from within.

I've always been drawn to ancestral stories – those whispered across time that reveal resilience, creativity, and heart. Whether it be stories of my grandmother of 'grit', raising six children on her own, able to craft pillows from straw and potato sacks; or of my grandfather, a well-respected, honourable man, lover of books and theatre, who cherished summer nights at the open-air cinema. Or that of my great-grandmother, known as a scribe and 'translator' of the written word for those needing help in her Italian village. These stories didn't just entertain; they shaped identity and belonging.

Even in my professional world, storytelling has remained a central pillar. I recall a conversation with a man involved in the braille translation of my book *Reece Give Me Some Peace!* He shared the story of a young girl – visually impaired yet proficient in braille – who proudly considered her ability to 'read in the dark' a superpower. She would sneak in late-night reading sessions, immersed in story without needing the light on. Moments like this remind us that storytelling isn't just tradition; it's a superpower woven into our DNA.

When I was awaiting the birth of my first child, one of the very first things I set up in the nursery was a bookshelf lined with an array of books and a wooden rocking chair, ready and waiting for shared story time. I still have the video footage of my three children, ages 1, 2, and 3, sitting on the lounge room rug looking up at me earnestly as I sat in that rocking chair sharing the manuscript of one of my soon-to-be-published picture books. Even without the illustrations, the story mesmerised them.

There's a magic in children's books that defies age and logic. As a mother to three young children – born within two and a half years of each other – storytelling became a sacred part of our nightly routine. And even before I became a parent, I spent years training parents and educators in how to use storytelling to strengthen connection, enhance language, and elevate emotional expression. Why? Because the benefits are enormous.

In my speech pathology work, storybooks were never just tools, they were doorways. Doorways into complex concepts made accessible through symbolic language and vivid imagery. And in my intuitive life coaching, storytelling takes on an energetic and spiritual dimension, used to shift frequency, release limiting patterns, and activate profound inner healing. Whether supporting a child's language development or guiding someone through their personal transformation, story becomes the bridge … from where we are, to where we're ready to go.

From ancient mythologies to Aboriginal Dreamtime, from sacred chants to fireside folktales, story has always been a way to transmit wisdom, identity, values, and collective memory. Long before written language, story was how we made sense of our world and ourselves. And while the forms have evolved, from cave paintings to digital animations, the essence of story remains the same – it is a human connector. A resonance that bridges soul to soul.

From a scientific lens, storytelling lights up multiple regions of the brain: language centres, emotional pathways, and even motor regions as we mentally simulate the actions being described. Studies show that when we hear a story, especially one rich in emotional and sensory detail, our brains release oxytocin, the neurochemical linked to empathy, trust, and connection. We literally begin to feel with the storyteller.

That's why we remember stories far more than facts. It's also why stories can shift perspectives, awaken emotions, and stay with us long after the telling is done.

The resonance of story reaches deeper than we realise; it transcends time, language, and even logic. It reminds us that wisdom doesn't have to be complex to be powerful … it just has to be felt.

As we explore storytelling in the context of raising empowered humans, it's important to hold it not just as a communication tool, but as an energetic portal. One that can nurture imagination, foster emotional literacy, shape belief systems, and even shift deeply embedded patterns of fear or disconnection.

In the legendary Persian tale *One Thousand and One Nights*, we meet Shahrazad; a courageous young woman who volunteers to marry a vengeful king known for executing his brides after one night. But Shahrazad doesn't just surrender to fate, she reshapes it. On their wedding night, she begins to tell the king a story so captivating that he delays her execution to hear how it ends. Night after night, she weaves new stories, pausing at dawn each time. Over 1,001 nights, her storytelling softens the king's heart, restores his humanity, and ultimately saves countless lives, including her own.

Shahrazad's legacy is one of emotional wisdom, strategic empathy, and the soul power of narrative. Her voice didn't roar; it resonated. And it reminds us that one empowered human, speaking from inner truth, can transform even the hardest hearts.

When we encourage children to tell their own stories, to create endings, to dream up characters, to rewrite narratives, they begin to remember their agency. They discover the power to narrate life, not just react to it. And that, right there, is the root of self-leadership.

Because how can we lead ourselves towards truth, towards purpose, towards healing, without first imagining that we are capable of doing so?

Imagination fuels resilience, building a bridge between challenge and creativity, helping children ask:

What if it could be different?

What if I try something new?

What story do I want to live?

This is how empowered humans are raised … by giving them space to imagine, feel, and create what's never been seen before.

Stories are not one-dimensional – they live in layers. There are the stories we speak aloud, sing in song, or carry quietly within. The stories we tell to teach, the ones we tell to connect, and the ones we tell ourselves … which often hold the greatest power. As we have already explored, a child's self-talk – *I'm not good at this* or *I'm brave, I can try again* – is a story. So is the tale a parent shares at bedtime or the narrative that unfolds in a favourite film. Every story holds a frequency. Some constrict. Some expand. And the stories we rehearse most often become the energetic rhythm of our reality.

This is why conscious storytelling matters; it's the invitation to become aware of which narratives are shaping our lives … and which ones we are ready to rewrite.

Because in the end, the stories we tell our children, and the stories we help them tell themselves, are among the greatest gifts we can offer for a life of flourishing, truth, and joyful expansion.

Heart-Powered Self-Leadership

So how can we help kids to superpower storytelling?

Story Mirror Journals

After reading or hearing a story, ask your child, *What part of this character reminds you of you?* or *What choice would you have made?* Let them write or draw their responses. This simple practice helps them build self-awareness, own their choices, and recognise their inner strength through the lens of narrative.

Create a 'Brave Book'

Encourage them to create a personal journal (or sketchbook) capturing times they felt brave, curious, kind, or even when they made a mistake and learnt from it. They can use drawings, simple sentences, or collage. Over time, this becomes a treasury of their own lived story, a reminder that they are always evolving.

Rewrite the Ending

If a child feels stuck, hurt, or frustrated by something that happened, invite them to retell it as a story and imagine a new, empowered ending. Ask, *What could the character try next time?* or *What magic would help shift this story?* This helps them step out of the 'stuckness' and into the role of conscious creator.

Craft the Craft: Stretch Their Storytelling Tools

Now and then, gently guide your child to enhance their storytelling with tools like adjectives, character voices, humour, or 'what happens next' twists. For example: *Tell me that part again, but like a scary movie!* This builds their expressive range in ways that feel safe and fun; no red pens, just creative joy.

Letters to the Future Self

Help your child write a gentle letter to their 'future self' one month or one year from now. They can include hopes, affirmations, reminders, or kind encouragement. This creates a bridge of continuity between their present self and their evolving self, and models intentional growth.

Hero's Journey Map

Draw a simple arc (like a rainbow) and help your child plot out a real challenge they've moved through, beginning, middle, and what they learnt. Let them illustrate or label each part. This mirrors the classic hero's journey and supports the inner narrative that *I grow through what I go through.*

Lifelong Flourishing

Daily Rituals & Rhythms for Families, Educators & Therapists

Story Spark Builders

Create a 'Story Spark Box' filled with prompts like: *a describing word* (e.g. *sparkling, soggy*), *a feeling* (e.g. *nervous, excited*), *a setting* (e.g. *on the moon, in Grandma's kitchen*), and *a twist* (e.g. *the animal could talk* or *everything was upside down*). Let your child pull one of each and build a story aloud (or in writing).

Encourage them to add descriptive language, dialogue, humour, or even sound effects. This helps them learn that storytelling isn't just about what happens, it's how you *share* what happens. It also builds confidence in using expressive tools like tone, rhythm, and pacing. Over time, this builds vocabulary, narrative structure, and sense of voice; all of which deepen self-leadership.

Storytelling Charades

Choose a few simple story themes or characters (e.g. a lost puppy, a magical forest, a grumpy pirate) and act them out as a family. The others have to guess the story. This playful activity builds non-verbal expression, creativity, and confidence in bringing story to life through movement, gesture, and emotion.

Tell It in Rhyme (or Song!)

Invite your child to turn a simple daily moment – like brushing teeth or walking the dog – into a short rhyme or song. You can join in too! This lighthearted practice helps children access rhythm, sequencing, and joyful play with language – all essential parts of oral storytelling.

What If … Reflection Prompts

Use open-ended *What if …* questions like *What if you were the mentor in someone else's story?* or *What if your heart could talk in a story, what would it say?* These spark introspection and foster a sense of purpose beyond performance.

'Story-Back' Ritual

After reading a book or watching a movie/show together, invite your child to 'tell back' the story in their own words; or even better, to make up an alternate ending. This strengthens memory and sequencing, while inviting creative ownership.

Story Basket or Book Nook

Create a cosy, visible home for books, whether it be a basket in the lounge or a nook near the bed. Rotate the selection weekly and invite your child to choose which book is 'this week's treasure'. That small act of curation builds agency, reverence, and personal connection to stories.

Drive-Time Dialogues

Turn car rides into story adventures. Share family memories or your own childhood tales or prompt your child to create a story using five things they spot out the window (e.g. a red car, a dog, a tree, a cloud, and a traffic light). These moments turn into rich, imaginative storytelling on-the-go.

Legacy in Motion

Reflect. Integrate. Empower.

Each day, we're both the narrator and the listener in our own becoming.

And as we guide children to honour the stories within and around them, we offer them a compass, guiding them with curiosity, truth, and possibility.

By embracing storytelling as an energetic and creative force, we help children:

- trust their voice, even in uncertainty
- reframe challenges as chapters of growth
- explore identity through playful imagination
- connect across generations through shared memory
- create meaning through both expression and deep listening.

Ultimately, story is not a script to follow, it is a sacred dance between intuition, imagination, and soulful leadership.

Their story isn't written **for** them. It's written **with** them.

But story doesn't only live in books. It's in the scribbled notes, the quiet reflections, the way kids put their thoughts into words – on paper, and out loud.

So next, we dive into how reading and writing can become powerful tools of expression.

Journal Prompts

- *What was my favourite story as a child, and what did I love about it? Are there any messages from that story I need to apply to my life right now?*
- *What story have I been telling myself lately, and is it expanding or limiting me?*
- *How often do I remember that I'm the main character in my life story; not just reacting, but creating?*

- *Where in my day could I invite more spontaneous storytelling with my child, without needing to 'add' anything extra?*

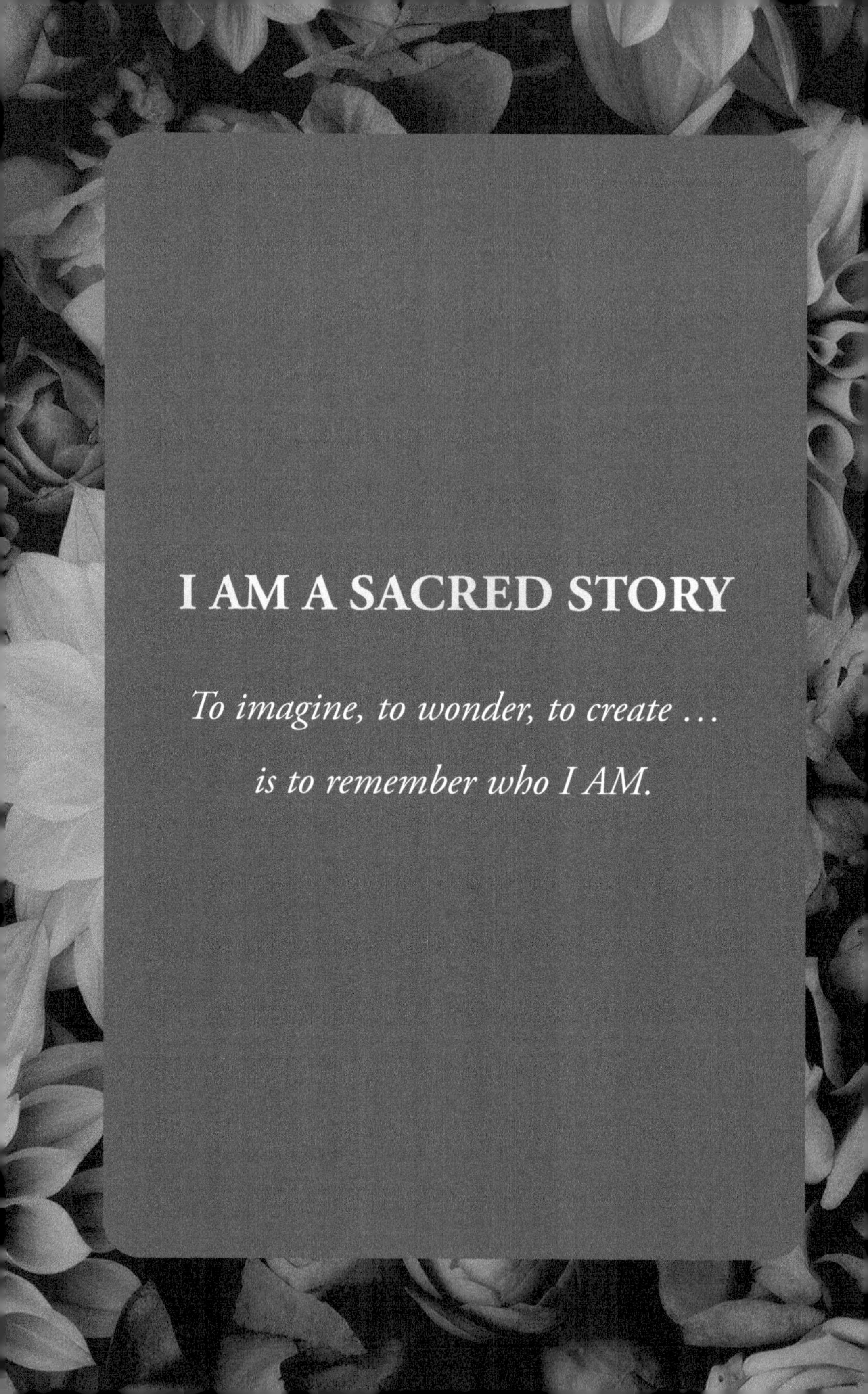
I AM A SACRED STORY
To imagine, to wonder, to create …
is to remember who I AM.

SHAPE TOOLS OF EXPRESSION

Nurture a Positive Bond with Reading and Writing

What if writing was a mirror, and reading a doorway, to imagination, healing, and the voice within?

It was the early weeks of my three kids starting at three different new schools. We were all still adjusting – everything felt fresh, unfamiliar, and slightly unsteady. That afternoon, I picked up my son from school, and as he jumped into the car, he said, 'Mum, it's the school swimming carnival tomorrow. I need new swimmers – the ones I have don't fit anymore.'

I glanced at the time. We had less than an hour before the stores would close. I let him know on the drive, 'We might not have many choices, so whatever they've got, we'll need to roll with it.'

At the store, the options were slim. The ones he liked weren't available in his size, and the only ones that fit were the traditional style speedos: the snug, brief ones. He looked at me in horror. 'Mum, I am not wearing those!'

I could feel his disappointment. 'Buddy,' I said gently, 'right now, this might be our only option. Let's just get them and see how it goes.'

We made the purchase, but the embarrassment hung heavy. On the way home, he sighed, 'Everyone at school is probably going to be wearing board shorts.'

Later, as I was preparing dinner, I noticed he still seemed unsettled. I washed my hands and went over to sit beside him. I didn't try to fix anything; I just sat.

After a moment, I asked softly, 'Why do you think they make speedos like that? Why not just have everyone wear board shorts?'

He paused, his mind starting to work it through.

I continued, 'Imagine a professional swimmer. Who do you think might swim faster: someone in board shorts or someone in speedos?'

He tilted his head. 'Speedos … less drag. They'd have an advantage.'

'Interesting,' I said simply, letting that idea land without pushing.

A few minutes later, he picked up his pencil and notebook and started writing. I left him to it. When dinner was done, he came over beaming, saying, 'Mum, I wrote a rhyme – like a rap song!'

'Awesome,' I said. 'Let's hear it.'

He launched into a rap about swimming in his speedos like a pro; leaving the others behind like 'chicken dinner'. His pride was radiant.

The next day, he wore those speedos, showed up with confidence, and came home with three ribbons.

I would describe that sequence of events as an unexpected alchemy of discomfort, reflection, and expression. The circumstances forged a *soul expression*. It was healing. It was self-leadership in action. And it also reminded me how powerful it is to hold space for a child, not to fix their feelings, but to witness them … and watch what rises from within.

It was beautiful to witness his chosen moments of emotional

resilience, and to couple it with writing as reclamation. The simple act of reaching for a pencil became a tool of transformation. A spontaneous rhyme helped him shape his experience, shift his state, and show up as the author of his own reality.

This is the heart of shaping tools of expression.

When children are empowered to *write through* their feelings, *read into* their strengths, and *create from* their truth, they begin to build a lifelong bond with language that goes beyond performance. It becomes personal. Purposeful. Powerful.

And in that space, self-expression becomes not just a skill, but a superpower.

Being able to find joy in reading and writing is not the case for all kids though. There's a quiet kind of heartbreak I've witnessed time and again, when a child's brilliance is misunderstood simply because it doesn't fit neatly into the standard boxes of reading and writing.

As a speech pathologist, I've worked extensively with children diagnosed with dyslexia, dysgraphia, and dyscalculia. Many of them radiate creativity, deep thinking, and emotional intelligence; but because they find spelling or handwriting difficult, they begin to question their own worth. The school system, with its heavy reliance on written output, often becomes a daily reminder of what they struggle with. And that wears away at self-esteem like a bruise that keeps getting bumped.

This chapter is for those children; and for the families, educators, and therapists walking alongside them. Whether you're navigating a learning difference, resistance, or reluctance, this is an invitation to look deeper and reframe literacy itself: not as a test of intelligence, but as a tool for self-leadership, creativity, and connection.

I remember delivering a masterclass to a group of allied health professionals about supporting children with literacy challenges. One attendee asked, 'How many minutes of homework should a child do each day to make progress?' I paused. The question made sense, but my answer wasn't what most expected.

'The prescription is not ten minutes, nor is it twenty or thirty. The prescription is fun.' I stated before continuing.

'When a child is deeply engaged, even for two minutes, it creates more neural connectivity than ten minutes of resistance. You don't need a lab-measured formula; the principle is clear: quality trumps quantity. A positive, playful relationship with reading and writing is far more impactful than clock-watching. And the key to creating that relationship? Start with the *why*.'

When my daughter was in kindergarten, she asked me – genuinely – 'Why do I even need to know how to read?' I didn't launch into a lecture. We were sitting on a bench inside a shopping centre, outside the supermarket, as I respectfully responded.

'Well, you love making muffins, right? To get the ingredients, you need to write a shopping list, read the signs in the supermarket aisles, and follow the recipe. Reading can help you do the things you love.' That clicked for her. It had meaning.

When we focus on functionality – on how literacy serves real life – we spark motivation, not resistance. And when we tap into a child's natural interests, whether it's baking, gaming, sport, animals, or animation, we can shape reading and writing into a co-creative process.

I've had countless parents thank me after sessions where 'homework' was simply to reconnect through joy. Like the time I asked a mum and her son (who was struggling with writing) to play PlayStation together. He'd write out the game instructions for her and read them aloud so she could learn. The next week? He came back beaming, having written over a page … and the energy between them was transformed.

In recent years, there has been a documented decline in both reading and writing skills among children and adolescents. A 2023 US national assessment showed that reading scores for nine-year-olds dropped to levels not seen since the early 2000s. In Australia and the UK, similar trends are emerging, with concerns about spelling, grammar, and comprehension falling behind expected milestones.

This isn't a place for blame; it's a wake-up call. They are reflections of how today's fast-paced, tech-saturated, overstimulated environments and shortened attention spans are shifting the landscape of learning. The message isn't to panic – it's to become more *conscious* of how we nurture the bond with reading and writing. Beyond academic performance. Literacy is deeply tied to brain development, mental health, and identity formation.

Yes, we can acknowledge that our current educational approaches or literacy policies may need reimagining. But in the meantime, the everyday relationship a child builds with words matters.

And then there's real life. In a world of autocorrect, predictive text, and tools like ChatGPT, many parents and educators are left wondering: Why even bother with handwriting or spelling anymore? If technology can do it for us, is it still necessary?

Here's the truth: The tools are helpful, but the *act* of writing is so much more than putting words on a page. It's a neurological workout. It enhances memory and comprehension. Reading builds focus, imagination, empathy. Writing helps regulate emotions, organise thoughts, and foster clarity.

These aren't obsolete skills; they are gateways to understanding ourselves and others.

And when children shape words in their own way, without judgment, they don't just build literacy. They build identity.

I've seen this with my own children. One was captivated by biographies and real-world stories, from the royal family to historical figures. Another loved escaping into the worlds of fantasy and science fiction. And my third? Manga, graphic novels, and soccer-themed adventures were his thing. Their differences taught me this: it's not about *what* they read – it's about *finding their doorway* into the world of words.

I'll also never forget the children's author I interviewed on my podcast; a brilliant author who shared that he didn't take notes during university. He wasn't disengaged. He was dyslexic, and he'd honed his auditory memory so well that he didn't need notes. His strength wasn't visible in traditional ways; but it was extraordinary.

This is the power of difference. Some of the most innovative thinkers I've worked with were once reluctant readers and writers. Not because they lacked intelligence, but because their brains were busy building new pathways.

The story is often told that young Thomas Edison came home from school with a sealed note for his mother. 'She said only you should read it,' he told her. Nancy Edison opened it, then read aloud through tears:

'Your son is a genius. This school can't support his brilliance; please teach him yourself.'

Years later, long after Edison had become one of history's greatest inventors, he reportedly found the note again. The real message?

'Your son is mentally deficient. He is no longer welcome at this school.'

Though historians say this version is likely fictionalised, one truth is clear: Edison's teacher *did* call him 'addled'. And it was his mother who chose to see beyond the label.

Nancy Edison believed in her son fiercely. She taught him at home, nurtured his natural curiosity, and gave him the freedom to learn on his terms. Edison would later say: 'My mother was the making of me. She was so true, so sure of me … I felt I had someone to live for.'

This story endures because it captures a timeless truth:

Children become what they are told. Words can wound – or they can awaken.

When shaped with love, reverence, and belief, words become the tools that shape a life.

And it begins with the stories we choose to tell.

We all have that power. To believe. To reframe. To nurture literacy not as a checkbox, but as a doorway to empowered self-expression.

I remember one Mother's Day when each of my children wrote me a letter. I was moved by the expression, purity, and depth with which they shared their thoughts and feelings. One of my daughters has a particularly extraordinary ability to write – her words hold a presence and precision in a way that is uniquely hers. How one expresses themselves in writing is often entirely different from how they communicate in spoken language. Like reading a book versus watching a movie; each carries a completely different energy. And for some children, writing becomes the clearest mirror of their inner world.

When we honour this, we create space for every child to discover their own authentic rhythm of expression.

So, collectively – it is time to focus on tools, not tests …

If your child struggles with reading or writing, remind yourself often:

- They are growing in their own rhythm.
- Their ideas matter, no matter how they come out.
- Your connection is more important than any worksheet.

Use affirmations like:

You're growing in your own way.

We'll find and use the tools that fit with you.

There's more than one way to be smart.

Seek support when needed, but seek it from professionals who honour your child's strengths. Use daily rituals like exploring bookstores, browsing the library, listening to audiobooks, reading environmental signs, or reading aloud together (even when kids can already read).

And when it comes to writing? Focus on capturing the *magic* of their ideas. Grammar and spelling can come later. Let their voice lead. Whether it's journalling, storytelling, comic making, writing cards, letters or rhymes, what is needed is to create a safe, joyful space where expression can flourish.

Because when we shape tools of expression with love and curiosity, we're not just raising literate children, we're nurturing sacred storytellers, ready to write the world they wish to live in.

Heart-Powered Self Leadership

So how can we help children cultivate reading and writing as sacred tools of expression?

Follow Curiosity Through Print

Encourage your child to explore reading materials beyond traditional books; such as magazines, comics, manuals, recipe cards, sports stats, joke books, even how-to guides based on their interests … there are books on everything! When children see reading as a tool to unlock what they care about, it becomes an act of self-driven discovery.

Read to a Pet (or a Plant!)

Reading aloud to non-judgmental companions – like pets, stuffed animals, or even a houseplant – can reduce performance pressure and increase fluency, while building emotional safety and confidence in young readers.

Start a Street Library or Book Swap Box

Support your child to decorate and manage a mini community library at home or school. This encourages responsibility, generosity, and belonging, while reinforcing that their voice and reading life matter to others.

'My Word, My Way' Journals

Offer your child a special notebook for them to write or draw anything: feelings, facts, made-up words, jokes, stories. Celebrate inventive spelling and silly grammar; this is about self-expression, not correction.

Book Buddies or Reading Circles

Encourage your child to share books with siblings or friends. Peer-to-peer reading builds confidence and relational connection, reinforcing that reading isn't just solitary; it's social.

Let Them Write the Rules (Literally)

Invite your child to write family rules, bedtime routines, or kitchen labels. This shows writing has real-world impact and builds authorship of their environment.

Lifelong Flourishing

Daily Rituals & Rhythms for Families, Educators & Therapists

Board Games as Bridges

Playing with words can be just as powerful as studying them.

Board games that involve reading, writing, or language-based thinking are fantastic for building:

- Vocabulary

- Reading fluency
- Turn-taking and listening
- Written communication
- Spelling and word creation.

Interactive Book Sharing

There are two main ways to share children's books: passively or interactively.

Passive sharing (e.g. reading aloud at bedtime) is calming and comforting; but,

Interactive sharing is dynamic, engaging children in questions, predictions, character feelings, and outcomes.

This builds vocabulary, empathy, attention, creativity, and a lifelong love of books – all while strengthening your connection.

Read Around the Day

Turn everyday moments into reading opportunities:

- Reading signs while driving.
- Reading a recipe while baking.
- Reading packaging or instructions together.

These organic rituals make reading relevant and functional.

Apps That Read & Grow With You

Apps like *ABC Reading Eggs* aren't just for screen time; they're springboards for shared exploration. Ideally, a parent or educator joins in so that the app becomes a co-experience. This builds emotional bonding, scaffolds understanding, and helps the child associate *reading with relationship*, not isolation.

Attend Author Events or Storytime Sessions
Bring your child to bookshops or libraries that host interactive story sessions or book launches. Meeting an author or engaging in live storytelling can inspire a child to see themselves as readers, and future creators.

Book-Love Walks
Take a walk and bring a favourite book. Halfway through your walk, sit down and read together in nature; whether that be a park or on the beach, etc. Let kids associate reading with calm and connection, not just classrooms and tests.

Creative Copycats
Invite children to 'copywrite' their favourite story ending; or rewrite it with a twist! This strengthens comprehension, creativity, and emotional connection to story.

Mailbox Magic
Set up a family mailbox (a decorated box or pouch), and take turns writing notes, questions, or stories to each other. This encourages writing in a low-pressure, love-infused way.

Legacy in Motion

Reflect. Integrate. Empower.

Whether our children are penning poems, crafting comics, sending and reading heartfelt notes, or composing emails one finger at a time, the way children shape and share words becomes part of their legacy. And when we model reverence for the written word, we remind them that their voice matters; on the page and in life.

What we nurture now echoes for generations.

The child who is empowered to write their feelings today becomes the adult who advocates with clarity tomorrow. The child who feels safe to read slowly becomes the adult who listens deeply, thinks critically, and creates imaginatively.

Our collective legacy is not measured by perfect penmanship or pristine grammar, but by whether we've helped children fall in love with their own voice.

Journal Prompts

- *What messages – spoken or unspoken – have I given my child about reading and writing?*
- *When have I witnessed my child express something powerful through writing or storytelling? What did it reveal about their inner world?*
- *In what ways can I co-create more joyful, functional, or meaningful literacy moments with the children in my life?*
- *How can I honour and nurture the unique rhythm of expression in my child?*

** ***See the Resources Section for more*** **

And so we come to the close of Section Three.

You've now received the third golden key – *The Frequency of Fun.* We've played, explored, imagined … and opened new doorways of possibility.

Now, let's follow that spark of wonder inward; into the power of aligned authenticity … where living a fulfilled life becomes a natural practice and rhythm.

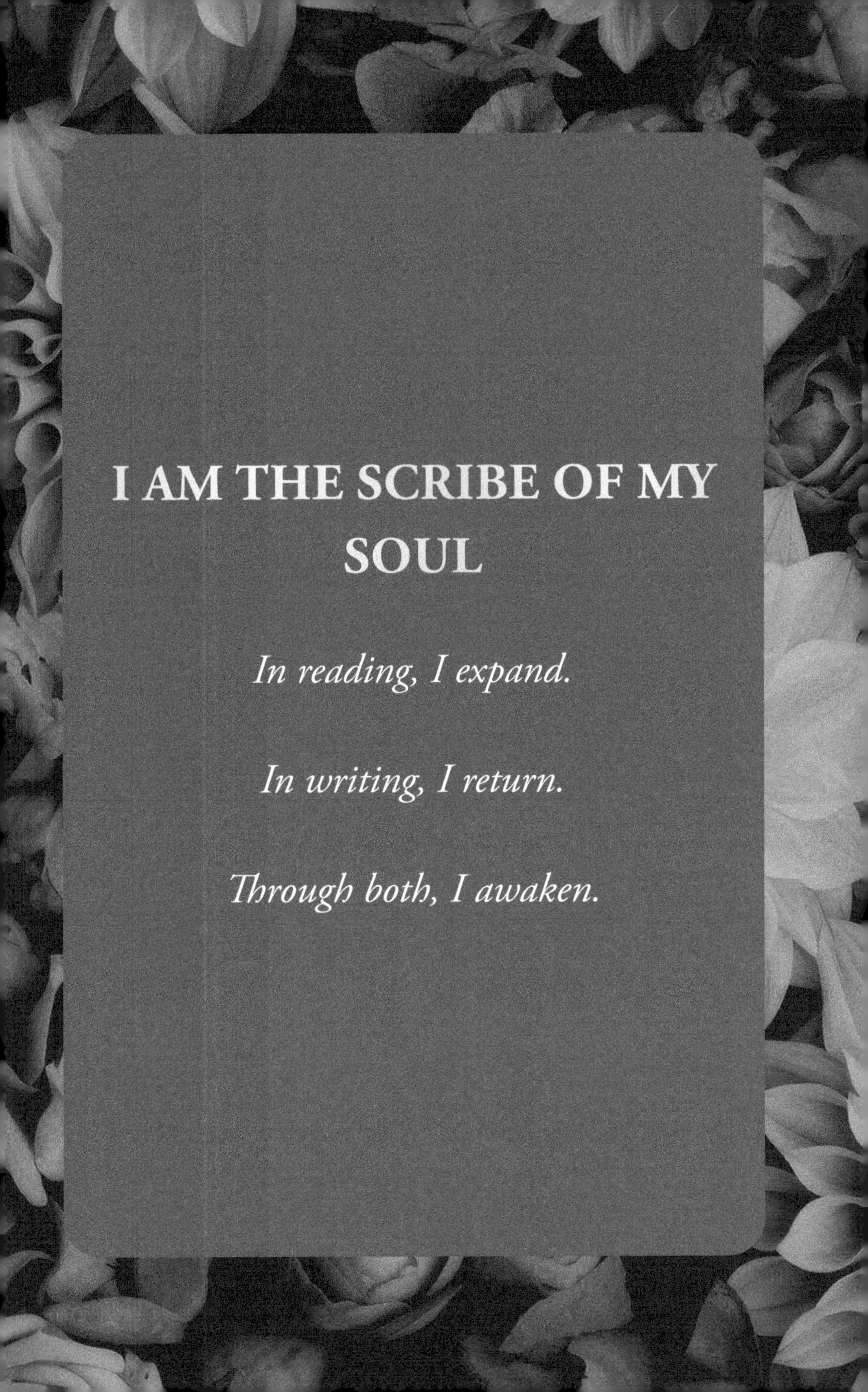

I AM THE SCRIBE OF MY SOUL

In reading, I expand.

In writing, I return.

Through both, I awaken.

GOLDEN KEY FOUR

THE FREQUENCY OF FULFILMENT

The Practice of Aligned Authenticity

fulfilment noun
/fʊlˈfɪlmənt/

A deep experience of contentment, within an ongoing process of becoming, rather than a final destination.

HIGHER SELF-EXPRESSION

Living Authentically from the Inside Out

What if your soul was never meant to fit in – but to be fully expressed, from the inside out?

I'll always remember a moment at a networking lunch, where I sat beside a woman who was telling me about herself and her work, facilitating equine therapy for children (this is a therapeutic approach that involves interactions between individuals and horses to support emotional, social, physical, and communication goals). I was excited to meet her, as I deeply appreciate the incredible benefits of this approach.

Within our conversation, she told me about a young Autistic boy who would attend sessions each week but never spoke during his sessions. He preferred to sit silently and watch the horses, week after week. On one particular day, the boy was in the company of a horse when she walked over and sat beside him.

Gently, she said to him, 'You know … the horse doesn't talk.'

From which the boy, maintaining his gaze on the horse, responded to her for the first time, using spoken language …

'It speaks with its soul,' he simply stated.

The woman paused her recounting, and I held the silence as I felt my body respond with small goosebumps rising along my arms in quiet recognition. Recognition of the deep truth offered by the young boy, and the sacred remembering it stirred.

His single, soul-filled sentence has stayed with me, as it is a reminder of something so many of us forget: expression isn't about volume; it's about truth. And that truth is felt within *our presence* and within the fluent 'spoken silence' of the soul.

Often, as humans, we can feel a deep longing within us, which may not be easy to articulate or understand; and that is the longing for our inner truth and authentic self to be felt and accepted, even when it's not spoken. It reminds me of an important distinction – that the opposite of depression is not happiness ... the opposite of depression is expression. *True*, heart-and-soul-aligned expression.

I grew up in a loving household, though it was 'strict' when compared to most of my school peers. So when I was 14, I was keen to start casual work alongside my schooling not just to earn spending money, but to carve out my own sense of autonomy. I preferred the freedom to choose, express, and explore beyond the confines of expectation.

I remember feeling the inner conflict early on: the difference between how my parents hoped or expected me to live and the quiet knowing of how I wanted to live. There were clear rules, clear roles ... and yet there was an inner whisper urging me towards something truer. Because just as we feel dismissed when someone ignores our voice, the soul too retreats when there is no space for it to land.

It's taken years to soften the tension between external approval and inner alignment. But to me, higher self-expression means listening when the soul speaks; and responding with action, reverence, and trust so life unfolds not through force, but through *flow*; guided by an inner compass that's always been there.

I enjoyed a chat with Vanessa Bell, whose life is a powerful testament to this truth. A former high-fashion model turned eco-entrepreneur, she is the founder of luxury knitwear rooted in regenerative farming and sustainability. Vanessa has redefined what success and self-expression can look like; by listening, aligning, and living from the inside out.

'I believe in DNA; how it links us physically and metaphysically,' she shared. 'Something in me reawakened when I stepped onto the land.'

That reawakening was more than career change. It was soul remembering. Vanessa now lives with her family on extensive acreage in rural Australia, where the rhythms of nature have become both mirror and teacher. She is a mother, a global advocate for sustainability, and champion of Australian Merino wool; in essence, she is an embodiment of intergenerational love and legacy.

But her journey hasn't been linear. She's worked across industries – from fashion and finance to wine and media – yet never stopped listening to what lit her up inside. That quiet, consistent inner pulse eventually guided her home.

'I didn't always know where I was going, but I knew when something felt right. I followed what brought me joy. That's always been my path.'

And at the heart of it all is her role as a mother. Her son is growing up on the land; riding horses across steep ridges, helping with cattle, and learning through real-world trust.

'He's been riding since he was two. He knows how to drive a tractor. He's been taught not just skills, but self-trust. We don't shape him. We give him space to become who he already is.'

Her message is clear: when we stop managing how we're seen and start honouring how we're *called*, that's where our truth begins to rise.

This is a beautiful reminder that authentic self-expression isn't loud. It's rooted … in remembering.

I shared another powerful conversation on my podcast with Kim Woods; a master astrologer, business strategist, and devoted mother. Kim's life is a bold blend of practical mastery and mystical devotion, shaped profoundly by the birth of her son who experienced developmental delays.

'The universe was like, oh, no, absolutely not, woman. That is not happening,' Kim reflected, recalling the cosmic redirection her life took when traditional systems failed to comprehensively support her son's needs.

Rather than accept limitations, she turned towards shamanism, sound healing, and vibrational medicine. Her personal and professional lives soon began to diverge; one steeped in corporate logic, the other in spiritual depth. For a time, she lived in both worlds.

'I would be channelling … I would clear things up energetically before I walked in,' she shared. Her clients didn't know, but they felt the results. Eventually, the split became too wide to hold. She left her consulting firm and stepped fully into her soul-led work.

'If I don't say the words *astrology* or *intuition* or *feminine wisdom* in the first two sentences, I am in conflict with myself.'

Kim's parenting has always been aligned with soul. She read her children's astrology charts as infants. She chose rhythm over rigidity. Her children were raised with a deep knowing of their own inner compass.

'They know they are souls. They know they are spirits. They have an inner compass. They have an inner authority.'

Now young adults, her children live by these truths; grounded in magic, advocacy, and self-leadership.

'Don't be afraid to be you,' Kim says. 'You'll find the doors open. People come to you. Opportunities appear. There are so many hiding in the spiritual closet; and you'll be surprised by how many are saying,

"Oh, you too?"'

Kim's words land with such resonance because when we let go of the fear of being seen, something shifts. Doors open, yes … but more importantly, we open. We become available to the life that's truly ours to live; and children feel this too. When they're supported in honouring their inner knowing, what unfolds can be extraordinary.

If you were to ask me for an example of a child (in the public realm) who is a shining example of soul truth in motion, it would be the remarkable story of Max Alexander, which is nothing short of magical. At just four years old, Max declared, 'I'm a dressmaker,' and began transforming ribbons and plastic wrap into gowns. By age five, he had launched his own label, Couture to the Max, and hosted a runway show in L.A. to a packed audience. Since then, he's created incredible couture pieces, using repurposed materials like coffee sacks and neckties, and has dressed celebrities, before earning a Guinness World Record as the youngest runway designer in history.

Of course, his parents have played a pivotal role of not just supporting his creativity, but helping him honour his soul's calling. It's a powerful reminder that when we nurture our children's inner voice, their higher self-expression becomes a gift to the world.

Heart-Powered Self-Leadership

So how can we help children live authentically from the inside out, embodying their higher expression?

As parents, educators, and caregivers, helping kids live from the inside out asks us to consider what it would mean to raise children to embody their authentic self (without performing to who they think they should be). Here are some ways to empower this.

Create Personal Values Art

Invite your child to choose three values that feel important to them, like kindness, fairness, or creativity, and create an artwork around them. This simple act anchors their sense of identity in what truly matters.

Embodiment Through Movement

Support your child to connect with their inner world through physical movement, whether it's free-form dance in the living room, gentle yoga stretches, playful nature walks, or simply swaying to music. Movement becomes a sacred language, especially when words fall short. It also helps kids nurture emotional intelligence and body-mind coherence, releasing tension, restoring clarity, and returning to their soul centre through rhythm.

Name Their Unique Light

Gently invite your child to reflect on their inner qualities by asking: *What do you think makes you you?* or *What do you love about how you show up in the world?* Let their answers be their own, without correction or comparison. These simple reflections affirm the parts of themselves that often go unnoticed (e.g. curiosity, honesty, imagination). When children are seen and celebrated for their essence, they begin to lead from it.

Create a 'Soul Shelf' or Sacred Space

Offer a small space, whether it be a shelf, box, or corner, for children to place objects that feel meaningful. A pinecone, a photo, a drawing, a crystal … anything that feels true. It becomes a mirror of their inner world and a grounding reminder of who they are.

Soul Time Rituals

Build regular moments of intentional stillness. This could be a warm bath with calming music, time spent under the sky, or simply lying on their bed with nothing but quiet. Soul time nourishes presence and helps them hear their own inner voice.

Truth Token Box

Help your child create a box to collect notes or objects that remind them of their inner strengths: for example, *I'm brave when I try* or *I listen to my heart*. Over time, this becomes a sacred archive of their own becoming.

Lifelong Flourishing

Daily Rituals & Rhythms for Families, Educators & Therapists

Children learn authenticity through atmosphere. These everyday practices help create an environment where presence is prioritised, self-trust is modelled, and technology is used with discernment. In a world that often pulls them outward, these rituals draw them back inward – reminding them to be more in connection with *themselves*.

Follow the Glow, Not the Goal

Pay attention to what naturally draws your child's interest, energy, or joy, even if it doesn't align with conventional success or your personal expectations. When you honour what lights them up, you affirm that their inner compass is valid. This teaches them to lead with authenticity, not just approval-seeking.

Anchor in the Real Before the Virtual

Before screens come on, ground into connection. This might look like a few mindful breaths together in the morning, sharing a hot drink outside, or simply a hand on the heart and a moment of eye contact. These rituals root your child in presence, so their sense of self doesn't dissolve into digital noise.

Make Media a Mirror, Not a Master

After screen time, gently open reflection: *How do you feel now?* or *What did you notice while watching that?* This helps your child begin to discern emotional impact and energetic shifts. The goal isn't restriction; it's deepening awareness so they can stay sovereign in a world that often pulls them into passive consumption.

Let Them Surprise You

Release assumptions about who your child is or what they'll love. Allow kids to try things that fall outside your story of them. A quiet child may love performance. An athletic child may find peace in poetry. Your openness gives them permission to discover undiscovered parts of themselves.

Model a Balanced Relationship with Technology

Your habits speak louder than your rules. Let your child witness you choosing presence: *I'm putting my phone away so I can really listen to you.* This models that tech is a tool, not a default. It also reinforces their worthiness of your full attention.

Invite Creative-Over-Passive Tech Use

Guide them towards using technology as a platform for expression (not just distraction). This could include making digital art, writing stories, coding a simple game, or even creating a family podcast. It reinforces that their voice, ideas, and creativity belong in the world.

Reclaim Real-Time Presence
Establish sacred, screen-free zones in your day; like mealtimes, the walk to school, or bedtime. These aren't rules to control, they're rhythms that restore. In those pauses, conversation flows, connection deepens, and the soul finds room to breathe.

Co-Create Digital Boundaries Together
Rather than dictating tech limits, invite your child into shared reflection: *What do you notice about yourself after being online?* or *When do you feel most like yourself?* This collaboration builds internal motivation and helps them take responsibility for their own energy, rather than waiting for control to come from the outside.

Legacy in Motion

Reflect. Integrate. Empower.

When we honour our soul's voice, we model what's possible for the next generation.

Every time we choose alignment over approval, presence over performance, or joy over obligation, we give our children energetic permission to do the same. We show them their truth matters, and that their inner knowing is the most trustworthy guide.

This is the kind of legacy that doesn't sit on a shelf. It's woven into conversations, choices, and quiet moments of self-trust; and it echoes in the child who dares to say, 'This is who I am.' and has the space to become it.

But for that kind of freedom to feel safe, it needs a container.

A sense of what feels right, what doesn't, and how to honour that truth.

And that's where boundaries come in …

As living maps – guiding children to protect their energy, trust their instincts, and speak their needs with clarity and care.

Next, let's explore how to raise empowered humans who see boundaries not as limits, but as sacred language for safety, self-leadership, and sovereignty.

Journal Prompts

- *What does soul-aligned expression look like in my daily life?*
- *What environments, rhythms, or relationships help me live from the inside out?*
- *How can I create more space for my child's inner voice to be heard, honoured, and expressed?*
- *What is one new way I can create space for my soul to speak?*

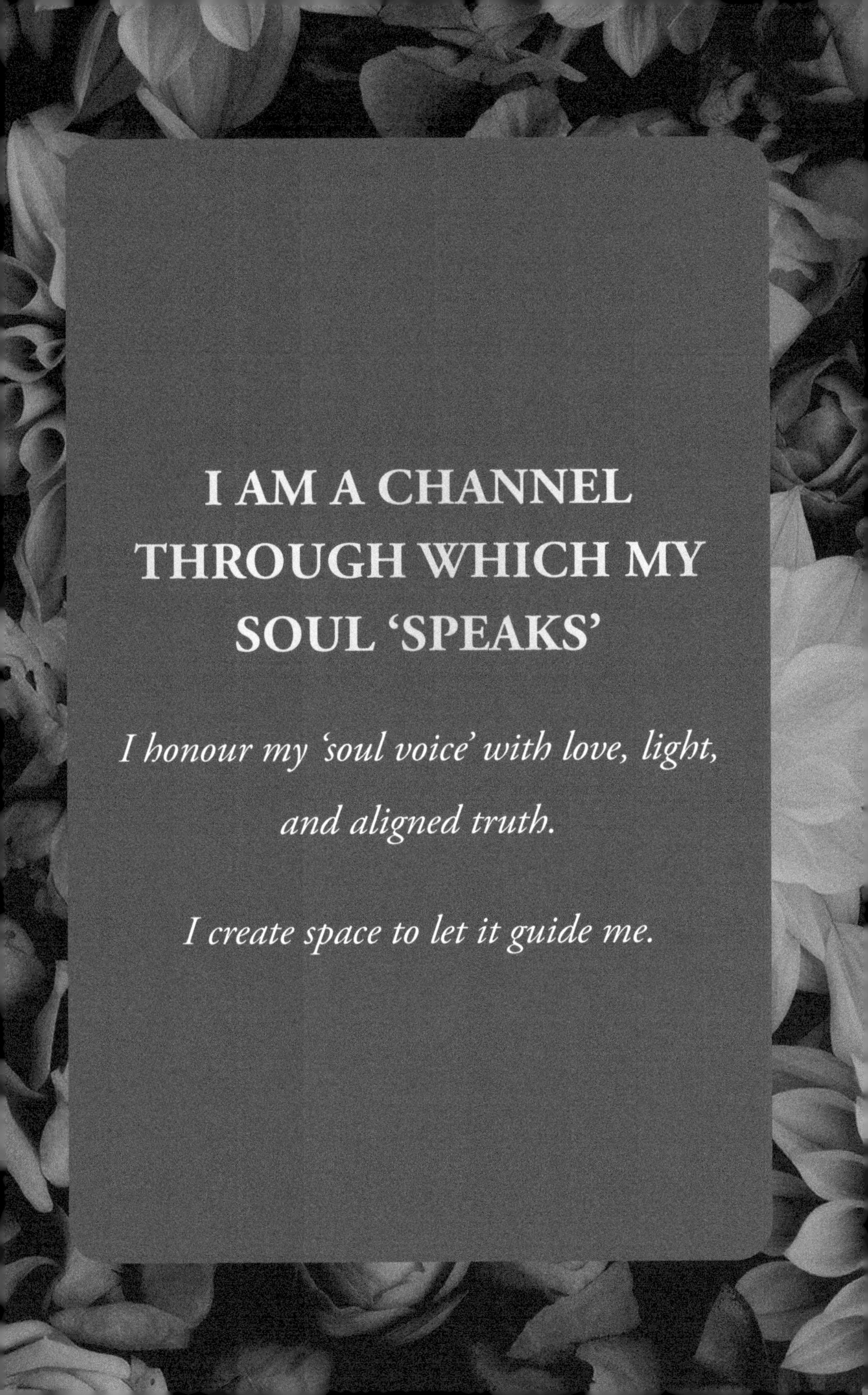

I AM A CHANNEL THROUGH WHICH MY SOUL 'SPEAKS'

I honour my 'soul voice' with love, light, and aligned truth.

I create space to let it guide me.

BEFRIEND BOUNDARIES AS LIVING MAPS

The Sacred Language of Safety and Sovereignty

What if boundaries aren't just limits we set … but living frequencies that teach children how to know and trust themselves?

My first job as a new graduate speech pathologist had me working for the Department of Education in Tasmania, Australia, across schools of various socio-economic backgrounds. This was eye opening and heart wrenching. I recall being on the phone with my mum after work one day in tears, heartbroken. There were kids with needs *far* greater than speech pathology services, who I wanted to do more for, to help more. But how?

This heartbreak and desire brought to the forefront patterns I hadn't realised I had, especially being a highly empathic individual (and there are many of us in the helping professions).

What were those patterns?

Over-functioning, over-giving, over-absorbing, over-identifying with a client's journey, difficulty saying 'no', and feeling guilt when prioritising myself over others.

Years of university allowed deep expansive learning across a breadth of human sciences. Practical clinical placements helped train me through the mechanics of putting the theory into practice; BUT … one thing that was not discussed – **energetic boundaries**.

How to be of **service – not sacrifice**.

That was something I learnt the hard way – through multilayered exhaustion, burnout, and what I call a 'sense-of-self crisis'. My own journey into energy healing, particularly through the ancient art of Reiki and my training in energy medicine, revealed profound insights. These wisdom traditions honour boundaries as expressions of the soul's integrity. They remind us that our energy field is sacred, and that the ability to say 'yes' or 'no' is foundational to wholeness.

I lost count of how many early-career and even seasoned allied health business owners and professionals I trained or coached who said, 'Nobody teaches you this stuff!'

And they're right.

In the traditional model, self-awareness, energy mastery, and boundary intelligence are rarely part of the curriculum. People speak about self-care in surface-level terms, like eating well and getting enough sleep (which, of course, matters), but beyond that is the need to nourish and protect the integrity of our whole selves, to recognise what depletes us and how to consciously restore and re-empower … and help our kids do the same.

Boundaries are constantly evolving, just as we are, and when it comes to the parenting world, boundaries have often been framed as rules or consequences – like tools for 'managing behaviour' – but true boundaries go *way deeper*.

Boundaries are not barriers; they are living maps that guide our (and our children's):

- Sense of self
- Energetic Safety
- Authentic Voice
- Right to belong without abandoning ourself.

When I refer to **Energetic Safety** I mean:

- physical safety (the body's sense of 'I am not under threat')
- emotional safety (my feelings are valid, and I won't be shamed for them)
- mental safety (my thoughts are heard and not ridiculed)
- spiritual safety (I can explore my sense of self, intuition, and beliefs without suppression)
- relational safety (I can be myself in connection and not lose my identity).

It is the **felt sense that your whole system – across all levels – is respected, attuned to, and allowed to exist without intrusion or distortion**.

For children, especially neurodiverse or sensitive ones, **energetic safety often precedes verbal safety**. They feel it before they can explain it. So, if a room, person, or conversation *feels* dissonant or 'off', their system may react long before they have the words to say why.

So, what is the truth about boundaries?

They are dynamic. Somatic (held in our body). Constantly evolving.

Consider a reframe on boundaries as a path to empowered 'selfhood'. As a sacred language of energy, body wisdom, and our evolving identity.

They begin in the body. So, kids who don't have the language to articulate boundaries … their body tells them:

This is too much.

I need space.

That doesn't feel right.

Fight/flight/freeze/fawn patterns are common responses; and overwhelm may present as shutdown, meltdowns, withdrawal, or avoidance.

It is encoded in our human circuitry of safety and regulation.

So, with the body as the first responder in sensing threat, safety, or overwhelm, children often express crossed boundaries through behaviour. This is important to remember as it removes the focus of boundaries being a tool of compliance, and supports kids to develop boundaries that reflect their sovereignty.

Neurodiversity and Boundary Expression

For neurodiverse children (and adults), boundaries may look and feel different. Some may struggle to express when a boundary has been crossed. Others might not recognise social cues that indicate another's boundary.

It's not a matter of defiance – it's a different **sensory blueprint** and **relational blueprint** (i.e. the internal pattern or map of how to connect with others).

Supporting neurodiverse boundary development means:

- observing behaviours as communication, not misbehaviour
- offering gentle, structured choice to support autonomy
- practising co-regulation: *I can help you find your edge by staying calm in mine.*

As we grow emotionally and gain more self-awareness, our understanding of what's okay for us, and what isn't, also changes. What once felt safe may now feel limiting. What used to be tolerated may now feel like an intrusion. This evolution matters.

Heart-Powered Self-Leadership

So how can we help children honour their needs, energy and voice?

Children are constantly developing their own boundary systems, and they learn by watching how we hold ours. Kids are in a developmental window of identity exploration and emotional expansion. This makes it a powerful time to help them feel safe in their own body, advocate for their needs, and know when their energy is being stretched or squashed.

Empower them with practices like:

Somatic (Body) Awareness

Use phrases like *Check in with your body – what is it telling you right now?* Practise body scans (progressively scanning your attention over your body), stretching, or gentle movements to locate and name their sensations.

Name & Validate Sensory Boundaries

Our sensory profiles are unique to each of us; that is, how we take in information from the world through our senses. For example, when a child says 'This feels scratchy' or avoids certain clothes, they're listening to their body. It's often not defiance (you can tell the difference).

So, acknowledge, 'That's okay, your body is telling you something, and it's important to listen.'

This helps children to:

- trust their inner signals
- feel respected in their choices
- build confidence in speaking up for their needs.

Normalise the Right to Say No (and Yes)
Reinforce the value that consent matters, even with affection. *You get to decide what feels comfortable for you.*

Create a 'Yes/No' Journal
Encourage children to reflect on moments during the week when they felt a strong '**yes**' or '**no**' inside their body. What happened in those moments? What helped them speak up, or what made it hard? This builds inner trust and strengthens their ability to honour their boundaries. Keep it simple with prompts like:

- *When did I feel a strong yes?*
- *When did I wish I'd said no?*

Let kids reflect on when they felt a strong yes or no in their week, and what helped them speak it.

Let Boundaries Be Fluid
Remind kids it's okay if their 'yes' becomes a 'no', or vice versa. Boundaries shift with context, maturity, and self-connection.

Lifelong Flourishing

Daily Rituals & Rhythms for Families, Educators & Therapists

Boundaries are taught not only through instruction, but through repetition, modelling, and rhythm. It's important to recognise how they might be expressed in the everyday.

I've popped a summary of various boundary types below.

Boundary Type	**Description**	**Everyday Expression in Children**
Physical	Personal space, body autonomy	Avoiding hugs, asking for space, fidgeting when crowded
Emotional	Protection of feelings	'I don't want to talk right now', crying, withdrawing
Mental	Thoughts, beliefs, opinions	'I don't agree', resistance to being corrected
Energetic	Sensory/empathic experience	Exhaustion after crowds, overstimulation, zoning out
Time	Valuing one's time and internal pacing/readiness	Struggling with transitions, needing downtime
Relational	Roles and social expectations	Wanting independence, rejecting adult emotional caretaking

And here are some everyday ways to integrate boundary wisdom …

Mirror Healthy Boundary Language

Model simple 'I' statements: 'I **feel** overwhelmed **right now**, so I'm going to sit quietly for five minutes.' Let children witness boundary-setting in action.

** Note the intentional wording of 'I feel' (not 'I am') and notice 'right now' as an indicator of the feeling of overwhelm being a *temporary*, not permanent, experience.

Support Neurodiverse Communication
Use visuals, stories, and sensory tools to help children who process information differently to articulate their energetic space. This may be spoken or non-spoken in form.

Draw Your Energy Bubble
Invite kids to use drawing or collage to show what their **personal energy space** looks and feels like. Use colours, shapes, or characters to explore what feels safe, cosy, and calm versus what feels invasive, loud, or overwhelming. This gives a visual language to boundaries and opens dialogue about what it means when someone steps inside their 'bubble'.

Boundary Role-Plays
Create short, playful role-play scenarios to practise common boundary-setting situations, such as:

- saying no to a hug or physical touch
- asking for a break or alone time
- responding to a friend pressuring them to do something they're unsure about.

These rehearsals help kids gain confidence, especially when paired with debrief questions like, *How did that feel in your body?*

Use Boundary Metaphors Kids Understand (relevant to their age)
Metaphors help children understand abstract ideas like boundaries. For example:

Your body is your home, what do you want to invite in today?
We all have an invisible bubble, yours matters.

These metaphors make the concept of boundaries relatable and empower children to develop agency in how they engage with others.

Legacy in Motion

Reflect. Integrate. Empower.

The ethos in my speech pathology clinic was simple: *create a space where kids and families feel safe – like they'd arrived 'home.'*

Where 'I need space' was heard.

Where 'I feel too much' was welcomed.

Where 'This is who I am' was celebrated.

Whether we're parents or professionals, our role isn't to control children's boundaries; it's to honour them. To offer environments where 'no' isn't punished, and 'yes' isn't coerced.

Boundaries, to me, are best described as energetic bridges; helping children sense where they end and another begins. And that's where real synergy starts.

So now, we explore how empowered humans can come together: to collaborate, co-create, and contribute – with compassion, purpose, and heart.

Journal prompts

- *How do I currently respond when a child expresses 'I need space' or 'this is who I am'?*
- *What does it mean to me to honour a child's boundaries rather than control them?*
- *How can I create an environment, at home or in my work, where children feel safe to say 'no' and trust that it will be respected?*
- *In what ways can I model compassionate boundaries in my daily life?*

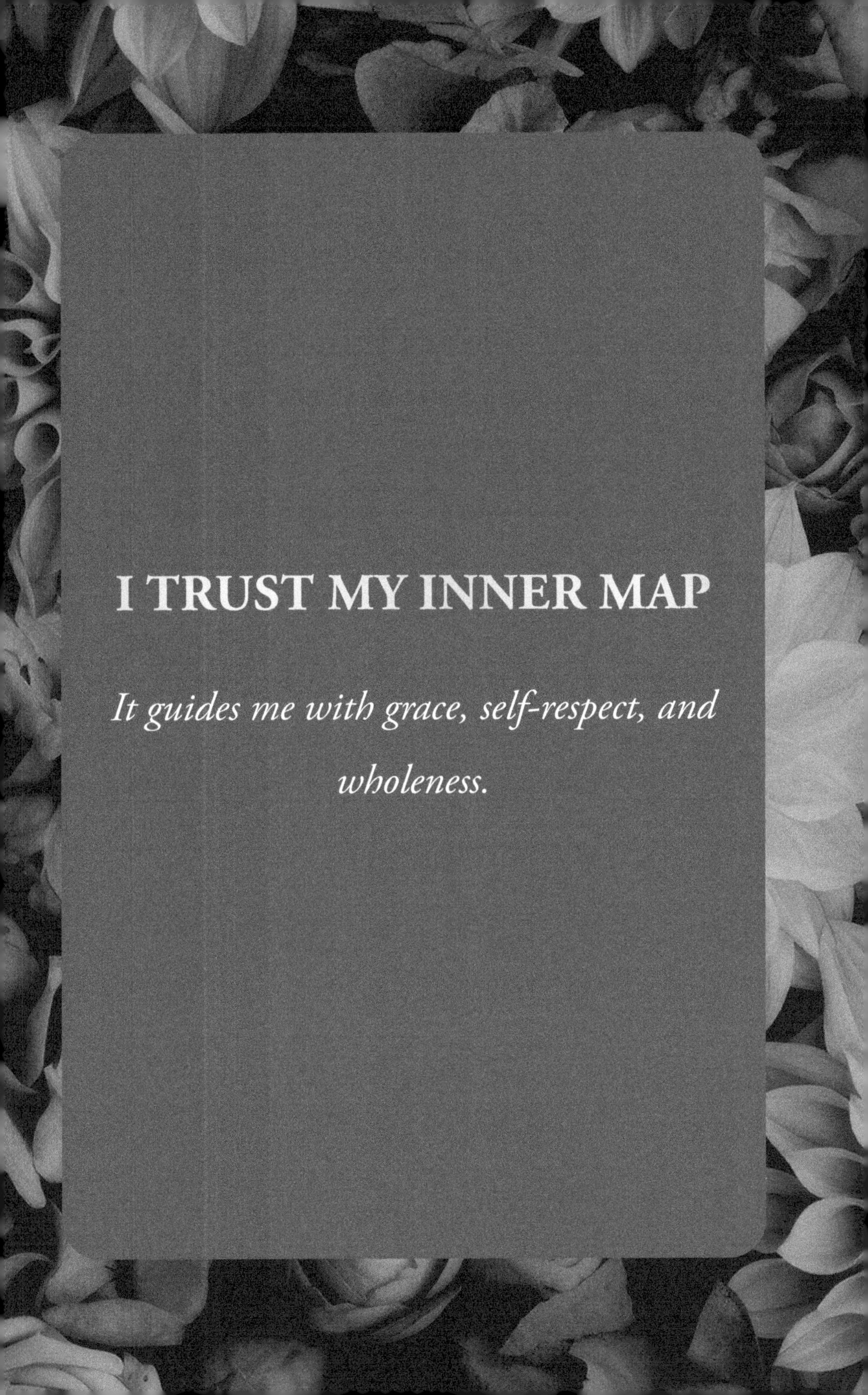
I TRUST MY INNER MAP
It guides me with grace, self-respect, and wholeness.

CHAMPION HEART-LED TEAMWORK

The Synergy of Collaboration and Co-creation

What if teamwork wasn't just about getting things done, but about cultivating purpose, presence, and heart-powered contribution?

As we sat around the dining table, sharing dinnertime banter and conversation, my daughter piped up ...

'Mum, I remember when we ate dinner in this room sitting on boxes.'

'Yes,' I replied, 'every chair we're sitting on, we put together ourselves, screwing in each leg.'

'And our Zia (Aunty) Bianca and Cousin Bea were here too, helping with the chairs ... and this dining table.'

I nodded, smiling. 'Yes – and remember our friends, who helped hire and drive the truck to move all our things?'

'And,' my son added, 'Uncle Geoff, Reece and Hamish (cousins) ... and their neighbour, came over to build our bunk beds before we even got to see our new home for the first time!'

'Oh, and we had to Google how to work our oven!' I recalled.

'We had no couch for months!' said my other daughter.

We all reminisced, laughing at the transitional adventures; especially the mountain of boxes (and a few too many empty pizza boxes ... yes, we embraced easy dinners as required!).

Looking back to those moments, during a time of massive life changes, something quietly powerful unfolded. My kids - my extended family, my friends, even strangers – all stepped up. They showed up asking, 'How can we help? What do you need?' Offering, 'Call me anytime.'

As I sit here now, I feel my heart swell with deep gratitude and quiet grace for the countless blessings we received ... and in truth, still receive.

Because honestly ... the mechanics of our world, the invisible threads that hold our lives together, are woven through the synergy of collaboration and co-creation. And that's the energy of heart-led teamwork.

Teamwork doesn't begin in a boardroom. It begins at the breakfast table; in the small, shared glances during dinner cleanup; in the quiet hand that reaches out when something spills; in the way a child is invited to feel they belong, simply because their presence matters.

We often think of teamwork as something that shows up when kids are older, or when they're assigned a group project at school or playing a team sport. But the truth is, it's cultivated long before that; in the rhythm of our homes, in how we solve daily problems, and in the way we treat each other when no one's watching.

True collaboration is caught, not taught.

Bear with me – I get the real-life challenges of collaboration ... even the most beautiful ideals of teamwork don't always land smoothly.

Maybe the group project ends in tears because one child tried to control everything.

Or cleaning the guinea pig cage becomes a war over who did it last time.

Or your child offers to help you wrap presents, only to get frustrated when the sticky tape sticks to everything but the paper.

Or a simple 'let's tidy up' becomes a negotiation over how much, how fast, and what *counts* as clean.

Or there's the classic car seat battle: 'It's my turn to sit in the front!' … again.

These aren't signs that teamwork is failing. They're signs that it's forming. That children are learning how to be with others while still being with themselves. That they're testing boundaries, finding their edges, and feeling safe enough to try.

And, to anchor this in some science, our kids' brains are still very much under construction. That part of the brain that helps with planning, empathy, and working things out with others? It's called the prefrontal cortex, and it's not fully developed until kids reach their twenties!

So, when children are navigating teamwork, especially through play or everyday co-creation, they're not just learning how to get along. They're building the neural wiring for trust, emotional regulation, and resilient relationships … all through the safety of connection and repetition.

It's easy to slip into autopilot – correcting, controlling, or just doing it ourselves – to keep things moving. But when we stay present in those messy moments, we teach that it's safe to get it wrong and try again.

We allow kids to state their case, consider other points of view, and learn how to repair connection.

We facilitate the dance of being in relationship, and of tuning to one another and choosing again, as we remember: collaboration is far more than just what we're building; it's really about who we're becoming as we build it. Together.

Everyday acts of collaboration are the foundation. Teamwork grows when children feel their contribution is *needed*. Whether it's feeding the dog, setting the table, or comforting a sibling, these are energetic imprints of belonging. It is so, so powerful, when a child sees that their effort *adds something* to the whole. It's here that they begin to understand what it means to share energy, not just responsibility.

This became so clear to me when the kids and I finally took our long-dreamed-of family trip to Japan. For years, my kids had been asking, 'When are we going overseas?' – with growing curiosity about the world beyond Australia. Japan had always been on our hearts: the food, the nature, the rich culture.

Life hadn't aligned yet … but then, it did.

From the very beginning – from announcing 'we are going to Japan!' – it was heart-led family teamwork. We booked the plane tickets together, selecting our seats with excitement. I gave the kids a brief for what kind of accommodation we were looking for, and they helped research and shortlist places. Once we made it over to Japan, it was shared energy all the way: navigating train systems, decoding menus with Google Translate, asking locals for help, and solving unexpected challenges – like 'cash only' cafés when we didn't have cash on us.

Rather than being passive participants, they were engaged contributors. Not because I pushed them to be, but because they *wanted* to be part of it. That's the essence of real teamwork … it feels like a shared adventure, not a chore; and it builds trust in one another, in ourselves, and in a greater guiding power.

Whether it's navigating Tokyo trains or planning a picnic, teamwork doesn't need a uniform or a scoreboard to be real. And while we often default to team sports as the poster child for collaboration, it's far from the whole picture.

Yes, sports can teach beautiful things – shared timing, collective goals, accountability, resilience – but not every child finds their rhythm in that space. Some find it on stage, bringing a story to life with their classmates. Others find it in music, syncing their instrument with a friend's. Some find it building a cubby house, creating a short film, or co-designing a Minecraft world. Teamwork shows up in the classroom, in the kitchen, in subtle moments of caregiving, and in spontaneous bursts of creative planning; like organising a surprise party for a loved one.

It's crucial for me to acknowledge as well, that for some kids – especially those with sensory sensitivities, communication differences, or who experience the world in a more nonlinear, intuitive, or energetic way – teamwork might look and feel a little different. It can take more time, more patience, and a whole lot more attunement.

Maybe they need extra time to process instructions or prefer quieter roles that don't involve lots of talking. Maybe transitions feel harder, or the emotional volume of group dynamics feels too loud some days. That's not a sign they're not a team player. It's a sign they're moving through the world in their own rhythm; our job is to listen for that beat.

Heart-led teamwork isn't about everyone doing the same thing, in the same way, at the same pace. It's about making space for every child to show up with what they've got, in the way that feels most true for them. And it's about helping them feel safe, seen, and supported as they contribute in ways that honour their energetic signature.

In essence, teamwork is relational energy – two or more people aligning their attention, presence, and shared purpose. When we only define teamwork by rules or winning or performance, we miss the deeper magic of how we attune to one another, move together, and co-create something bigger than ourselves.

That's the synergy and the sacredness of heart-led teamwork.

Heart-Powered Self-Leadership

So how can we help children champion heart-led teamwork?

'Lead One Moment' Invitations

Each child is gently invited to lead one part of a shared family or classroom activity; this could be as simple as choosing the morning song, setting the table theme, or deciding how to start the clean-up. Before leading, they reflect on two short prompts:

How will I bring the team together?

What kind of energy do I want to lead with?

This helps children practise leading from a place of inner alignment and care and reminds them that leadership isn't about being the loudest voice; it's about setting a tone others feel safe to join.

'Lead from Within' Cards

Create or draw 5–10 cards representing heart-led team qualities such as *kindness*, *problem-solving*, *being the calm one*, *helping others feel seen*, or *bringing joy*.

Before a shared activity, each child chooses one to embody …

Today, I'm leading from within by being the ___.

They carry that quality with them during the task, like an invisible badge. Afterward, they can reflect on how it felt and what impact it made. This invites children to discover the many quiet, powerful ways leadership can flow from within.

'What Would a Leader Do?' Challenge

This is a gentle pause tool when there's a 'sticky spot' … maybe someone's not helping, or there's tension in a game. You want to encourage children to ask themselves:

If I were the heart-led leader of this team right now, what would I do next?

This helps children step into perspective-taking and self-regulation without blame. They're invited to connect to their inner compass, make empowered choices, and act from integrity. Over time, they begin to internalise the question as a self-check-in tool for everyday situations.

The Heart Teamwork Checklist

Below is a self-guided checklist to help children reflect on how they're showing up as part of a team, whether in the home, classroom, or playground.

Before We Start:

- Did I take a deep breath to feel calm?
- Am I ready to listen, not just talk?
- Do I remember we're on the same team, even if we're different?

While We're Working or Playing Together:

- Did I take turns and let others share ideas?
- Did I notice if someone was left out?
- Did I say something kind or encouraging?
- Did I ask for help without blaming?
- Did I use a calm voice, even when I felt big feelings?

If There's a Disagreement:

- Did I pause before yelling or walking away?
- Did I try to understand how the other person felt?
- Did I share my feelings without blaming?

After We're Done:

- Did I say 'thank you' or 'good job'?
- Did I notice what I did well today?
- Is there anything I want to try differently next time?

Lifelong Flourishing

Daily Rituals & Rhythms for Families, Educators & Therapists

Small, consistent practices make heart-led teamwork feel real, lived, and organic.

Listening Before Leading

For educators in classroom or group activities, invite students to **pause and hear each other's ideas** before jumping in to 'fix' or lead. Assign a 'Heart Listener' role; someone who checks in to see if every voice has been heard. This builds emotional intelligence and collaboration.

For families, at the dinner table or during shared decisions (like planning a weekend outing), encourage children to be **mindful of** and **ask what others think** before offering and focusing only on their own ideas. You can model with prompts like: *What do you think your brother/sister would enjoy?* or *Let's hear everyone's idea before we decide.*

This helps children strengthen the practice of listening deeply as an act of respect and shared power.

Micro-Moments of Repair

Whether in the home or the classroom, reinforce that disagreements/differing viewpoints are a natural part of collaboration. When tensions arise, it is important to guide children to pause, reflect, and revisit the shared goal with respectful language.

Use phrases such as:

Let's take a breath – what's really important here?

How might we come back to kindness and move forward together?

We can disagree and still stay connected.

In both spaces, children learn that repair is a powerful form of trust-building, reinforcing resilience, emotional responsibility, and the art of reconnecting.

Role Rotation with Reflection

Whether in group projects or group therapy formats, rotate roles weekly (e.g. note-taker, presenter/spokesperson, peacekeeper, timekeeper). Afterward, invite a reflection:

What did you learn from that role?

How did it feel to lead from behind the scenes?

This can be done at home too, applied to shared chores or family planning:

This week, you lead the dinner plan/shopping list/outing idea. Next week, it's your sibling's turn.

Discuss how leading doesn't always mean being in charge; it means bringing care and clarity to whatever role is needed.

Acknowledgement Post-its

I love the use of Post-it notes, stuck on mirrors, walls, or fridges with authentic heartfelt messages. They have a different 'flavour' to sharing spoken acknowledgement.

In the context of heart-led self-leadership, it could be for example:

I noticed you helped quietly with the chairs; thank you.

Thank you for making space for everyone to speak.

You thoughtfully prepared dinner for us all – thank you!

The Post-it notes are for all to use and are a powerful way to build a culture of seeing others' leadership, not just our own.

The Pause of Integrity

Encourage the understanding that sometimes the strongest move is to pause before reacting, especially when emotions run high or peer pressure kicks in.

Use language like:

Take a breath and ask – does this feel true for me?

Is this kind? Is this needed? Is this aligned?

I wanted to say yes straight away, but I needed a moment to check in with myself.

I'm proud of how you paused and thought it through; that's your inner compass at work.

The pause of integrity nurtures conscious responsiveness instead of reactive behaviour; it helps strengthen decision-making rooted in inner wisdom, not outer approval.

Legacy in Motion

Reflect. Integrate. Empower.

Heart-led teamwork is a process of becoming; so, the legacy we leave is not what we built, but *how* we built it, together.

With love.

With attunement.

With truth.

When children experience the magic of true teamwork, they learn that they're never alone in this world and begin to see life as something to co-create.

And that knowing becomes especially powerful when change arrives in life, as it always does.

Transitions, big or small, can feel uncertain. But when kids are grounded in connection and supported by trusted others, they grow.

So, next, we will unfold how to guide children through life's many seasons … with trust, resilience, and reverence for the wisdom that change brings.

Journal Prompts

- *What's one moment this week where your child showed true, heart-led teamwork?*
- *Where in your family rhythm could more collaboration flow in?*
- *How do you model heart-led teamwork even when it feels challenging?*
- *What does your child teach you about collaboration and contribution?*

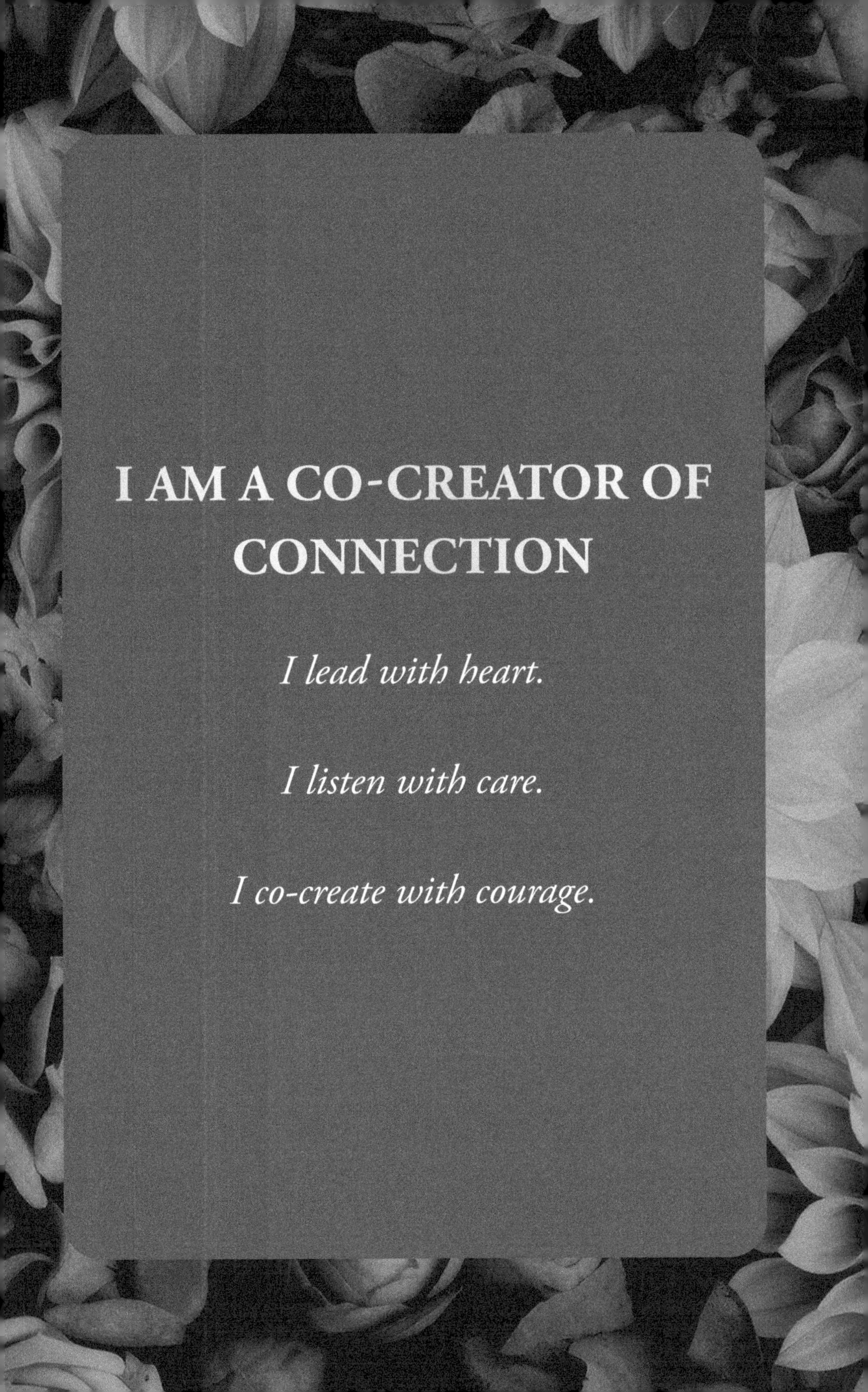

I AM A CO-CREATOR OF CONNECTION

I lead with heart.

I listen with care.

I co-create with courage.

WELCOME THE SEASONS OF CHANGE

Guiding Life's Transitions with Trust, Resilience, and Reverence

What if change isn't disruption, but a sacred rhythm woven into what it means to be human?

My young daughter seemed mildly troubled one evening as she sat on her bed, getting ready to sleep. I looked into her eyes.

'Hey … what's happening?' I softly asked.

'I have another wobbly tooth,' she responded.

I nodded. 'Yes … is it sore?'

She shook her head. 'I don't want my tooth to fall out.' Large tears formed in her eyes before rolling down her cheeks.

'I want to keep my tooth …' she sobbed, heartbroken.

Change is a full-body experience, flowing through us like a wave – sometimes energising, other times unsettling. Life is an ever-turning cycle of beginnings, endings, and rebirths; what I call the sacred seasons of change. Children experience these seasons deeply and often, from losing a baby tooth, to starting school, to navigating friendship changes, puberty, and unexpected transitions in family life. Yet, we don't always realise how these 'everyday changes' can trigger subtle and cumulative grief responses in both children and adults.

Grief is traditionally associated with major losses. But what if grief is actually a natural response to *any* meaningful change – whether it's the end of a phase, the loss of familiarity, or a shift in identity? In this way, grief isn't a one-off event, **it's a spectrum of emotion that lives alongside change itself**.

My invitation in this chapter is to reframe grief not as something to avoid or fix, but as an emotional messenger that calls us into presence, healing, and adaptation. And at the heart of that process is one powerful self-leadership skill: **adaptability**.

Adaptability doesn't mean ignoring what's hard. It means *meeting change with creativity, flexibility, and truth*. It means grieving what was, embracing what is, and growing into what could be. I know this is easier said than done; however, I also know that in very challenging seasons of change for me and my family, honouring that cycle and the process therein helped strengthen our resilience, our grit, and our devotion to *embodied self-reverence*.

Modern neuroscience views grief as a neuro-emotional process involving memory and safety centres of the brain, while spiritual traditions see change as a sacred invitation to let go and grow. As I would often say to people asking me how I was doing: 'I'm growing with the flow'. Together, science and spirit remind us: **how we respond to change profoundly shapes our emotional wellbeing, adaptability, and self-leadership**.

Change is *not linear*. It ebbs and flows, and it deserves spaciousness.

I had the honour of interviewing Stephenie Rodriguez on my

Chatabout Children podcast. In 2019, Stephenie contracted cerebral malaria during a business trip in Nigeria. What followed was a coma, sepsis, and the loss of both her feet, and she became a bilateral amputee. She had a 2% chance of survival.

She now trains as a para fencer for the Paralympics, amongst her continuous journey and cycles of medical operations and deep healing. She is a globally recognised TEDx speaker, resilience expert, tech entrepreneur, and devoted mother on a mission to positively impact a billion lives. In my view, she is the embodiment of fierce empathy, reinvention, and the power of purposeful leadership.

'Resilience is the ability to come through difficult situations with grace and elegance,' she shared in our conversation. 'It doesn't mean it won't get ugly – but you still rise.'

She expressed what it means to become an athlete later in life, learning to fall – and rise again – with humility, humour, and strength.

'One of the last things I had to do in physio was to learn how to fall. It was the most abstract lesson … but learning how to rise again was everything.'

As a solo parent, Stephenie models resilience not through control, but through compassion. She raises her son with radical trust, encouraging him to pursue his dream of being a recording artist. Her guiding phrase?

'Find the yes.'

This simple mantra guides her parenting, her leadership, and her recovery. It's a mindset she believes every child can benefit from: problem-solving with creativity, persistence, and personal agency.

'We can teach our children to think in solutions, not just problems. That's how we build resilience.'

In a world rapidly shifting through technological, emotional, and social change, Stephenie reminds us that adaptability is an art form.

One shaped by truth, trust, and the courage to dream – again and again.

Heart-Powered Self-Leadership

So how can we help children welcome the seasons of change in life?

Empowering children to navigate change begins by helping them tune into their inner world, especially when the outer world feels uncertain. As we can all relate to; change can trigger feelings of vulnerability, confusion, or grief, and it's often our instinct to protect children from discomfort. But when we instead model *trust*, *presence*, and *curiosity*, we give them permission to do the same.

Empower kids with these supportive practices:

Body-Led Resets

Use movement to help shift emotional energy: shaking, stretching, 'change dances', or slow walks to integrate new rhythms.

Name What's Happening

Use language like: *This feels like a change, and it's okay to have feelings about it.* By naming change and normalising emotion, we model acceptance over avoidance.

Introduce the Concept of 'Mini-Griefs'

Help children understand that it's normal to feel a sense of loss even in small transitions, like finishing a favourite book series, changing teachers, or saying goodbye to a friend who moves away. Grief is not just for big events, it's the body and heart recalibrating to a new rhythm.

Use Identity-Affirming Language

When your child says 'I'm not good at this', gently reflect: *Maybe you're still finding your way with … (insert specific ability here), and that's okay; you're learning, and it takes courage to keep trying.*

How we speak about challenges shapes a child's evolving sense of self, and a growth mindset is nurtured through words that honour progress, not perfection.

Celebrate Endings with Meaning

Honour the conclusion of things – school years, friendships, phases – with simple rituals that acknowledge change, closure, and gratitude. It might be a candle lighting, a memory book, or a spoken affirmation practised with *heartfelt feeling*: *Thank you for what was. I welcome what's next.*

Practise Emotional Weather Reports

Encourage children to check in with their internal landscape: *What's the weather like inside you today?* This playful approach teaches awareness without judgement.

Model Vulnerability

Let children witness how you move through your own changes, whether with joy, fear, or a mix of both. When you say, 'I'm feeling a bit nervous because this is new, but I trust myself to grow through it,' you model grounded confidence.

Build Agency in Everyday Choices

Change often comes with a sense of loss of control. Build self-trust by offering age-appropriate choices: for example, *Do you want to choose the playlist in the car today?* or *Do you want to pack your bag tonight or in the morning?* These small decisions can build a sense of inner stability during times of flux.

Lifelong Flourishing

Daily Rituals & Rhythms for Families, Educators & Therapists

When change becomes a regular and welcomed guest in the home or classroom, children develop a flexible nervous system and a resilient spirit. Below are some practices that intend to integrate and support adaptability and emotional flow, offering stability and spaciousness in these fast-evolving times.

Seasons of Me Journal

Create a family or class journal where each member can reflect weekly on their 'season'.

Are they in a season of planting (starting something new)?
Harvesting (enjoying results)?
Resting?
Letting go?
This builds language around change and self-awareness.

Moon-Aligned Rituals for Growth

The moon cycle teaches us that every ending brings a new beginning. Aligning with its natural rhythm can help children (and adults) feel supported through change. Each full moon can be accompanied by a ritual of releasing something that no longer serves: an old habit, fear, or item. This can be done using a 'letting go bowl' or writing it on a piece of paper and burning or burying it (safely). Affirm together: *As I release, I grow stronger.*

When the new moon arrives, invite each person to plant a small intention, something they'd like to grow into, try, or embody.

Write it down and place it somewhere visible or in a special box. Affirm together: *With each new beginning, I grow closer to who I'm becoming.*

These monthly rituals can support emotional clarity, energetic balance, and a deeper connection to inner wisdom and the rhythms of the cosmos.

Memory Sharing Evenings

Regularly share favourite memories from a past chapter (e.g. 'remember when ...?'). This nurtures joy, perspective, and the understanding that we can carry the beauty of the past into the now. For my family, sharing dinner together most evenings allows for these golden memories to resurface with replenished reminiscence.

Nature Walks of Noticing

This is a favourite. Walks in nature where you are immersed in presence and interconnectedness. During a time of much transition for my family, nature walks were a comforting and nurturing process. Together, we researched various local walks and created a vision board of the walks we had done and the ones we were planning on next. This allowed an appreciation of what was, and positive anticipation for what was to come.

Depending on the age of your kids, they may like to collect natural items to reflect how nature changes and adapts; otherwise, just noticing and appreciating what surrounds you as you walk anchors the understanding that all life flows in cycles, and we're part of that.

Legacy in Motion

Reflect. Integrate. Empower.

Change is not the exception; it's the essence of life.

When we raise children who understand that change is not to be feared but *felt*, processed, and responded to, we raise humans who can move through life's transitions with inner steadiness and soulful strength.

Whether it's the loss of a loved one, the shift of a friendship, or the quiet grief of leaving a familiar routine behind, every season of change invites growth.

The key is not to rush it. But to meet it, moment by moment, with reverence.

This empowers our children to learn to ride life's waves, knowing they carry the wisdom of the tide, and naturally beginning to tune into subtler realms of wisdom.

Because sometimes the most profound guidance doesn't always arrive in waking hours ... It whispers through our dreams.

Next, we open the doorway to the sacred space of sleep and symbolism – where healing, messages, and inner recalibration speak in the language of soul.

Journal prompts

- *How do I respond to change, and what do my children learn from it?*
- *What small transitions in our life deserve more reverence?*
- *What emotional tools am I modelling during times of loss or shift?*
- *What legacy do I want to leave around navigating life's changes?*

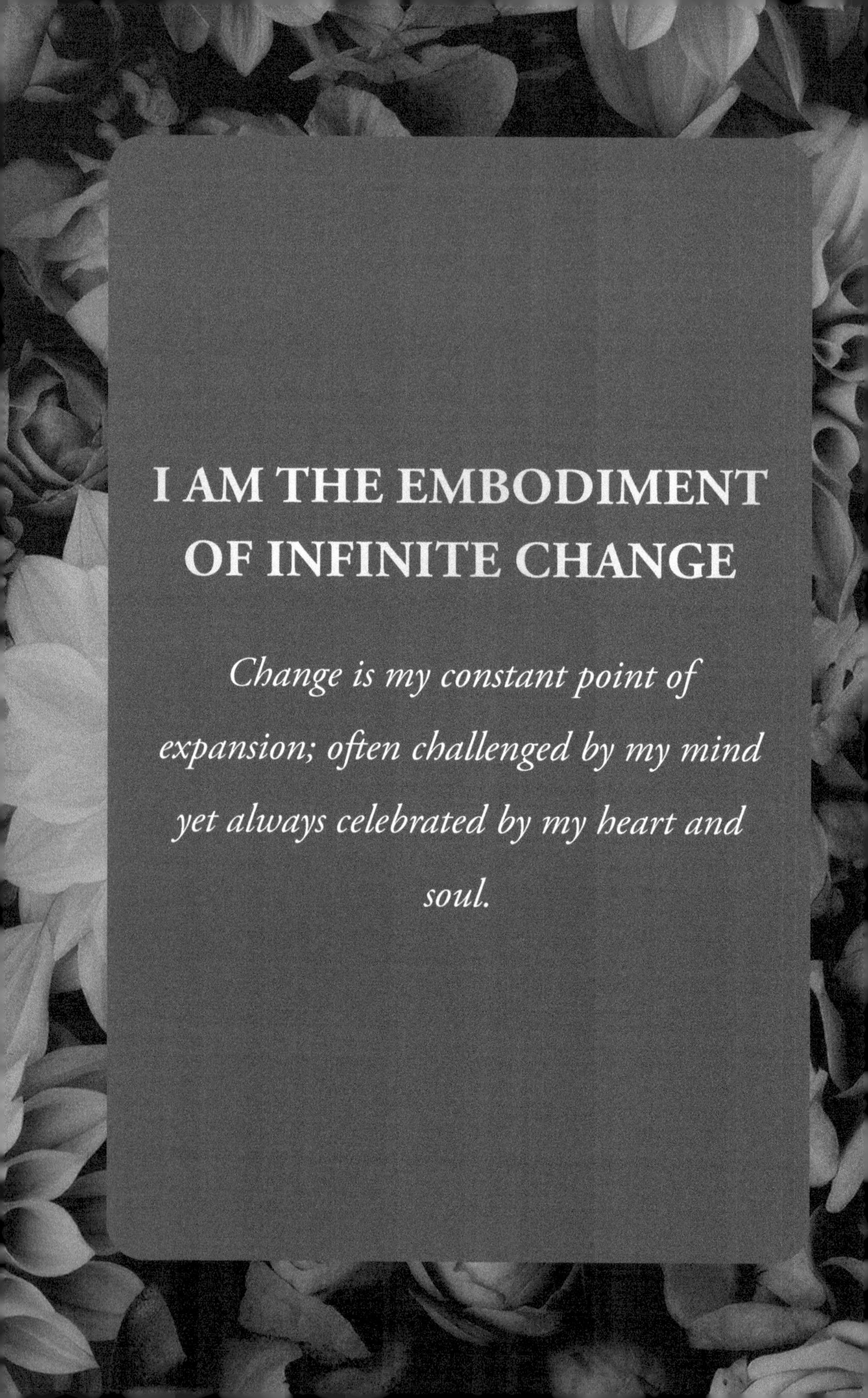
I AM THE EMBODIMENT
OF INFINITE CHANGE
Change is my constant point of expansion; often challenged by my mind yet always celebrated by my heart and soul.

DREAMS AS DIVINE DIALOGUE

Unlock Inner Wisdom, Healing, and Recalibration

What if your dreams are not just echoes of the day … but profound whispers from your soul?

I find dreams to be a fascinating and sacred part of what it means to be human. An interface between the conscious and subconscious, the seen and unseen. Yet, in modern society, I find we don't really give them much attention, often labelling them as 'just a dream', 'weird', 'random', etc., because they may not make much logical sense to us.

Many very sensitive and intuitive children (I was one of them) have very vivid, rich dreams, feeling 'really real'. Sometimes I would share them with my parents, but dreams weren't really something we talked about much. So, for a long time, I wasn't quite sure 'what to think' about some of them, deeming dreams as something that just happens to us when we sleep.

In later adult life, I became more intentional and interested in the dialogue of my dreams, which has been a very powerful way to more consciously consolidate learning, integrate healing, and nourish a healthy relationship with myself on all layers. I experienced a shift from dreams being somewhat meaningless to 'meaningful medicine'.

With a willingness to pause, to ask, and to listen, I discovered that dream time is not separate from waking life. It is a continuation of it, in a different frequency. A language. A communication. A profound divine dialogue. And our kids can benefit from it too; knowing the dream world is a place of **revelation, not randomness**.

I recall one of my kids one morning recounting a recurring dream they had. This led to further discussion and exploration, with a general chat about how you can work with your dreams. This brought about a 'wow' moment from them, with the comment … 'So it's like you can do a google search inside yourself?!' I loved this analogy … yes, dreams are our sacred search engine.

Across cultures, from Ancient Egypt to Indigenous dream walkers and Tibetan dream yoga, dreams have long been honoured as gateways to wisdom. Visionaries like Albert Einstein and Nikola Tesla all credited dreams with sparking ideas and insights. Far from being forgettable stories, dreams are bridges to inner guidance, self-understanding, and world-shaping innovation, something many of us are just beginning to remember.

Within neuroscience and psychology, dreams have been studied, especially during the stage of sleep known as REM (rapid eye movement).

During this time:

We process emotions – The part of the brain linked to emotions (the amygdala) becomes more active, helping us work through feelings.

We store memories – The brain's memory centre (the hippocampus) organises new information and connects it to what we already know.

We think differently – The logical part of the brain (the prefrontal cortex) slows down, which is why dreams can feel imaginative or symbolic.

So, yes, dreams can feel confusing, inconsistent, or surreal, and without a framework of trust and curiosity, they are often dismissed.

But here's the truth:

Dreams don't always make *sense* - they make *meaning*. And meaning is deeply personal.

When children engage with their dreams, by remembering them, talking about them, drawing them, or asking questions, they begin to **develop a relationship with their inner world**. This connection is the root of all meaningful self-leadership.

Heart-Powered Self-Leadership

So how can we help children awaken their sacred relationship with dreams?

Firstly, how you prepare your child for sleep is important. As you can appreciate, the nervous system holds the **residue of the day** ... joys, tensions, screen exposure, sensory input, and emotional exchanges. If left unprocessed, it can lead to:

- restless sleep
- difficulty falling or staying asleep
- heightened or fearful dreaming
- moodiness the next day.

You want to ensure you have **soothing rituals** before bed, to help children **shift from survival mode into safety**, activating the parasympathetic 'rest and digest' state. This is especially important when supporting neurodiverse children who may have vivid dream experiences.

This could include:

Dream Nest Ritual (Nightly Wind-Down)

- **Set an intention aloud**: 'Only kind dreams are welcome in my sky.'
- **Brush off the day**: Gentle hands down the body while saying, 'We're brushing off what's not ours.'
- **Call in guardians**: Choose to call in loving protectors that align for you/your family, e.g. animal spirits, stars, angels.
- **Hold a natural object**: This may be beside the bed (crystal, feather, shell, etc.)
- **Breathe your intention into your 'dream cloud'**: Gentle belly breathing together; holding the intention with eyes closed.

Use soft lighting, weighted blankets, or calming scents to create a sensory-friendly bedtime space and consider a dream light or soft projection nightlight to comfort children with nighttime sensitivities.

Ask children *What would you like to dream about tonight?* This gives children **ownership of their dreamscape**, instead of being passive recipients.

Creating a daily waking ritual is also important:

Morning Dream Sharing (Integration)

Keep a notebook journal for drawing or writing dreams. Also have stickers available that can be used within it. Having this bedside is important so dreams can be recorded/expressed on waking.

Soon after waking time, ask gentle questions like:

- *What did your dream feel like?*

- *If your dream was a message, what might it say?*
- *What showed up? Colours, numbers, names?*

Use a **dream catcher board** on the wall with magnets or symbols to track dream themes: flying, water, animals, friends, etc.

Talk about symbols and feelings, without needing to 'fix' and **do not overanalyse**.

Especially for intuitive or sensitive children, these practices help build energetic boundaries and transform any fear into curiosity. Nightmares can shift from being scary to sacred, showing what wants to be acknowledged, healed, or released.

Dreamtime Tips for Energy Mastery

For vivid dreams:

The next day, help your child gently ground – go barefoot on the grass, splash in some water, or get moving with playful stretches. It helps to 'land back in the body' and feel balanced again.

For unsettling dreams or nightmares:

Invite your child to light a candle (or imagine one) in the morning, saying something like: *Thank you, dream. You're free to go now.* It's a simple ritual that helps release any lingering energy.

For intuitive or sensitive kids:

Let them know they can say 'no' in their dreams; or call in someone loving for support. That could be a grandparent, a pet, or even a superhero they trust.

Dreams give children a beautiful space to explore what they're feeling, imagining, and remembering deep inside. When we help kids make sense of dreamtime, we're actually strengthening their emotional awareness, intuition, and sense of personal power … one night at a time.

Helpful Sleep Hygiene Tip!

Use the power of sound frequencies/soundscapes when preparing for sleep and dreaming. I use various apps to access sound frequency tracks I feel are most relevant for that day/evening.

	What It Does	When to Use It
Delta Waves	Deep sleep and body rest	During sleep
Theta Waves	Boosts dreaming and emotional release	Before or during sleep
432 Hz Music	Calms nerves, helps with peaceful sleep	Wind-down time or bedtime routine
528 Hz Music	Opens the heart, emotional soothing	Evening relaxation or meditation
Gentle Rain or Nature Sounds	Soothes the senses, masks background noise	Bedtime, especially for anxious kids
Binaural Beats	Helps brain shift into sleep state	Use with headphones before bed

****Avoid Before Bed****

- Fast music or songs with words.
- Loud or unpredictable sounds (like crashing waves).
- Screens and stimulation right before sleep.

Lifelong Flourishing

Daily Rituals & Rhythms for Families, Educators & Therapists

Here are gentle, energy-aware principles and rhythms to help deepen your child's relationship with dreams. Especially for neurodiverse kids, dream work affirms that **their way of sensing is valid and magical**, while nurturing a lifelong connection to the symbolic, mythic, and intuitive realms.

Switch from Analysis to Curiosity

Dreams speak the languages of **symbol**, **emotion**, and **metaphor**. When we stop trying to 'figure them out', we start to **feel them through**. Children (and adults) don't need to understand everything to *trust* something. When you give a dream space to *be*, it begins to *speak*.

Interpretation isn't about decoding a symbol like a puzzle; it's about recognising *how the dream reflects something alive in your inner world.*

Let Meaning Unfold Over Time

Some dreams make no sense today, but weeks later, something clicks. A real-life moment mirrors the dream's emotion or sequence. That's the nature of non-linear insight.

Keep a dream journal (even one word per night) to build trust. Over time, patterns appear.

Make Dreams Feel Sacred Again

The reason dreams are often dismissed is because we treat them like 'junk mail'. But when a person feels their dream *matters*, they're more likely to: remember it – reflect on it – share it.

Even a child saying 'I dreamed of a purple giraffe eating pancakes' can be a doorway into their emotions, their imagination, their unspoken needs.

Dream Guardians and Boundaries

Some children (and adults) may experience vivid, intense, or scary dreams. Offer them **dream tools of sovereignty**:

- Draw or create a **dream guardian** (e.g. animal, light being, tree).
- Write a 'dream rule' to place under the pillow: *Only kind dreams may visit tonight.*
- Use calming touch to 'seal the dream field' with golden light.
- Teach them to 'zip up their energy field' (visualising a cocoon or light cloak).
- Reassure them they can **invite only what serves their highest good** in dreams.

This builds energetic boundaries and a sense of **agency over the subconscious realm**.

Anchor Just One Part

Even if your child forgets most of the dream, **remembering one image or feeling** is enough. That fragment is a *seed.* (e.g. 'I remember I was flying.') You can then ask questions such as:

- *Did it feel like a dream that wanted to teach you something?*
- *Did it feel like a gift, a game, or a mystery?*

Remember some kids may feel deeply but not be able to articulate the words to describe their feelings, so bridge that gap using a variety of ways they can express: drawing, stickers, writing, etc.

(Check out the *Dream Reflection Journal Template* in the resources section).

LEGACY IN MOTION

Reflect. Integrate. Empower.

We reclaim the superpower of what it means to be human when we honour dreams as sacred. And this in itself reinforces that this superpower lives within us. May this chapter reignite your remembrance that empowerment doesn't end at bedtime, as:

- dreamtime is a sacred space for connection, healing, creativity and guidance
- your child's dream world is valid, vibrant, and valuable
- families grow stronger when they make space for the invisible
- you don't need to 'understand' every dream. You do need to listen and love the one who dreamed it.

Journal Prompts

- *How do I support restful, intentional sleep for myself, and for my family?*
- *What was my own relationship with dreams as a child? Did I feel safe to share them, or did I learn to dismiss them?*
- *What do I believe dreams can offer, not just to me, but to my children?*
- *Have I ever received insight, clarity, or healing from a dream?*

So, we draw Section Four to a close.

You've now received the fourth golden key – *The Frequency of Fulfilment.*

We've explored what it means to raise humans who live and express in alignment ... honouring their truth, sharing their gifts, and feeling at home in who they are.

Now, we rise into the final key – *The Frequency of Flourishing.*

Where sacred self-celebration meets service ... and empowered humans shine their light for the good of all.

I AM THE LISTENER OF
MY DREAMS
Where the divine speaks.
Where my soul remembers.

GOLDEN KEY FIVE

THE FREQUENCY OF FLOURISHING

The Activation of Self-Celebration & Service

flourish: verb

/ˈflʌr.ɪʃ/

The graceful dance between the inward journey of self-awareness and outward act of contributing to the world

CELEBRATE SUPPORT AS SOVEREIGN

Dynamically Align with Heart-Led Sincerity

What if true support is a cycle of sacred exchange – where we give without rescuing, and receive without losing ourselves?

Working in a professional 'title' of support – holding space for families, empowering children and adults, and weaving multidisciplinary care – naturally placed me in a rhythm of giving. Giving felt second nature. Nurturing felt instinctive. Yet beneath that rhythm, a quiet tension pulsed: the act of receiving – genuinely, openly – felt far more difficult.

Whether it was a compliment, a gift, or a heartfelt thank you, I often felt a need to deflect or dilute it. Not out of modesty but almost out of obligation. If a parent said, 'Thank you so much; you've been incredible helping Johnny with his reading,' my first response was often to redirect the credit. I would say something like, 'Oh, it's really not me – it's Johnny doing all the work, and it's your support at home ...'

And while those words carried absolute truth, what I came to realise is that my reflex to correct the compliment carried a thread of discomfort in being seen.

Because the fuller truth is this: yes, Johnny did the work. He showed up with effort and openness. His family reinforced that effort at home. But *I* was also part of that equation.

I held the space.

I offered tools.

I was a catalyst – someone who ignited possibility, created momentum, and mirrored belief.

And both roles matter. Both are worthy of acknowledgement and recognition.

So now, when gratitude is offered, I pause. I receive it fully. I let it land in my nervous system. And *then* – if I feel called – I add the nuance: 'Thank you, I really appreciate that. It's been an honour to support Johnny's growth – he's worked with commitment.'

This way, I remain open to the energy of appreciation, while also naming the collaborative truth. It's not about taking credit. It's about being part of a shared current of growth; and allowing ourselves to belong in the rhythm of giving *and* receiving.

Because here's the quiet thread so many of us carry: when our identity becomes over-attuned to supporting others, we can lose rhythm with the equally sacred act of *being supported.* And over time, that imbalance sends subtle signals to our children, our partners, and our own nervous systems. Signals that say: 'I'm more comfortable giving than receiving. I'm more at home holding others than being held.'

But sacred support – support that honours sovereignty – is reciprocal.

It breathes.

It listens in both directions.

It doesn't mean we need to take up more space than others.

It simply means we belong in the exchange.

Fully. Worthily.

I came to realise … *what if the way we receive support was just as powerful as how we offer it?*

Energetically, this is vital. When we reject receiving, we create static in the field. We deny others the gift of giving. And **we teach our children, consciously or not, that to be strong means to be self-sufficient, rather than self-aware**.

Rebalancing this flow is not about keeping score. It's about coming into resonance. Giving from overflow, not depletion; and receiving with openness, not apology. And when we do, we model what sovereign support really looks and *feels* like – something that nourishes *both* people in the exchange. A rhythm of shared respect.

So what about the dynamic of asking for support?

There's a deep cultural shame embedded in our society when it comes to asking for help, or receiving it. Somewhere along the way, support became synonymous with weakness.

I've seen it time and time again in schools: a visiting therapist or specialist doesn't feel like a lifeline to a child, but a spotlight. Some children feel exposed, different, or even judged by their peers. Not because support is inherently negative, but because of how our systems, language, and environments have framed it.

But when the reason for seeking support is meaningful, when it's rooted in something a child wants to grow into, everything changes. Shame dissolves. Resistance softens. And what emerges is *agency*.

Because when the why is strong enough, the will to rise becomes self-generating.

I remember working with a highly anxious teenage boy who lived with a significant stutter. At school, conversations felt like walking a tightrope, and he avoided interaction in the community as much as possible.

But then something shifted. He discovered a YouTube creator who stuttered and owned it. Someone who used their voice, unpredictability and all, to share powerful messages.

My client in watching this creator, saw possibility. At the core of it all, he saw himself. And with that came a spark of purpose, and his why became clear:

He wanted to get a casual job and start earning his own money.

He wanted to contribute ideas in class.

He wanted to speak his truth without fear hijacking his breath.

So, he (and his parents) reached out to me for support.

Together, we didn't just work on speech fluency; we worked on the 'muscles' of aligned confidence. We moved through what I call the 'stages of self-trust'. Step by step; from asking a question at the shops, to ordering food at a café, to making phone enquiries.

Each moment building not just smoother speech, but deeper belief: **my voice is worth hearing**.

And as his voice emerged, so too did his world. He began forming friendships, rooted in authenticity. He didn't need rescuing. He needed resonance. And that's what sovereign support looks like.

Support not done to him, but claimed, chosen, and lived with him. This, of course, opens an essential realisation …

What if asking for help isn't a weakness, but a sacred strength?

A wisdom that remembers personal growth isn't a solo mission, it's a sacred unfolding, shaped by the quality of connection we allow into our lives.

It's a sovereign choice; an empowered alignment with the people, energies, and environments that honour who we are and who we're becoming.

I caught up with Carrie Kwan, co-founder of Mums & Co and

mother of two. I feel Carrie exemplifies what it means to *celebrate support as sovereign*; both as a lived practice and a guiding philosophy. Deeply committed to championing women-led ventures, Carrie doesn't just talk about support, she builds it. Through Mums & Co, she's created what she calls a 'psychologically safe space', where ambition, livelihood, and wellbeing are not competing forces, but equal pillars of empowered living.

'If one area isn't firing – your ambition, your income, your wellbeing – the rest can't thrive either.'

This has us reimagine support as an energetic agreement rooted in mutuality. Sovereignty, in Carrie's world, includes intentional interdependence. Her personal and professional 'advisory boards' aren't indulgences; they're essentials.

'I have a business advisory board … but I also have a personal advisory board. And that could be your partner, your co-parent, etc. … if they need to step in at times when I can't be there (like at the 15th kids' Christmas party that month!) … It's about knowing who's in your corner.'

Her message is simple and powerful: we don't have to carry it all to be sovereign; we simply need to walk alongside those who honour our path. This support is both sacred and soulfully shared.

And this, leads to the next question …

What if our connections weren't just company, but catalysts?

Psychology, neuroscience, and spiritual wisdom agree – **we become like the people we spend the most time with**. It's not just poetic, it's physiological.

Our brains mirror. Our nervous systems co-regulate. Our energies entrain.

What this means is simple but profound:

The people we surround ourselves with shape how we feel, how we think, and how we grow.

When we share space with people who live with sincerity, speak with compassion, and embody their truth, it strengthens those same qualities within us.

This is why the company we keep, for ourselves and our children, matters. Not because we seek perfection, but because **resonance is real**; and the people around us are either amplifying our soul's direction … or pulling us off course.

As children grow into themselves, their circles shift. Friendships evolve and emotional needs deepen. And the ability to discern becomes one of the most important self-leadership abilities they will continue honing through life as they attune to:

Who doesn't pull me off my path, but walks beside me, with reverence?

Who doesn't dilute my truth, but helps me hear it more clearly?

We often celebrate independence as the ultimate sign of maturity. But I've come to see something more nuanced …

Maturity is not about doing it all alone, it's about knowing who to call into your corner, for ultimately, the people we surround ourselves with don't just shape how we feel; they shape how we grow.

That is the act of celebrating empowered support. It is sovereignty in action.

Heart-Powered Self Leadership

So how can we help children celebrate support as sovereign?

Learn to Ask for Help Without Shame

Embody the reframing for children that asking for help is a strength, not a shortcoming. Create space where it's normal to say, 'I'm struggling with this; can you help me?' This builds self-awareness and dismantles shame.

Reflect on Giving and Receiving

After moments of support, prompt a little reflection: *How did it feel when you helped?* or *What did it feel like when they helped you?* These gentle questions build emotional intelligence and deepen understanding of connection.

Practise Saying No Respectfully

Empower children to use their voice when something doesn't feel right. Model and role-play how to say 'no' with kindness and clarity, helping them understand that boundaries are part of loving relationships.

Create Personal Check-In Moments

Guide your child to pause and ask themselves, *What do I need right now?* This strengthens inner listening and helps them discern between seeking support and honouring space.

Use Stories and Role-Play

Bring in stories, books, or imagined scenarios that explore giving, receiving, and boundary-setting. Afterward, invite them to discuss what they noticed or felt. This helps build empathy and practical insight.

Develop 'Holding Space' Muscles

The deeper reality is that sometimes being a good friend means simply being present, not fixing. Use phrases like: *You don't need to make them feel better; you can just be there.* This nurtures compassionate presence that is attuned with stillness, resonance, and belief in the other's inner wisdom.

Encourage Self-Support Rituals

Encourage the development of small practices that regulate and nurture your child, like journalling, quiet time, art, or breathing exercises. These anchor their capacity to self-soothe and return to inner balance.

Relationship Sensing – What Does My Heart Say?

Encourage children to pause after interactions with various people and check in with their body: *Do I feel more relaxed or tighter? Do I feel seen or small?* Over time, they begin to recognise energetic resonance and dissonance.

Energetically, every relationship is an exchange. When a child is attuned to how they feel around others, they begin to understand what safety, sincerity, and synergy feel like. These aren't abstract ideas; they're embodied truths. The right people feel like open windows. The wrong ones? Like tight shoes.

Lifelong Flourishing

Daily Rituals & Rhythms for Families, Educators & Therapists

Model Graceful Receiving

When offered kindness or a compliment, pause, smile, and say 'thank you' with presence, not awkwardness or deflection. Let children see that receiving is an act of self-respect and trust. It requires vulnerability, but also energetic clarity; allowing help from those who uplift, not override. Children model this from us: when they see us receive, they learn it's safe to be held.

Narrate the Cycle of Support

Point out everyday examples where support flows naturally: *You helped your sister this morning, and she shared with you later; see how we all support each other?* This normalises the interconnected rhythm of giving and receiving.

Invite Instead of Impose

When children are struggling, ask: *Would you like help, or do you want to give it another go?* This approach honours their autonomy and empowers choice while still offering safety.

Guide From Heart, Not Obligation

Shift from duty-based language ('you have to share') to soulful intention: *Is there a kind way you'd like to offer something right now?* This makes generosity a choice of the heart, not a rule.

Set Up Mutual Support Rituals

Create space for reciprocal care like: *How can we support each other today?*, check-ins, or rotating family responsibilities where everyone has a role in giving and receiving.

Validate Boundaries

When children express 'no', respect it and let them witness you doing the same with others. This builds a culture of trust and teaches that true support includes honouring limits. Also remember to model your own boundaries and the language you use (e.g. *I want to help, but I need a minute to get ready* or *Thanks for asking, I can help after lunch.*)

Speak in Terms of Energy, Not Effort Alone

Acknowledge emotional contribution, not just tasks: *You gave so much of your heart today helping your friend.* This helps kids recognise the energetic currency of connection.

Language of Letting Go

Support kids in finding compassionate closure, so they feel comfortable with what words to use:

e.g. *I'm grateful for our time, but I feel like I need new space now* or *We don't grow in the same direction anymore, and that's okay.*

Support Tokens

Children can create small cards or symbols they can use to signal *I need support* or *Can we talk?* This supports nonverbal communicators and builds respectful awareness.

Legacy in Motion

Reflect. Integrate. Empower.

Support is something we grow *with*, so when we honour support as a sovereign exchange, where giving uplifts and receiving empowers, we seed a new standard for connection. A standard where sincerity, discernment, and mutual growth become the norm.

As we know, our children *feel* our frequency. They calibrate to the way we ask for help, the way we receive support, the way we allow ourselves to be held.

And when our energy says *I honour my worth. I welcome support that aligns with who I am. I walk alongside others, not behind them*, that becomes a legacy they carry forward; and that builds the foundation for something even more powerful – knowing when:

To speak up.

To honour a boundary.

To express a need.

To take up space – with love and clarity.

Which brings us to our next marker in raising heart-led self-leaders:

The power of sacred self-advocacy – the soul language of self-regard.

Journal Prompts

- *Who are the people in my life that support my sovereignty?*
- *How can I model aligned support without over-functioning?*
- *Where in my circles of relationships (family, friends, etc.) do I see the need for sacred letting go?*
- *How can I help children tune into the difference between support that expands and support that entangles?*

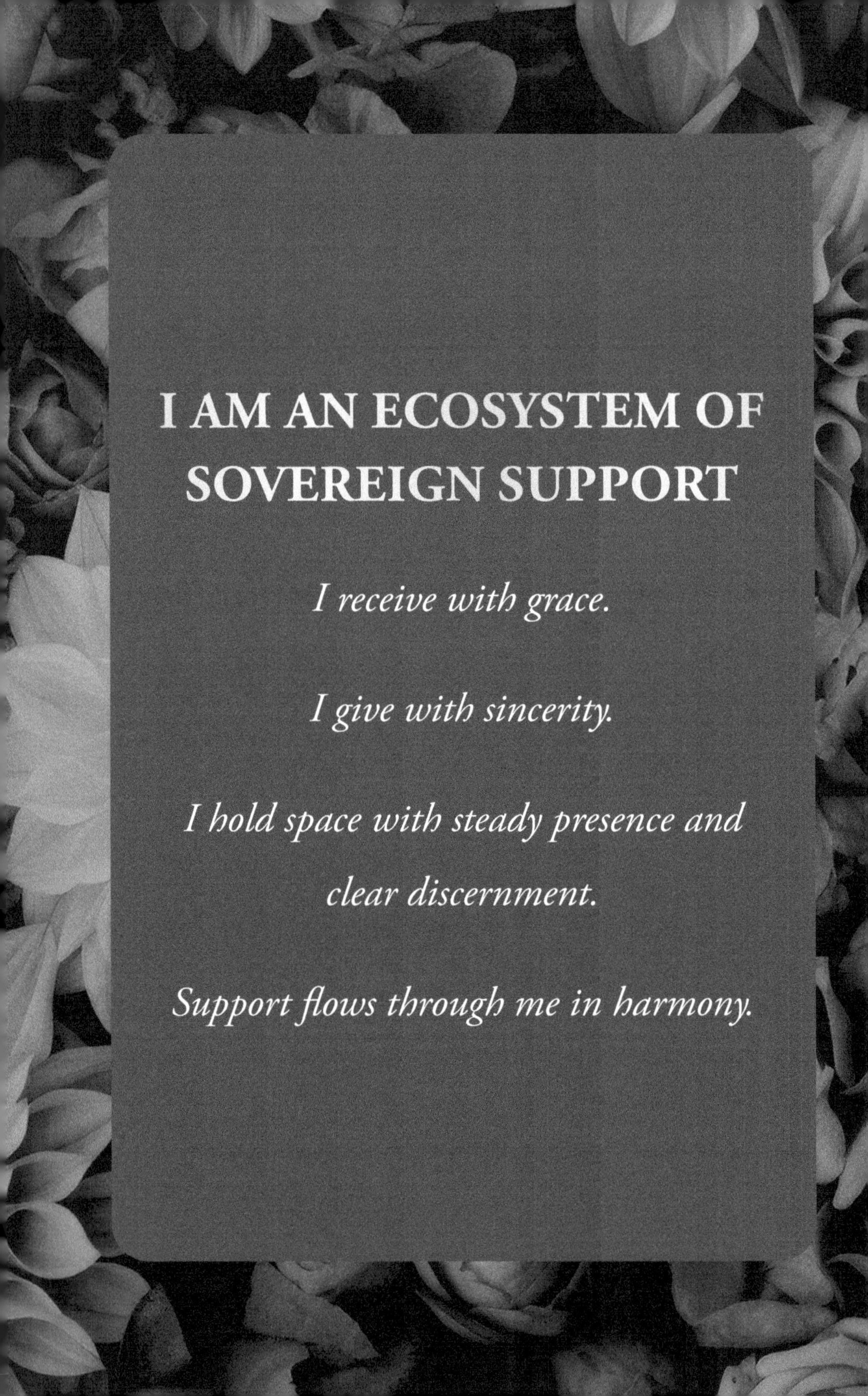
I AM AN ECOSYSTEM OF SOVEREIGN SUPPORT
I receive with grace.
I give with sincerity.
I hold space with steady presence and clear discernment.
Support flows through me in harmony.

SACRED SELF-ADVOCACY

Speaking the Soul Language of Self-Regard

What if your voice flowed from a reservoir of self-respect, not the weight of self-questioning?

'If Denmark didn't get so cold, I think we'd move there!' I announced to the kids.

For a season in my life, I found myself quietly obsessed with Denmark. I was captivated by the consistent research declaring it the happiest country in the world for over 40 consecutive years. What were they doing differently, I wondered, especially in how they approached family, education, and the shaping of young lives?

Curiosity led me to interview the vice president of the LEGO Foundation in Denmark on my podcast. It was one of the most joy-filled conversations I've had. His words literally vibrated with the energy of play, spontaneity, and lightness as he spoke of joy not as a luxury, but as an essential element of learning and life. And that struck something in me – not just as a parent, but as a human deeply invested in how we raise empowered, heart-led contributors to the world. Because joy isn't frivolous; it is formative – building emotional safety, flexibility, and the freedom to express without fear. And when a child feels free to be in the energy of joy and play, they also feel free to speak. To try. To lead. And to serve.

I also reached out to Jessica Joelle Alexander, author of *The Danish Way of Parenting*, to dive deeper into what made Danish childhoods so rooted in wellbeing. What stood out most in our conversation wasn't a single technique or strategy – but a way of being. She spoke of how Danish schools explicitly teach empathy. How 'hygge' isn't just a lifestyle trend – it's a cultural rhythm of connection, presence, and belonging.

But perhaps most striking was her description of **respect**.

From the moment of their birth, she explained, Danish children are raised with an embedded respect. Not fear-based obedience. Not top-down authority. But genuine mutuality. There was no sense of a parent being the 'boss' of the child – instead, the home felt more like a round table, where every person, regardless of age, had a place. A voice. A space that mattered.

As she spoke, I imagined that table: soft light, warm voices, and the unspoken knowing that *you belong here, just as you are*.

This, to me, is sacred self-advocacy in action. Not taught through lectures but modelled through culture. When a child grows up in a space where their inner world is respected, where their presence carries weight, they don't need to fight to be seen; they already *know* they matter.

And that knowing?

It becomes the root system of sovereignty.

A child raised this way doesn't need to dominate to feel powerful; they walk with quiet dignity, attuned to themselves and those around them. This is how joy and justice meet; and how self-leadership is born, through deep, mutual regard. What warmed my heart the most was the idea that respect is not earned through age or status; it's offered as a baseline for being.

When a child is raised in a space where they are inherently regarded, where their words carry weight and their presence is honoured ... it creates **the soil where self-worth grows** as their embodied essence is rooted. And this brings us to understanding that one of *the most* vital expressions of self-worth in motion ... is **sacred self-advocacy**.

As I reflect on self-advocacy, it is clear that it is often very misunderstood; not as *the natural birthright that it is*, but something earned through struggle. The words *self-advocacy* often carry an unspoken association: to 'stand up for yourself', to 'fight for what's right'. For many, it conjures a forceful, even defensive, energy. But my conscious addition of the word *sacred* in this chapter title is an invitation to recode that energy completely.

Sacred self-advocacy isn't about fighting; it's about faithfully standing in the truth of who you are. It's a solid, steady presence rooted in reverence – for the self. It 'speaks' the language of sovereignty: *I matter. My truth is safe here. I am allowed to be.* It's not an outer skill. It's an inner state – an energetic embodiment of self-worth.

As you can imagine, my work as a speech pathologist has gifted me insight into the lives of many individuals and families, each navigating the impacts of communication differences and challenges on their unique journey.

For children with communication differences or challenges, sacred self-advocacy isn't just harder – it's often more crucial. When a child struggles to express their needs clearly, be it through language, speech, or social understanding, their capacity to advocate for themselves can feel fragile. But it's also precisely in those places of vulnerability that the seed of self-leadership must be nurtured.

Because for these children, every act of expression – no matter how small – is sacred ground. A gesture, a glance, a pause before a word. These are more than micro moments of communication; they are moments of becoming. When we teach children that their voice matters, regardless of how it sounds or how long it takes to form, we teach them that *they* matter.

And yet, this is where things get tender. As adults, especially parents, our instinct is to help – to fill in the words, solve the problem, speak for them. We rush in with love, but sometimes in that rush, we unknowingly override their sovereignty. We take the reins, and in doing so, we remove the very opportunity for them to discover their own strength.

Empowerment doesn't always come from doing – it often comes from *waiting*.

From making space.

From asking, 'What would you like to say?', and then holding that space, however long it takes, with reverence.

Sacred self-advocacy, for *all* children, and especially those who communicate differently, is not built by pushing them forward – but by adjusting our pace and walking beside them.

Across the years, I've supported individuals of all ages with developing the art of self-advocacy through communication. For many primary school children, it was about building confidence to help their teacher better understand 'the best way I learn' or knowing how to respond to peers who perceived or treated them in an unfavourable way.

For older teens, it has been preparing for job interviews and learning how to express their capabilities clearly while communicating how they work best. And for young adults, it was empowering them through life transitions such as independent living and learning how to navigate daily demands of housing, appointments, work, etc., with clarity, confidence, and self-respect; all while embracing their unique communication style.

This in essence is direct and explicit training in sacred self-advocacy … however, there is more to it.

It was my first session meeting an adult client with communication differences. She was in her late thirties and had been in various allied health therapies her entire life. She attended with her mum: an incredibly warm, friendly, bright, and sociable woman whose presence immediately filled the room.

Her mum launched straight into sharing the details of her daughter's daily routine and life dynamics. It painted a wonderfully comprehensive picture; and at the same time, I found myself wondering what the client herself might want to share, in whatever way she could. So I asked her.

With single key words and short phrases, the client communicated what lit her up most in her weekly schedule. She also expressed some frustration that she couldn't read but only recognised some common words, she wanted to learn more.

As this exchange unfolded, I gently and respectfully paused her mum a few times from 'filling in' her daughter's communication.

'I'm doing my best to not interrupt … it's just so hard!' her mum said. (And yes – it absolutely would be, especially when 'filling in the communication gaps' has been a pattern for the mum for over thirty years.)

Then she added, 'I just want to say, I know my daughter would like to learn to read, but it's probably too late …'

I smiled gently and replied, 'Maybe. Maybe not. I do wonder though if you'd be happy to stay open to the possibility – that she *can* learn in a way that works for her and aligns with her interests and strengths.'

'Of course!' the mum replied with interest.

We continued with regular sessions, and together we set goals, with one goal being the ability to read core words related to her areas of interest, and another to formulate and express her own opinions, needs, and wants.

The progress that unfolded was extraordinary. Being in the joy of her passions, she began to learn how to read in ways that resonated with her unique strengths and abilities. More than that, she developed a voice – a voice that was heard, valued, and celebrated.

Yes, her mum was 'retrained' to pause, to wait, to offer space for her daughter to communicate in everyday scenarios. And in doing so, she couldn't believe the result.

'It's like a new discovery,' she said. 'A whole new side of her.'

But it wasn't new. It was the side of her that tapped into the inherent self-worth that had been there all along, waiting for space to rise. It highlights that sacred self-advocacy is the expression of one's truth, nurtured in a context or environment that allows it to unfold.

And this begs the questions:

What if self-advocacy didn't always have to begin from crisis or defence?

What if it was seeded in childhood, through everyday rituals of self-awareness, self-regard, and safe expression?

What if advocacy wasn't something children learnt to do only when their needs weren't met, but something they practised daily, in the way they breathe, move, and speak?

I'll leave those reflective questions with you …

Heart-Powered Self Leadership

So how can we help children embody sacred self-advocacy?

Sacred self-advocacy begins long before a child learns to argue a point or assert a need. It begins in the everyday moments where they are invited to notice what feels right in their body, express what matters to them, and speak their truth; no matter how gently.

Below I offer embodied practices to nurture children's capacity to tune in, speak up, and stand strong in who they are.

Breathe Before Words

When a child connects to their breath, they connect to their centre. Before tricky conversations or decisions, guide them: *Let's take three deep breaths so we can hear what your heart wants to say.*

When the breath is shallow, the voice shrinks. But when the breath is full, the voice can rise. Simple rituals like humming, singing, or even playful lion's breath help children awaken their throat centre and feel the resonance of their voice as something alive, safe, and powerful.

Tune into Inner Yes and No ***(yes, it is this one again!)***

Guide and remind children to feel the difference between a body-based 'yes' (open, expansive, grounded) and a 'no' (tight, withdrawn, uneasy). Invite small daily check-ins (e.g. *Close your eyes … what does your belly say about this?*).

Create a Mini Library of Self-Honouring Phrases

Children can learn kind, clear statements that honour both themselves and others.

Try phrases like:

I'm not ready for that yet.
I hear you, and I feel differently.
This is important to me.
I can claim my space and still care.
I trust my knowing.

Model Confident Calm

Children learn what self-advocacy feels like by witnessing it. Let them see you say no with kindness. Let them hear you ask for space, voice emotion, and change your mind with grace.

Practise 'Truth Circle' Moments

Set a weekly time where each family member shares one feeling, one need, or one boundary and is simply heard, without correction or fixing. It normalises truth-telling as connection, not confrontation.

Celebrate Expression in All Forms

Whether a child expresses through drawing, dance, words, or silence, affirm their self-awareness. *Thank you for sharing that* can be a powerful phrase to validate their courage.

In this way, self-advocacy becomes less of a reaction, and more of a rhythm. The rhythm of *sacred* self-advocacy – walking through life attuned, empowered, and anchored in the truth of one's own being.

Lifelong Flourishing

Daily Rituals & Rhythms for Families, Educators & Therapists

Even the most loving, well-intentioned adults can unintentionally override a child's growing voice. It often stems from a beautiful instinct – to protect, to solve quickly, to maintain harmony. And yet, both neuroscience and developmental wisdom remind us: agency isn't taught through instruction alone. It's cultivated through space-making, respect, and the slow, sacred practice of letting a child lead.

Here are gentle shifts we can make in everyday life to support sacred self-advocacy:

Wait for Their Voice

Instead of answering on their behalf, create a pause: *Would you like to share, or would you like me to help?* Give them the first invitation and honour their response – verbal or not.

Coach Don't Rescue

In moments of challenge, resist jumping in to fix. Sit beside them, breathe together, and ask: *What could you try?* Empower their problem-solving before offering your own.

Validate Their Inner World

Dismissive phrases like *Don't be silly* or *It's not that bad* may seem harmless, but they chip away at emotional self-trust. Try instead: *That sounds hard. Tell me more.*

Honour Truth Alongside Kindness

Politeness is valuable; but not when it silences truth. Model ways to be both respectful and real: *It's okay to say no, kindly. Your feelings still matter.*

Notice and Name the Pause

When a child hesitates, don't rush in. Try saying: *I see you're thinking. I'll wait.* This affirms their process and shows you trust their timing.

Debrief With Compassion

After an event where their voice was overridden (intentionally or not), reflect gently: *Did you feel heard? What would you want to say next time?* Invite learning, not shame.

Offer Support Without Control

Use empowering prompts like:

Would you like to practise how you might say that?

How can I support you in sharing what's important?

These questions teach collaboration and ownership.

In the day-to-day rhythms of life, these micro-moments matter. They are the threads that weave self-regard, voice, and autonomy into a child's nervous system and knowing. When we practise these shifts consistently, we create a culture of sacred listening, and inner trust in their voice.

Legacy in Motion

Reflect. Integrate. Empower.

When a child feels safe to show up, with their voice welcomed, something beautiful takes shape.

Kids begin to carry themselves with quiet certainty.

Their choices become more aligned.

Their boundaries more natural.

Their empathy more available.

Sacred self-advocacy gives rise to a kind of leadership that radiates from within. These are the children who listen deeply, speak with care, and know how to stand in truth without needing to overpower. They navigate challenge with resilience because they trust their own inner compass.

This is the heart of what we're growing, not just independence, but integrity. And every moment we honour a child's perspective, every time we model presence and mutual respect, we nurture this sacred architecture within them, and the power of self-regard in action.

But sacred self-advocacy isn't where the journey ends. It's where it softens – opens – and makes room for something just as vital: deep celebration.

So now, we step into the practice of joyful reverence, where celebration becomes a way of being and a way of seeing. Not for performance or praise, but for the miracle of showing up, again and again, in authentic wholeness.

Journal Prompts

- *What did I learn about using my voice as a child, and what do I want to do differently now?*
- *How do I respond when my child struggles to express themselves, and how can I offer more space?*
- *What does sacred self-advocacy mean to me, and how can I model it in everyday life?*
- *What would it look like for me to create more rituals of voice and choice in my home, classroom, or therapy space?*

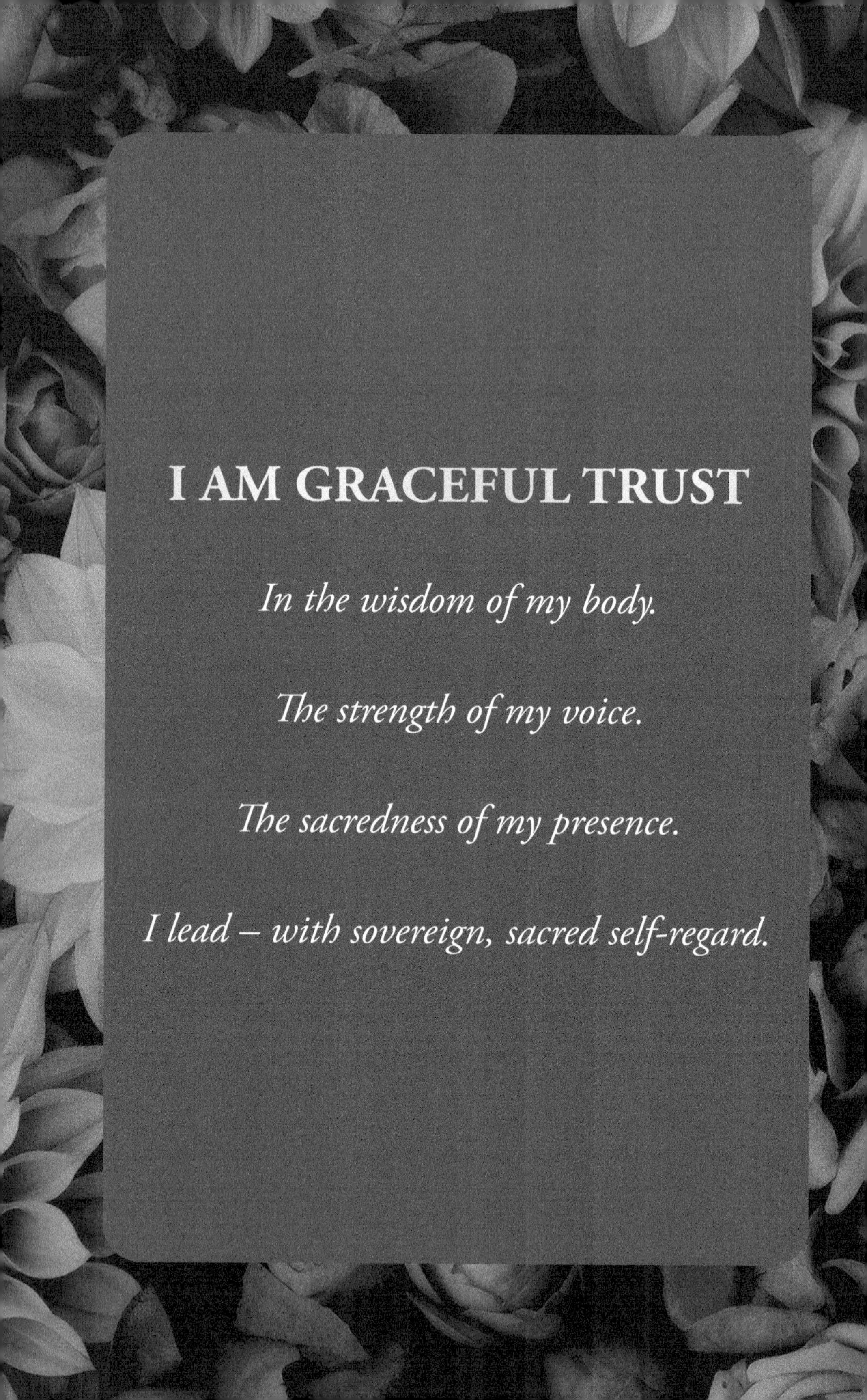

I AM GRACEFUL TRUST

In the wisdom of my body.

The strength of my voice.

The sacredness of my presence.

I lead – with sovereign, sacred self-regard.

THE PRACTICE OF DEEP CELEBRATION

Cultivate Joyful Reverence

What if celebration is a frequency, quietly shaping how we live, love, and lead?

It had been a long day – a day that had thrown some big, very unexpected curveballs. As I was preparing to head home, my phone lit up; it was a message from one of my close friends. A simple check in:

Here if you want to talk xx

In that moment, something softened in me. Amongst the swirl of chaos and unexpected turns, I felt an overwhelming wave of gratitude.

Yes, things had 'gone sideways' that day; but ultimately, I realised I still held the remote control. And I could choose what button to press … wallow in self-pity and perceived victimhood, or practise deep celebration, graceful gratitude and quiet reverence.

So, I chose.

On the way home, I stopped at the supermarket and gathered a few items: some essential oil bath salts; a bunch of beautiful roses; and some organic chocolate (of course!). That night, I ran a warm bath – calling it **my bath of blessings** – and soaked with a sense of reverence for all the good flowing in my life.

As I rested in that water, I remembered a truth that re-empowered my core:

I am supported. I am loved. By something greater than any challenge life might present in my path.

And that, I realised, was cause for **celebration**.

There's a quiet strength in celebration that often goes unnoticed. In a world that spins fast, where achievement is praised but inner joy is often overlooked, celebration can feel like a luxury. But what if it's actually a necessity? Not just for our happiness, but for our, and our children's, flourishing.

Societal messages will have you believe celebration is just for birthdays and significant milestones; but I like to embrace the energy and frequency of celebration as a way of being. It doesn't have to be loud; it has to be felt.

I touched on the energy of joy previously, but I feel the need to emphasise that joy is one of the highest measurable frequencies we can embody. In fact, on the Map of Consciousness developed by Dr David Hawkins, joy calibrates even higher than love. That's not to say it's better, but it holds a unique, elevated vibration that carries lightness, expansion, and deep alignment with our truest self. Joy is a state of reverence for life itself, and this frequency opens the doorway to deep celebration.

For a number of years, I've ended each episode of my *Chatabout Children* podcast with the words: 'I celebrate you.' It's not just a nice sign-off. It's an intentional energetic transmission. A frequency sent through sound and word to uplift the listener, no matter what kind of day they've had, or where they are on their journey.

When we begin the day (and end it) through a lens of celebration, the world meets us differently. Our awareness expands. So instead of seeing problems, we're more likely to see possibilities; and instead of bracing ourselves for the next challenge, we soften into moments of grace, where even the smallest things, like sunlight on skin or a child's laugh, feels profoundly sacred.

And when comparison sneaks in, as it often does, celebration becomes a powerful circuit breaker. In my book *Flourish for Mums*, I wrote about the moment I learnt to shift out of comparison by actively celebrating the very person or thing that had triggered the spiral. This works beautifully with children too. When they notice themselves comparing – whether it's someone's new shoes, higher grade, or faster run – they can learn to pause and to say *and feel* internally: *Wow. I celebrate that.*

This shift isn't about pretending everything is perfect. It's about interrupting the thought loop that leads to self-diminishment, and consciously choosing to honour what they see, without draining their own energy in the process.

Science supports this shift ... sharing that celebration activates parts of the brain related to reward and connection, releasing dopamine and oxytocin. This activates motivation, wellbeing, and emotional resilience. It's a small act with a large ripple effect. So why not choose celebration as a lens to wear and adopt it as a way of seeing? This invites the flow and energy of celebration into life without reserving it only for individual achievement.

We can celebrate the rise of the moon, the pattern on a butterfly's wing, a friend's courage, or a stranger's kindness. Celebration becomes a sacred witnessing. A remembering that we are part of something vast, beautiful, and interconnected.

I recall a conversation with a woman based in Europe, who was deeply invested in the global wellbeing of future generations. She was conducting research and had reached out to interview me about my philosophies and practices around raising empowered humans. At one point, she asked a powerful question:

'What would be the one thing that could make a quantum difference for current and future generations?'

Without hesitation, I responded, '**Celebration**. Celebrating one another. Celebrating ourselves. Celebrating the life that pulsates through us and around us.'

It sounds so simple, doesn't it?

And if you pause for a moment and truly imagine it, you'll feel the shift. It evokes a sense of joy. And in that frequency, it becomes almost impossible to think a hurtful thought about yourself or someone else. **This is reverence beyond what we can even fathom**. A living, breathing devotion to life itself.

When a child is taught to celebrate others sincerely – not from obligation, but from a genuine heart-space – it recalibrates comparison into communion. So instead of *Why them and not me?*, it becomes: *How beautiful for them. I trust in what is for me.*

And when they celebrate nature, or a moment of stillness, or the awe of the cosmos, they are learning to live in reverence. This reverence softens the edges of self-focus and strengthens the soul's sense of union and belonging.

But perhaps the most radical and restorative celebration is the one we rarely speak about: celebrating ourselves.

Not for being perfect. Not for doing more. But simply for being. I've touched on this in various ways throughout this book; but ultimately activating sacred self-celebration means choosing to see ourselves as inherently worthy of joy. Not later, not when we've 'earned it', but now.

It's the moment we look in the mirror and don't rush to correct but pause to smile, and the choice to speak kindly to ourselves when no one is listening. Basically, it's the deep, cellular remembering that we are enough as we are.

And this matters.

A child who moves through life more rooted in self-worth, and less shaken by the approval of others, is growing in the soil of lifelong flourishing. Joy, then, is not just a feeling; it becomes a field. A lived frequency we carry, share, and return to.

So let us show our children that celebration can be quiet and powerful. That to celebrate is to sanctify life … and that by cultivating this inner and outer reverence, we are not escaping reality; we are re-enchanting it.

Heart-Powered Self-Leadership

So how can we help children cultivate joyful reverence and the practice of deep celebration?

Celebration Circuit Breaker Tool

Help children to notice when they're comparing themselves to others; and instead of spiralling, acknowledge your child's immediate emotion (e.g. frustration) and help them shift into celebrating the other. Create a cue card or bracelet that reminds them: *I celebrate others. I celebrate myself. I trust my path.*

Mirror Moments: The Daily Self-Celebration Ritual

This is a daily practice of looking into a mirror and saying:

'I celebrate you. I love how you …' *(followed by something kind and true)*

Although it may feel uncomfortable to start with, it does become more genuine and heartfelt, reinforcing healthy self-talk, self-respect, and self-leadership from within.

Soundtrack of Celebration

This is a fun and quick way to set the frequency to joy, where children (or families) create a playlist of songs that evoke feelings of joy, empowerment, and reverence. It can be used:

- as a morning activation ritual
- during transitions (e.g. home to school)
- to reset energy after a tough moment.

Daily 'I Celebrate Me' Journal

Encourage a simple journalling ritual to affirm self-worth and sacred self-celebration for your child. The journal prompt can simply be: *Today, I celebrate myself for …*

The response can be as short as one word or one sentence. Great for bedtime reflection; and also great for your child to be able to flip through in any moments of feeling self-doubt or uncertainty.

For younger children: They can draw it out and add stickers or symbols to represent what they're celebrating about themselves.

Lifelong Flourishing

Daily Rituals & Rhythms for Families, Educators & Therapists

Soul Sabbaths

Once a week, have a family 'slow day' or 'digital detox window' where the focus is rest, nature, and connection. It helps recalibrate energy and models soulful pace and joyful reverence.

Celebration Declarations

Invite children to create short affirmations or spoken word pieces that begin with: 'Today I celebrate …' This can be used in class sharing circles, therapy check-ins, or family dinner rituals.

Celebratory Breath Pause

Practise a mini pause ritual throughout the day to anchor in celebration. This could be done by taking three slow breaths and silently affirming: *I celebrate this moment.*

This works really beautifully after completing a task, receiving help, or noticing nature.

Children can pair it with a hand-over-heart gesture; and this uplevels the practice, turning the celebration into a somatic, embodied experience of *presence and self-appreciation.*

Cup of Celebration

I have shared this ritual quite a few times now publicly and coined it as the *Cup of Gratitude* ... and the cup of celebration is the same premise.

Choose your favourite mug/cup and make it your cup of celebration (or gratitude). Do the same for your kids – have them choose a cup or special glass to represent this ritual. The way it works is that for each sip from your cup, close your eyes and *feel* truly grateful for an aspect of yourself.

So, this isn't about your circumstances or what material items you have. This is purely celebration about you. This means for every sip from your cup, you internally repeat your chosen statement of celebration (about you). For example, *I celebrate my sense of humour; I celebrate my creativity; etc.*

Letters of Celebration

One of my favourite practices is writing *Letters of Celebration.* I've used them in many ways: marking the beginning of a new life chapter, honouring a meaningful transition, or celebrating the life of a loved one who has passed.

As a family, we've embraced this ritual on special occasions like Mother's Day, where the children have written heartfelt letters to their grandmother, remembering and cherishing the joyful moments they shared.

It's a powerful way to weave gratitude, memory, and love into words; and to keep celebration alive in both presence and remembrance.

Legacy in Motion

Reflect. Integrate. Empower.

Celebration is not a detour from real life; it is a way to walk through it with sacred presence. When we choose to live as celebrants of the everyday, we raise humans who carry within them a natural reverence for life. These are the children who pause to marvel, who honour others with sincerity, who speak to themselves with kindness, and who create futures rooted in joy and flourishing.

This is how legacy is lived … not by what we accumulate, but by the frequency we pass on.

Let us be remembered for what we celebrated – the glimmers, the grace, the growth. And in doing so, we gift the next generation a permission slip to live with wonder, dignity, and delight.

The choice is ultimately yours; you can choose for celebration to become your living prayer. One that says: *I honour this life … and I choose to uplift it.*

And from that space, something sacred and magical awakens … a desire to share the overflow and be of service. So from here, we move into how that overflow becomes soulful devotion; where legacy is lived and passed on through the everyday.

Journal Prompts

- *If I treated celebration as a sacred daily practice, what moments today would I honour and why?*
- *When do I find it easiest – and hardest – to celebrate myself? What beliefs might be influencing that?*
- *How does comparison show up in my life, and how might I transmute it through authentic celebration?*
- *What does 'joyful reverence' feel like in my body, and how can I invite more of it into my everyday rhythms?*

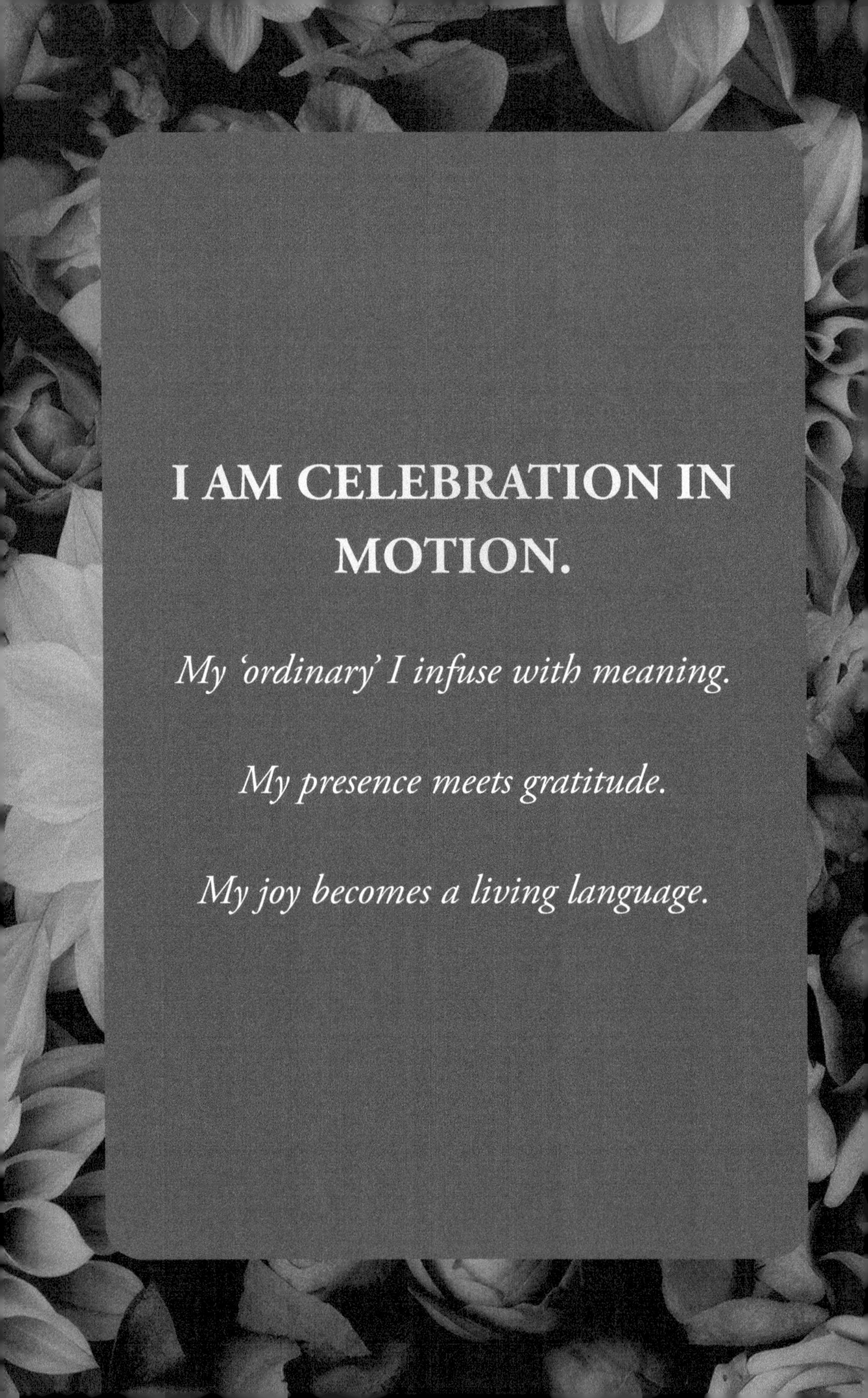

I AM CELEBRATION IN MOTION.

My 'ordinary' I infuse with meaning.

My presence meets gratitude.

My joy becomes a living language.

INSPIRE SERVICE

Transforming Personal Growth for Collective Good

What if the truest form of giving … was actually becoming more of who you are?

Back in 2021, months after the release of my book, *Flourish for Mums: 21 Ways to Thrive with Self-Care and Acceptance*, I was in the beautiful energy of connecting with various people and organisations in the community, sharing the wisdom and power of what deep, nurturing, self-care truly was; whilst reframing the way we practised it.

Amongst all the activity, the book was also honoured with a national award in the Australian Business Book Awards. This momentum energised the next natural step … writing another book – to expand on the 'flourish' series, to encompass the family ecosystem. I eagerly mapped out the framework for the book (which at that time, had the working title of *Flourish for Families: 21 Ways to Raise Empowered Humans*). My publishers were on board, and the publishing contract was posted out to me, ready for me to sign.

On receiving the contract … something tweaked. I couldn't sign it. I let it remain on my desk for two weeks before I wrote to my publisher, informing them that now was not the aligned time for me to write it and release it into the world.

Why?

Because I knew in my heart that there was a whole new personal growth curve awaiting. A chapter of life that held with it an array of incredible unknowns. One I had to navigate as best and as gracefully as I possibly could. One I had to embrace, and journey through, with absolute trust that the all-loving universe would help me to *know* the right timing to action the writing of the book … if it was *'mine'* to ever even write at all.

As I moved through those turbulent times, one thing that kept me grounded was knowing this: every challenge, every unexpected curveball, every moment of inner chaos was there to help me grow new 'cells of sacred sovereignty'. It was like the soil of my personal growth was being replenished so I could plant deeper, more sustainable seeds of wisdom.

And in doing so, I wasn't just honouring my own journey … I was living the very essence of *Raising Empowered Humans*; because our children learn empowered service not by being told, but by witnessing how we rise, how we serve, and how we stay true to ourselves.

And then, that moment arrived; the sacred intersection of inner knowing and divine timing. I was ready to share. The world was ready to listen. And so, I wrote *Raising Empowered Humans*. This lived experience reminded me: raising empowered humans begins with becoming whole.

This palpable process of transforming personal growth for collective good is an ongoing one for us all. When we expand beyond ourselves in service, we evolve who we are; individually and collectively. True service isn't about fixing, saving, or proving. It's a sacred act of alignment, where self-expression meets collective upliftment.

I am inspired daily by the stories I hear and the people I meet who have done and are doing exactly that … giving rise to a collective flourishing future.

Being of service doesn't mean you have to be on a global stage, or running a business, or leading a company. It is how you choose to show up in your everyday. It is a gentle yet pure energy of heart-activated contribution. And when our children witness that, feel it, and absorb it, they come to understand that who they are matters … and that their light, no matter how small it may seem, can brighten the world. Tuning in to how you can contribute in your everyday with presence, humility, and a heart rooted in love is both a beautiful and a divine weaving of wonders.

Sometimes, the most meaningful acts of service aren't planned or polished … they're born in ordinary moments, when we simply follow the nudge to act with kindness, presence, or generosity. That heart-led impulse can ripple far beyond what we ever imagined.

I remember a simple moment that began with a smile across the street …

A few years ago, I had noticed a neighbour in the street often playing with his young grandson in the front garden. Their joy in simply being together radiated. On this particular day, as I saw them, I felt inspired to gift them my children's books to share and enjoy; and so I did.

The following day, I received an order for a few copies of *Kisses in Your Heart* – from that neighbour's wife. The following week, she contacted me to let me know she was a pastoral care worker in a palliative care hospital, sharing the book with children who were grieving the loss of a loved one. She shared her gratitude for the contribution the book was making to their healing journey.

The week after that, I received a phone call from a woman who was grieving the loss of her close friend, who had been at that same palliative care hospital. She explained that her friend had several grandchildren, and she, along with her friendship group, wanted to make a sizeable donation of *Kisses in Your Heart* copies to the hospital to help more children in their healing journey. I was deeply moved by this.

Days later, she contacted me again to let me know that the order would be doubled – her friend's husband also wanted to contribute.

I have always held a certain trust that my books will find their way to where they are needed and to whom they are meant for. But this brought me to tears of deep gratitude – for the power of being inspired by the whispers of the heart and the collective good that they can radiate.

I loved catching up with and interviewing the incredible Karen Weaver. A multi-award-winning author, publishing powerhouse, entrepreneur, and mother of six, Karen has built an empire not through force, but through flow. Her life is a testament to what it means to lead from the heart, walk with intention, and live in service of both self-growth and collective upliftment. When Karen speaks – the heart listens.

My conversation with Karen served as a reminder that empowered parenting and soulful ambition are not separate paths. They are, in fact, the same; and she credits her deep-rooted clarity to her upbringing.

'As a child, I was allowed to be curious and adventurous,' she recalls. 'I knew unconditional love.' That inner foundation, she says, meant she didn't have to do a lot of 'undoing' later in life. Instead of fear, she was given trust, and that trust became her compass.

Now a global entrepreneur and author of over 40 books, Karen is also an advanced Law of Attraction practitioner who lives by the truth: 'Where there's a will, there's always a way.' Her motto is not just a saying – it's a lived mantra. As she shares: 'Some days I don't [do it all], and that's okay.'

Her parenting is not perfectionist, it's poetic. She builds her life around presence; 'I prioritise joy very highly,' she says. And this joy isn't about escape; it's about essence. 'Where there's joy, there is success.'

Karen's vision of service is deeply interwoven with how she raises her children. Rather than placing pressure on them to 'be' something, she invites them to explore who they already are.

'They know that if they want something, they can get it,' she says. 'But I show them how to journey for it.'

In her household, wants are not denied nor indulged, they are honoured as invitations for personal growth. This concept of the 'journey' is crucial.

As Karen describes it: 'I want them to journey for it, not just have a tantrum and receive.' In this way, she plants the seeds of emotional maturity and self-leadership.

Her eldest son, once studying engineering, now runs his own publishing company – after breaking his leg and unexpectedly working with Karen during recovery. 'He caught the publishing bug,' she laughs. It was the perfect example, she says, of how the universe reroutes us in divine timing.

Service, for Karen, is sacred action. 'Too many moms think they have to sacrifice themselves completely for motherhood. But what are we teaching our kids? If they see us pursuing our dreams, aligned with our values, they learn from our actions.'

Her closing advice to parents and caregivers was as humble as it was revolutionary:

'Be the best version of yourself – not someone else's version. Show your kids they are loved. Hug them. Let them grow. Give them space.'

This is what it means to inspire service …

Not by telling others what to do, but by simply being who we are … without the forcing of outcomes, but rather by nurturing our frequency – with joyful intention and devotion to the good of all.

And in doing so, we raise our children as light-bearers for a new world.

Heart-Powered Self-Leadership

So how can we help children live a life of heart-led service, rooted in self-leadership?

Here are energy-aligned ways to empower service-minded children:

Root in Self-Awareness

Help children notice what lights them up, so they begin to recognise their authentic motivations – that's the starting point of meaningful service.

Empower with Purpose

Invite children to see their everyday actions as part of something bigger. When you ask 'How did you help today?' or 'Who did you help uplift?', you're teaching them that their presence carries impact, and that even small acts matter.

Let Them Lead (in Small Ways)

Offer opportunities for children to take initiative – whether it's organising a book corner, leading a classroom greeting, or suggesting a family kindness challenge. These moments build confidence and show them that leadership and service often go hand in hand.

Model Curiosity & Compassion

Let children see you asking questions, listening deeply, and responding gently to others' experiences. These behaviours signal that understanding and kindness are not just reactions; they are choices that create connection.

Celebrate the Invisible Gifts

Shine light on the quiet acts: comforting a friend, standing up for someone, making space for another's idea. These subtle expressions of heart-centred care are the seeds of true leadership.

Encourage 'Why Does This Matter?' Moments

Support children in linking their actions to impact: *Why did that feel important?* or *How might that ripple out?* This cultivates an internalised sense of purpose and helps them see themselves as stewards of the collective.

Use the Language of 'We'

Instead of asking, *What do you want to be when you grow up?*, try asking: *What do you think the world might need – and how could your gifts help?*

This simple shift gently awakens children to a sense of purpose that expands beyond self-image … towards contribution, connection, and co-creation.

Honour Curiosity + Responsibility

When children notice something confusing or unjust, try asking: *How do you feel about that?* or *Is there anything we could do?*

There may not always be something that can be *physically* done to help, but our ability to stay grounded in loving compassion is a powerful contribution in itself.

It's so important for children to understand and own this … so they retain a deep sense of agency, even in moments of uncertainty.

Micro Moments of Contribution
Encourage everyday acts of kindness: writing a thank-you note, picking up litter, helping a neighbour.

Let kids feel the joy of giving without pressure or praise.

Include Them in Your Service
If you volunteer, support others, or donate – bring your kids along. Let them witness your authentic care in action, even if imperfectly done.

Model Sovereign Service, Not Martyrdom
Children absorb energy more than words. When we give from joy and choice (not resentment), they learn that service is expansive, not exhausting.

Lifelong Flourishing

Daily Rituals & Rhythms for Families, Educators & Therapists

So, what are some ways we can inspire service in our day to day? Have a go at some of these …

Morning Heart Check
Begin the day with a centred question: *How do you want to show up for the world today?* This intentional pause cultivates agency and invites children to step into their day with clarity and kindness.

Sparks of Service Journal
Encourage kids to jot down or draw one act of kindness or contribution each day. Over time, this creates a narrative of identity; not just of what they do, but of who they are becoming in service to others.

Impact Language That Uplifts

Use language that ties effort to impact. Instead of a general remark such as 'nice work' be specific; for example, *Your words helped your friend feel safe* or *That action brought calm to the group.* This kind of feedback anchors their self-worth in contribution, not comparison.

Create Collective Rituals

Establish simple, shared practices like a weekly gratitude circle, a kindness jar, or a service-themed family dinner topic. These rituals reinforce that belonging, intention, and contribution are woven into daily life.

Reflect Out Loud

Share your own self-growth moments openly: *I lost my patience today, and tomorrow I will do better.* This transparency normalises the ups and downs of human growth and models that service includes self-accountability.

Empathy Pause

Before reacting, encourage children to ask: *What might they be feeling?* This small practice cultivates the emotional wisdom needed for deep and inclusive leadership, and helps transform conflict into compassion.

Honour Each Voice

In family and classroom conversations, ensure every child is invited to speak and be truly heard. When children feel valued, they're more likely to extend that respect to others, becoming inclusive leaders of collective care.

Close the Day with Connection

Within your winding down routine, include the reflection: *How did you bring light today?* or *What moment made your heart feel full?* These questions plant seeds of conscious contribution, anchoring the day in meaning.

Global Community Service Reflection

Choose a cause that impacts the local community or the global community and learn about it together, discussing: *Is there a way we would like to be of service? If so, how could we help?* Even small awareness builds global citizenship.

Legacy in Motion

Reflect. Integrate. Empower.

Service isn't something we wait to give when we've 'made it' or figured it all out. It's how we choose to show up right now – right here – in the everyday mess and magic of life. It's in the way we listen, the way we love, and the way we offer what's real and true.

When we honour ourselves, trust our light, and grow from the inside out … what naturally flows from us becomes an offering. An act of service fuelled from personal growth.

That's how our kids learn what it means to contribute from the heart. We don't have to do it all. We just have to show up – with loving honesty, and the courage to be seen.

What begins as small, authentic acts of kindness becomes a soulful imprint; one that inspires meaningful contribution for generations to come. Because true service is about being more of who we are … and allowing that to ripple outward.

And when that ripple is lived consistently, it becomes something even greater:

A legacy.

And that leads us to our final chapter of this book. One that shares how to raise humans who shine their light in the world with clarity, courage, and care; so their presence becomes a gift that is felt, long after the moment has passed.

Journal Prompts

- *Where in your life are you already in service, but haven't named it that way?*
- *What does true, aligned giving feel like in your body?*
- *How do you want to model the energy of service to the children in your life?*
- *What's one small act of kindness you could offer this week – from your heart, not from obligation?*

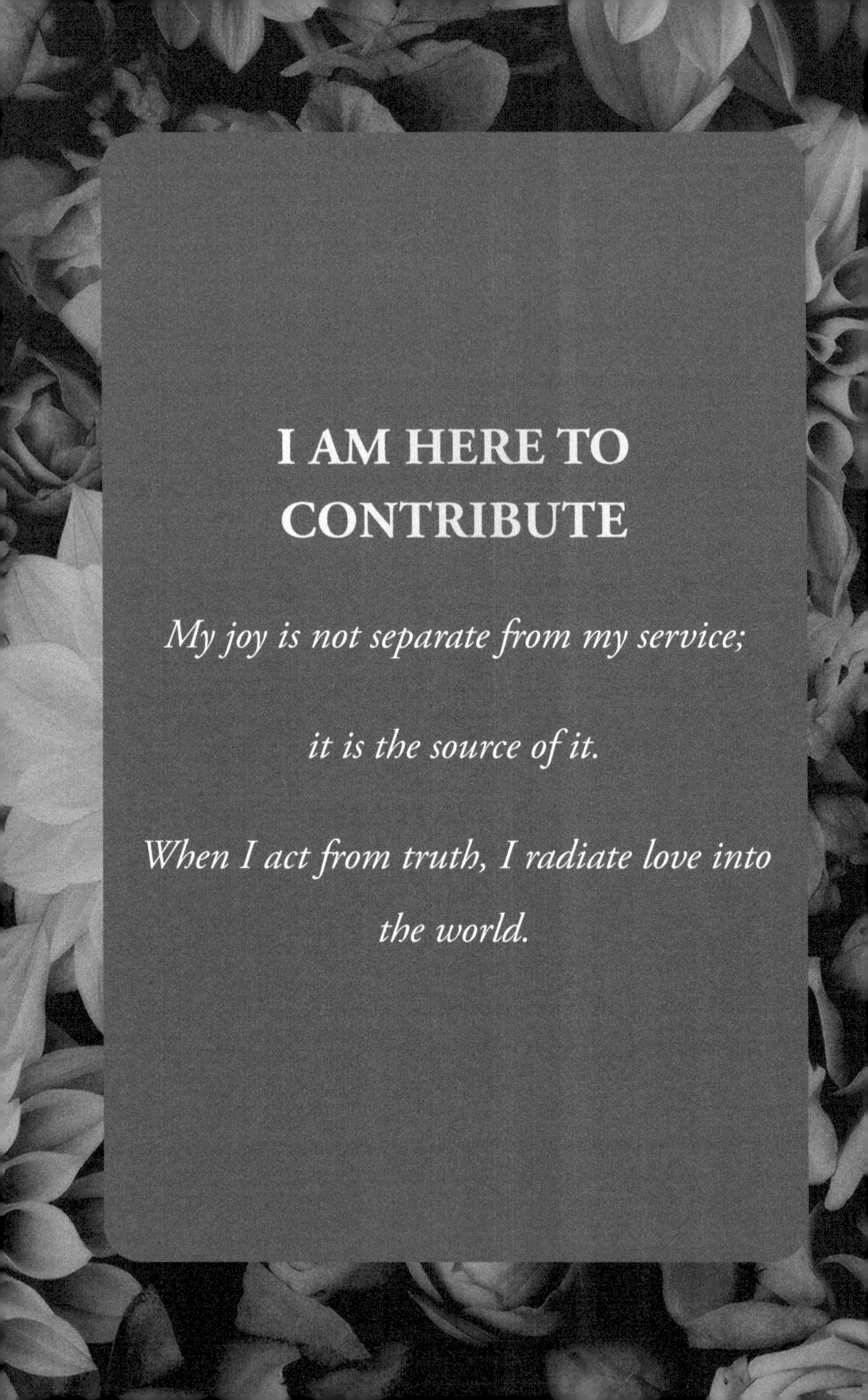
I AM HERE TO CONTRIBUTE
My joy is not separate from my service;
it is the source of it.
When I act from truth, I radiate love into the world.

LIGHT UP LEGACY

Raising Humans Who Shine Their Light in the World

What if legacy isn't something we leave behind, but something we live into, moment by moment?

My mother was a philosopher and deep listener of life. A graceful presence and a poet. A pillar of strength and gentleness … a grounding force and a gentle guide. Many of our conversations in her final months were quiet yet deeply profound, rich with love, reverence, wisdom, and reflection. I recall one moment vividly. She looked at me with clarity and softness and said, 'There's still more I want to do in this life.'

It wasn't said with regret. It was more like longing wrapped in love; an ache towards purpose that hadn't yet finished singing. That truth held its own kind of radiance. It reminded me that legacy isn't something we leave when we die. It's something we live, moment by moment, breath by breath.

Legacy isn't a far-off ideal or a someday dream. It's right here in how we show up today. That quiet exchange with my mother echoes through my life, nudging me to live in a way that honours the light now, not later.

Just before writing this chapter, I photographed the first oranges and lemons picked from my small but determined trees and texted the images to my siblings in celebration. They responded with shared celebration. I then asked the kids what we should make with the oranges. Without hesitation, they said, 'Nonna's biscuits!'

I smiled. That truly warmed my heart with happiness as I felt the echo of my mother alive in their memory, in our kitchen, and in the scent of citrus and the sweetness of tradition. Legacy made simple, made sensory, made real, with love being held and carried forward in my children.

True legacy … pulses beneath the surface.

It is energetic.

It is lived.

And then there are those everyday moments that become soul memories.

I recall a 'Mum date' with my son, our very first three-hour bushwalk together. He was confident in both his ability and endurance, proudly insisting (at six years old) that he would carry our shared backpack by himself. 'I've got this, Mum,' he reassured me. And he did.

We walked in peaceful rhythm, elevated among the trees with the stillness of water glistening below. At one point, he stepped ahead, turned back to me with bright eyes, and said, 'Mum – when I'm older, I'm gonna tell my friends – *and* my kids … if I have kids – that I came on this bushwalk …'

He paused, then beamed, 'With *my* mother!'

His voice rang with pride, presence, and love. And in that simple moment, I was reminded: this is what life is about. Legacy lives in these shared moments; where hearts open, connection deepens, and light expands between generations.

This is how we light up our legacy.

Not by waiting. But by weaving it now. And letting our kids weave theirs, every single day.

I was gifted the honour of speaking with David Meltzer on my *Chatabout Children* podcast. David is a man whose presence alone radiates what I call 'legacy in motion'. Whose heart-led mission and high-level accomplishments co-exist in the most grounded, generous way. While many know him from the business world, as the co-founder of Sports One Marketing or the CEO behind the agency that inspired *Jerry Maguire*; what truly resonated was the frequency he embodied.

His mission?

'To empower over one billion people to be happy.'

That mission flows as energetic service in action, across every touchpoint of his every day; and our conversation reflected exactly that – heart-centred, humanity-first wisdom for parents, children, and changemakers alike.

'We're here to plant seeds under trees we may never sit under,' he said, crediting his single mum, who raised six kids while working two jobs, as his first model of legacy. Her impact wasn't loud, but it was lasting. 'Not every child is ready to receive our wisdom now … and that's okay. Plant the seed anyway.'

David also offered a powerful reframe of accountability, not as blame, but as a return to personal power. When faced with challenge, he asks himself:

What did I do to be responsible for this?

What did I energetically attract?

How am I participating in the perception of this moment?

His goal by asking these questions?

To clear interference. 'I don't spend days in pain anymore. Just minutes and moments,' he shared.

He also introduced the concept of the *Ferocious Buddha*; a way of being that holds both fierce drive and peaceful surrender. 'Be productive, accessible, gracious … but let go of the result. That's where suffering begins.'

For children growing up in a results-driven world, this offers deep liberation … and perhaps most potent was his reflection on the dis-ease he observes in young people today.

'We need to raise them in a world of more than enough. Not "not enough". Not even "just enough for me". But more than enough for all – a world of giving, receiving, and witnessing, where value multiplies.'

This reminds us that scarcity is taught. But so is trust, and so is wholeness, so the practice then becomes *alignment.*

'I already am happy, healthy, wealthy, and worthy. I just need to stop interfering with it,' he said.

That is the real legacy; not what we leave behind, but what we help rise up.

The call to *Light Up Legacy* becomes deeply practical and very necessary. It means to raise humans who carry an internal flame; not one lit by external approval, perfectionism, or pressure, but one kindled from within.

In a time when so many young people are grappling with anxiety, confusion, and spiritual fatigue, what they need isn't more fixing or performance, it's space to remember their inherent worth and power.

Self-leadership begins with grounding, not goals.

When we raise children to connect with their hearts – to listen inwardly to name what they feel, and to make choices aligned with who they truly are – we're raising *whole*, resilient humans who know how to navigate life from the inside out.

Legacy, in this context, isn't a burden of expectation, it's the permission to live with *meaning*. It's the daily imprint of presence, love, values, and conscious being.

It's knowing: *I matter. I can choose. I can serve. I belong.*

So, to *Light Up Legacy* is to raise children who:

See their life not just as a timeline, but as a living expression of contribution.

And when legacy is modelled this way – not as a destination, but as a way of being – it becomes the seed of lifelong flourishing. A true coherence: mind, body, spirit in alignment.

And that is how we raise the next generation to flourish.

Heart-Powered Self-Leadership

How can we help children light up their legacy from within?

Helping children *light up their legacy from within* means creating consistent, loving conditions for inner awareness, self-trust, and aligned action.

Drawing from the various wisdoms already shared; here is a summary:

Reframe Accountability

When things go off course, invite children into compassionate self-inquiry with gentle questions like:

- *What part did I play?*
- *What am I feeling right now?*
- *What can I choose next?*

This keeps them connected to their inner authority, not out of guilt, but through awareness and grace.

Ferocious Buddha

Introduce the concept of the *Ferocious Buddha* as a playful and powerful inner guide – the part of them that can hold both courage and calm, action and peace.

Invite children to imagine what their *Ferocious Buddha* would say when things feel overwhelming.

This helps them meet big emotions and reminds them that strength and stillness can live in the same breath.

Use Mirror Mantras

Support their self-communication with affirming phrases they can speak aloud; especially when doubt creeps in.

Try: *I am already enough* or *I am learning as I grow.*

Saying it to their reflection makes it real. Over time, the mirror becomes a friend, not a critic.

Keep a Seed Journal

Invite your child to jot down, or draw, one small act of light they shared that day: a kind word, a brave choice, a creative spark.

These daily 'seeds' are reminders that legacy grows through little moments.

Feel & Listen Within

Support your child in tuning into their inner world. Help them name what they're feeling, *What am I feeling right now?*, and gently guide them to listen deeper: *What feels true for me today?*

This simple practice builds emotional fluency and inner trust, helping them stay connected to themselves even when the world gets loud.

Reflect on What Matters

Guide children to explore what lights them up: *What do I care about?* or *What makes me feel peaceful?* These reflections help them live from values, not just habits.

Offer Small Choices Daily

Let children choose what to wear, how to set the table, or which project to pursue. These micro-decisions build autonomy and intuitive confidence.

Celebrate Learning from Mistakes

Shift the story around failure. Use moments of struggle to model curiosity: *What did I learn?* or *What might I try next time?* Normalise learning from any 'mistakes' along the way, as the root for growth.

Encourage a Kindness Practice

Prompt one small, intentional act of kindness each day. It could be as simple as a compliment, helping a friend, or writing a thank-you note. These become daily acts of legacy.

Support Respectful Expression

Let kids practise saying what's true, setting boundaries, sharing thoughts, with both honesty and respect. That's how we raise heart-led, compassionate communicators.

End the Day with Gratitude or Wonder

Create a calming bedtime ritual by asking: *What's one thing that lit you up today?* It might be a moment of laughter, a kind gesture, or something they noticed in nature.

Gratitude grounds the heart. Wonder keeps it open.

This gentle pause helps kids end the day not in rush or worry, but in connection – with themselves, and with what matters most.

Lifelong Flourishing

Daily Rituals & Rhythms for Families, Educators & Therapists

Raising empowered humans is an honouring of our children's unique essence. It integrates in daily life through various means, already shared throughout these pages.

These include flourishing family practices such as:

Model Heart-Led Living

Let your kids see you speak your truth with calm, honour your needs without guilt, and make aligned choices; even when they're hard. When you live from the heart, you give them permission to do the same.

Create Emotional Safe Zones

Hold space for your child's inner world; without rushing to fix or dismiss it. Practise deep listening. Instead of *You shouldn't feel that way*, try: *Tell me more.*

Even when their worries seem small to you, take them seriously. Validation builds trust, and teaches them that their feelings are safe, seen, and worth honouring.

Ask Reflective Questions

Rather than jumping in with all the answers, invite your child into their own inner knowing. Ask things like: *What feels right to you?* or *What would your heart say?*

These simple, open questions nurture intuition, build self-trust, and teach kids to listen inward before looking outward.

Celebrate Process & Integrity

Shift the spotlight from outcomes to inner effort. Acknowledge how your child handled a tough situation or showed kindness, not just what they achieved.

Pause before praising. Instead of a quick *Good job*, try: *That looked like it took a lot of thought. How did it feel for you?*

This simple shift rewires motivation, moving it from seeking approval to honouring inner alignment.

Offer Meaningful Roles & Responsibility

Give children real ways to contribute; let them lead a class ritual, help a younger sibling, or plan a family meal. When their efforts are valued, they feel capable and trusted. Purpose builds pride, and responsibility becomes a source of belonging, not burden.

Integrate Mind-Body Practices

Include short breathwork, yoga, music, or nature walks. As you are well aware now, these help to regulate the nervous system and reconnect to self.

Anchor Service & Legacy Language

Talk about service as a privilege, not a pressure. Shift from *You should help* to *You get to make a difference.*

Infuse everyday language with a sense of purpose. Try phrases like:

- *You're shaping your legacy with that choice.*
- *That's one way you shine your light.*
- *What do you feel proud to stand for today?*

These small shifts plant powerful seeds, helping children connect action with meaning, and identity with contribution.

Instil Abundance

Model a mindset of 'enough'. Choose thoughts, words, and actions that reflect possibility; not scarcity. So, instead of focusing on what's missing, speak into what's *available*, what's *working*, and what's *growing*.

Abundance isn't about having more, it's about seeing from a place of trust, gratitude, and potential. And kids feel that frequency deeply.

Hold Space & Let Them Lead Too

Give children the time and trust to unfold in their own way. Their light doesn't need to be pushed; it needs to be seen, nourished, and believed in. Remember: they're not just here to learn from us. Invite their wisdom too.

Ask things like: *What do you think we could do better as a family?* or *What would make this space feel more supportive?*

Empowering them as co-creators builds self-respect, shared trust, and a deeper sense of belonging.

And from that place, their legacy isn't something they try to live – it's something they can't help but become.

Legacy in Motion

Reflect. Integrate. Empower.

Legacy is not a far-off destination. It's *spoken into being, seeded in the now*, and remembered in the heartbeats of ordinary days.

It's in the moments we pause to listen deeply. The times we choose curiosity over correction. The courage we model when we speak from truth.

This light is nurtured through *permission* to be fully seen. For raising a child who shines in the world isn't about shaping them into something … **they're already someone**.

It's about making space for who they truly are.

Allowing them to lead with coherence, with presence, with integrity.

And as for legacy?

It's not something heavy we hand down. It's the light we pass on.

Journal Prompts

- *What kind of legacy am I living right now – and is it aligned with my truth?*
- *If my child were to describe how it felt to be with me, what would I want that feeling to be?*
- *What are the 'seeds of light' I most want to plant in the hearts of my children/the children I work with?*
- *How can I embody my truth more fully today – so that my legacy is something lived, not just spoken about?*

So here we are …

The final golden key has landed in your hands, and in your heart – *The Frequency of Flourishing.*

This one is special. It's the key that doesn't just open a door … it radiates through everything.

Empowered humans who celebrate themselves fully, naturally uplift others.

Their service becomes sacred. Their self-worth becomes luminous.

And life becomes a space to shine; and to express what's real.

You've journeyed through the full circle now – from *Foundations* to *Flourishing* – unlocking self-leadership, wisdom, and possibility at every turn.

I hope you feel that.

I hope you *own* that.

This isn't just a book. It's a remembering, and a reconnection.

For the ripple that begins with you … echoes through generations.

Thank you for the honour of having me walk this path with you.

May your days be filled with light, laughter, and love; as you raise humans who lead, and live … with truth, intention, and heart- and soul-led guidance.

LEGACY IS HOW I SHOW UP NOW
Present.
True.
Radiating from within.

Humans attuned to their higher divine self see life on Earth as a field of pure and blissful harmony – where joyful love is the default resonance.

The time is now for:

New ways of doing.
New ways of being.
New ways of discerning.
New ways of deciding.
New ways of serving.
New ways of creating – new pathways.
New portals …
to a NEWLY EMPOWERED HUMANITY.

May we flourish together,
Sonia xo

BONUS GIFT…

THE CURATED PODCAST PLAYLIST

Your Golden Toolbox for Raising Empowered Humans

I've lovingly created a **handpicked playlist of *Chatabout Children*®** podcast episodes.

This curated list deepens and extends your experience of the themes shared throughout these pages.

Each episode has been selected for its alignment with key messages shared, and includes:

- a short summary of the conversation
- a direct, clickable link for easy access
- the chapter or topic it beautifully complements.

This bonus resource saves you time and brings the most resonant insights straight to your ears; whether you're walking, resting, or needing a moment of inspiration.

Access your bonus gift and more at:

www.soniabestulic.com/goldentoolkit/

OR

Scan this QR code

May these conversations uplift, empower, and support your flourishing; and that of the children in your life.

DID YOU ENJOY THIS BOOK?

There's so much more waiting for you …
Learn about Sonia and explore how you can work together to raise empowered humans –
who know their worth, trust their truth, and shine their light in the world.

ABOUT SONIA BESTULIC

Sonia Bestulic is a globally respected leader in human potential, communication, and conscious parenting. A multi-award-winning and bestselling Children's and Adult Author, International Speaker, Holistic Speech Pathologist, and Intuitive Life and Business coach; she holds a rare gift: bridging ancient wisdom, modern neuroscience, and soul-led living into one powerful presence.

With nearly three decades of professional experience, Sonia has empowered thousands of families, professionals, and children through her integrated approach to energy mastery, self-leadership, and human flourishing.

A creative and visionary entrepreneur, Sonia has worked both nationally and internationally across various health and education sectors including a role as Clinical Educator at Sydney University. In her twenties, she founded and led her Speech Pathology company in Sydney, Australia, for over 18 years; whilst also founding her transformational consulting, coaching, and training company *Flourish with Sonia*. A name that, on the surface, reflects her personal presence, but on a deeper level symbolises the essence of her life's work: to empower people of all ages to flourish by reconnecting with their inner wisdom. The name *Sonia*, meaning 'wisdom', is more than just her name – it's the heart of her mission, guiding everything she offers, the way she connects, and the transformational experiences she guides and creates.

In 2025, Sonia received the prestigious *Global Thought Leader of the Year – Bronze Award* for her visionary impact across health, education, and personal transformation; whilst also receiving a global level *Honorary Mention* for *Wellness and Wellbeing Services.*

Sonia has delivered hundreds of masterclasses to parents, educators, and medical professionals; has mentored hundreds of allied health practitioners; and coached numerous entrepreneurs across the globe. She has also contributed countless hours to community education and has been called upon as a consultant for global companies. She is recognised as a resident expert for Parent TV, and her work has been featured in international media including *The CEO Magazine, Mamamia, Practical Parenting,* and more.

She has authored children's and adult books including:

- *Flourish for Mums: 21 Ways to Thrive with Self-Care and Acceptance* – an award-winning and bestselling book for mothers embracing deep and sustainable wellbeing.
- *Reece, Give Me Some Peace!* and *Kisses in Your Heart* – both award-nominated and nationally acclaimed children's books acknowledged for their contribution for gifting kids the best literary start in life.

Sonia also contributed chapters in various anthologies such as:

- *Old Worlds, New Worlds, Other Worlds* – The Children's Book Council of Australia
- *The Freedom in Forgiveness* – Series by Karen Weaver
- *Intuition and Action* (Puma Edition) – *Hear us Roar* series: KMD Books

Back in 2018, Sonia launched her podcast, *Chatabout Children*®, renowned for its evidence-based, value-packed content, loved by parents/caregivers, educators, and all professionals who work with children. Sonia has shared her growing expertise whilst also interviewing thought leaders, innovators, and changemakers across the globe, weaving real-world guidance with soul-deep insight. Her podcast is rich with evergreen content; while also featuring a special *Flourish for Mums* series, and a *Raising Empowered Humans* series.

Sonia co-founded *The Allied Health Sanctuary*, a revolutionary global community supporting allied health professionals and business owners with heart-led clinical coaching and high integrity self-leadership. In addition, she co-founded *Flourishing Ladies*, through which she hosted national and international events to empower women to lead lives of authentic freedom, fulfilment, and aligned pure power.

But behind every title and accomplishment is lived experience.

Based in Sydney, Australia, Sonia is a devoted mother of three children (all born within 2½ years), making her work grounded in her personal story and journey of navigating the full spectrum of human growth with grace, grit, and intuition. When Sonia is not officially wearing one of her professional hats, she relishes in quality time with her kids: conversations with nature; bushwalks; travel; and eating good quality chocolate. And … she is also known to enjoy creatively cooking whilst singing and dancing to Disney songs.

She has been described as 'someone whose presence heals the heart and soothes the soul', with her mission deeply rooted in service; to help co-create a high-vibration, heart-led, and humble humanity. Sonia's current creative initiative is that of building a global movement through transformational entertainment and education to awaken the light, leadership, and intuitive wisdom within every child.

Sonia is most often sought out as a keynote speaker, educator, and intuitive guide, delivering compelling talks, transformative training, and soul-infused wisdom for audiences of all sizes. She continues to work with a select number of 1:1 clients, offering holistic speech pathology and/or intuitive life and business coaching support for families, C-suite professionals and entrepreneurial leaders seeking energetic alignment, communication mastery, and soul-aligned leadership in life and business.

Sonia lives and leads with compassion, clarity, and creative power – reminding us all that the greatest act of transformation begins within.

WANT TO CONNECT WITH SONIA?

Sonia's website is the best place to learn more, send an email, and subscribe to her updates.

soniabestulic.com

or

Scan the QR Code below

Email: sonia@soniabestulic.com.au

You can also reach out and connect on LinkedIn and sign up to her newsletter: *What Did you Forget?*

INTERESTED IN 1:1 SUPPORT?

Sonia offers a limited number of private sessions for individuals, families, and leaders seeking personalised guidance, energetic attunement, and soul-aligned strategy.

To explore availability or join the waitlist:

Email: sonia@soniabestulic.com.au

Or go to:

soniabestulic.com

TUNE IN TO CHATABOUT CHILDREN®

It's easy to access the podcast! Go to Sonia's website or tune in from your favourite podcast player.

soniabestulic.com.au/chatabout-children-podcast/

or

Scan the QR CODE below

Email: sonia@soniabestulic.com.au

KEEN TO INVITE SONIA TO SPEAK?

Sonia Bestulic is more than a speaker – she's a soul-led presence. Her talks awaken clarity, spark transformation, and connect hearts with higher purpose.

Whether on stage, in boardrooms, or with communities, Sonia weaves ancient wisdom, modern science, and soul-led truth into every word she shares.

Invite Sonia to speak at your next event, summit, retreat, or gathering; and co-create an experience your audience will remember.

soniabestulic.com.au/keynotespeaking/

or

Scan the QR CODE below:

Email: sonia@soniabestulic.com.au

LOOKING FOR MORE BOOKS BY SONIA?

Sonia is an award-winning author, gifting people of all ages to live a life powered by love.

For signed copies of her books:

soniabestulic.com

or

Scan the QR Code below

Email: sonia@soniabestulic.com.au

MEDIA ENQUIRIES

Sonia has featured across numerous national and international media platforms, regularly contributing thought leadership on parenting, education, kids' self-leadership, energy mastery, and conscious communication.

She is available for:
Media interviews and expert commentary.
Podcast guest appearances.
Keynotes, workshops, retreats, and event panels.

For bookings and enquiries:

soniabestulic.com
or
Scan the QR Code below

Email: sonia@soniabestulic.com.au

RESOURCES

Centre. Clear. Cohere.

Ritual for Frequency Stability

Total Time: 5–10 minutes
Can be done in the morning, evening, or mid-day reset.

Step 1: Centre
(1–2 minutes)
Reclaim your core signal.

Sit or stand.
Close your eyes.
Place one hand on your chest, the other on your belly.
Breathe slowly. Ask inwardly:
'What is true for me right now?'
Don't edit. Don't explain.
Just feel. Let the answer rise – emotion, image, or stillness.
This step reconnects you to your original tone.

Step 2: Clear
(2–3 minutes)
Release field noise.
Say inwardly or aloud:
'I release what is not mine to carry.'
'I return to my frequency.'
Now visualise a subtle golden or white light washing through you – gently sweeping out noise, other people's emotions, fear loops, confusion.
On each exhale, imagine letting go.
Even 3 deep breaths here makes a difference.

Step 3: Cohere
(2–4 minutes)
Lock in your chosen frequency.

Now ask:
'What tone do I choose to hold today?'
Pick one word: *Calm. Joy. Precision. Openness. Sovereignty.*
Let this become your tuning fork.
As you breathe, imagine your body gently ringing with that word – like a bell being struck from within.

Optional Anchor Phrase to Use Throughout the Day:
'I am stable in my signal.
I respond – not react.
I remember my tone.'

Repeat anytime you feel pulled 'off centre'.

Grounded Embodiment Guide

Grounded embodiment is the art of living fully present in the body, honouring both spirit and Earth. These practices help children and families stay rooted in calm awareness while nurturing their intuitive gifts.

Barefoot Earth Walks

Take off your shoes and walk on grass, soil, or sand together. Breathe slowly. Ask, 'What do I feel under my feet?' This grounds energy and builds body awareness.

Movement as Expression

Create space for spontaneous movement or dance. Let each person express how they feel with their body, not words. This enhances emotional expression and integration.

Mindful Eating Together

Bless your food before eating. Eat slowly. Share what the food feels like in the body. This cultivates gratitude and embodiment through nourishment.

Stillness Time

Sit together in silence for 3–5 minutes. Place hands on hearts or thighs.

Breathe together. Ask, 'Can I feel my breath?' This builds nervous system regulation.

Speak from the Belly

Practise speaking slowly and clearly. Encourage kids to imagine their words coming from their belly. This grounds communication in truth and confidence.

Anchor Objects

Give each person a grounding object (a smooth stone, wooden bead, etc.). Let them hold it when feeling floaty or anxious. This helps reconnect with the present moment.

Reflection Time

End the day with a reflection: 'What helped me feel calm today?' or 'What helped me feel strong in my body?' Celebrate their inner awareness.

Energetic Self-Leadership Guide for Kids

This guide is designed to help children develop heart-led self-leadership through the lens of energetic awareness and integrity.

Each practice supports emotional intelligence, self-awareness, and relational wisdom, helping children flourish from the inside out.

1. Bubble Breaths (Regulating My Energy)

Helps kids self-regulate when they feel overwhelmed or emotionally dysregulated.

How To Do It:

- Sit or stand comfortably. Close your eyes if you'd like.
- Take a deep breath in like you're filling a big bubble in your belly.
- Exhale slowly as if you're blowing that bubble into the sky.
- Repeat 5 times. Each breath helps calm your energy field.

Reflection Prompt:

Ask: 'What does your bubble look like?'

'What feelings are you breathing out today?'

2. Energy Field Scan (Body Check-In)

Supports somatic awareness – knowing where emotions live in the body.

How To Do It:

- Lie down or sit still.
- Start at your feet and move your awareness upward, scanning for any sensations – tightness, tingling, warmth, etc.
- Put your hands where you feel the most 'buzz' or tension. Breathe into it.

Reflection Prompt:
Ask: 'Where is your energy calm today?'
'Where does it feel noisy or heavy?'

3. Mirror of Forgiveness (Letting Go)

Teaches how to release stuck energy tied to guilt, resentment, or blame.

How To Do It:

- Stand in front of a mirror. Gaze softly into your own eyes.
- Say gently: 'Even if I made a mistake, I am still worthy of love.'
- Now think of someone you feel upset with. Say: 'I let go of holding this hurt. I choose peace.'

Reflection Prompt:
Ask: 'What happens inside when you say those words?'

'Is there more space in your heart now?'

4. Heart Portal of Compassion (Expanding Love)

Fosters deep empathy by helping kids tune into others' perspectives energetically.

How To Do It:

- Sit with your hands on your heart.
- Think of someone having a hard day. Imagine sending them a soft golden light from your heart.
- Breathe in love. Breathe out understanding.

Reflection Prompt:
Ask: 'What do you think that person needs right now?'
'Can you send it from your heart?'

5. Energy Cleanup (After Conflict or Overstimulation)

Releases chaotic or stuck energy after a busy day, emotional experience, or disagreement.

How To Do It:

- Pretend you're brushing off invisible dust or static from your arms, legs, chest, and back.
- Say: 'I clear what's not mine. I keep what feels true.'
- End with a grounding breath and wiggle your toes into the floor.

Reflection Prompt:
Ask: 'What feels different in your body now?'
'What's one word for how you feel?'

Emotional Mastery

A Parent & Child Companion Resource

Insights for Parents & Educators

1. Tune into the Body's Signals

Emotions often arrive as physical sensations before they become words. A racing heart, tight chest, or tummy flutter can be the first cue. Teach children to ask: 'Where do I feel this in my body?'

2. Acknowledge Without Attachment

Swap 'I am angry' with 'I'm feeling anger right now'. This subtle shift helps children separate their identity from their emotion; and invites self-compassion instead of shame.

3. Validate the Whole Range

Every emotion carries wisdom.

- Sadness = Processing
- Anger = Protection
- Joy = Expansion

Empower your child to see each feeling as a part of their inner guidance system.

4. Let Nature Co-Regulate

The elements offer simple, embodied ways to shift energy:

- Water: Release emotions in a bath or swim.
- Earth: Ground through sand, soil, or tree touch.
- Air: Open windows, take wind walks.
- Sunlight: Soak in solar clarity and warmth.

5. Use Stories & Symbol to Support Expression

Films and books create emotional language. Ask:

- 'What did that character feel?'
- 'What helped them feel safe or strong?'

Stories often give children emotional words they don't yet have.

The Kid-Friendly Emotional Mastery Map

Use this before bedtime, after school, or anytime emotions feel big. *(Parents/ Educators: Let your child lead. You're there to listen, hold space, and be present).*

My Breath is My Magic Tool

When I feel tight or tangled inside

- *I breathe in like I'm filling a bubble.*
- *I breathe out like I'm sending that bubble into the sky.* I can do this anywhere – nobody even has to know.

My Emotions Are Like Waves

What kind of wave is my feeling right now?

- Big crashing wave (anger)
- Slow drip (sadness)
- Sparkly splash (joy)

Now I ask: *What helps me ride this wave with kindness?*

Nature Knows What I Need

When I feel full inside, I ask my heart:

- Do I need **water**? (bath, swim, cry)
- Do I need **earth**? (grass, tree, sand)
- Do I need **air**? (breeze, window, breath)
- Do I need **sunlight**? (stand in the light)

Feelings Want to Move, Not Be Fixed

I can draw it.
I can dance it.
I can whisper it to the wind.
There's no wrong way to feel. There's no wrong way to share.

I Can Say …

- 'I feel ___ in my ___.'
- 'This feeling is visiting me now.'
- 'I don't have to fix it – I can just feel it.'

My Feelings Make Me Powerful, Not Problematic

They are *not too much.*
They are *not wrong.*
They are *my wisdom.*
I'm a wave rider.
A breath tamer.
A heart listener.

Dream Reflection Journal Template

A Companion Resource for Children

This companion resource balances **open-ended prompts** with **simple guidance**, encouraging insight while honouring mystery.

Dream Reflection Journal Template

Name:____

Date:____

Did you sleep well? ○ Yes ○ A bit restless ○ Not sure

1. **What do you remember from your dream?**
(You can write, draw, or even just list images or feelings.)

2. **What was the most powerful part of the dream?**
(Choose one thing that stands out the most.)

- A place

- A person or being
- A feeling
- A symbol or object

Something else: ____________________

Why do you think it stood out to you?

3. **How did the dream make you feel?**

Check or circle any that apply:

- Calm
- Curious
- Sad
- Angry
- Scared
- Excited
- Confused
- Loved

Other: ____

4. **What might this dream be trying to show or teach you?**

(There are no wrong answers. It could be something simple like 'I miss someone' or 'I need more fun.')

5. **If your dream were a story or movie, what would its title be?**

"____"

6. **Do you want to carry something from this dream into your day?**

- A message
- A feeling
- A colour
- A reminder
- Nothing this time
- Not sure yet

Describe what you'd like to carry:

The Wholeness & Growth Model

The 4 A's Framework

This model offers a simple and powerful way to hold both acceptance and self-betterment in harmony – for kids, parents, and educators alike.

1. Acknowledge

'This is what I'm experiencing right now.'

Whether it's a behaviour challenge, an emotional state, or a life circumstance; acknowledging it honestly (without sugarcoating or shame) is step one.

This says: 'What's here is real, and it matters.'

For kids: 'Looks like you're feeling left out right now.'

For adults: 'I'm noticing I feel reactive when I'm tired.'

2. Accept

'Even with this, I am whole.'

This is the radical love piece. It says: your worth is not in question. You are not broken.

Acceptance doesn't mean you don't care – it means you are safe to grow from a place of compassion, not criticism.

For kids: 'It's okay to feel mad. That feeling doesn't make me a bad person.'

For adults: 'I can be overwhelmed and still be a loving parent.'

3. Align

'What matters most here?'

From this foundation of worth, we invite alignment with values.

What feels true?

What energy do I want to bring?

What does integrity look like in this moment?

For kids: 'What kind thing can we do, even though we're upset.'

For adults: 'What's the most loving choice for my nervous system and theirs?'

4. Act

'Here's the next small step.'

Only after acknowledging, accepting, and aligning do we take action.

But now it's not from guilt, fear, or fixing.

It's a conscious movement from inner wisdom.

For kids: 'Let's try asking for a turn instead of yelling next time.'

For adults: 'I'll take three deep breaths before responding.'

Why It Works

This framework protects the child's core belief: 'I am enough.'

It makes space for growth, without reinforcing shame.

It supports self-awareness and personal responsibility without bypassing emotion.

Closing Reflection

Growth is not about becoming worthy.

It's about letting more of our wholeness be expressed. This is how we nurture empowered, heart-led humans.

Graceful Reflection

Journalling Guide

Graceful reflection, especially through journalling, is one of the most potent practices for building emotional intelligence, self-awareness, and heart-led self-leadership in children. It helps kids slow down, observe, process, and reframe their internal world.

Here's how and why it's so powerful, grounded in both research and real-world application:

Opt for your child to handwrite if possible … here's why:
Neurological Benefits of Handwriting

1. **Deeper Cognitive Processing**: Writing by hand activates multiple brain regions related to memory, language, and emotion (like the hippocampus and prefrontal cortex). It's been shown to enhance conceptual understanding and emotional integration compared to typing.
2. **Improved Emotional Regulation**: Studies have found expressive writing helped reduce stress and anxiety by allowing emotional processing through narrative formation.
3. **Stronger Connection to Self**: The kinaesthetic act of moving the

pen slows down the thinking process and grounds the nervous system, allowing children to tune into their inner experience with more presence and clarity.

What If My Child Prefers Typing?

No need for guilt or pressure. Typing can still be highly effective for:

- Quick expression of intense feelings (especially helpful for older kids).
- Building a sense of ownership over their reflections.
- Practising consistency – kids may be more willing to type if writing is tiring.

Tip: If your child types, encourage:

- A quiet space to deepen presence.
- Slow, mindful breathing before and after.
- Occasional prompts like 'What did I learn about myself today?' or 'What's something I'm proud of?'

For Kids Who Struggle with Both Writing and Typing

There are beautiful alternatives that still allow for the benefits of journalling:

1. **Voice Journals (Audio Reflections)**

- Encourage your child to speak their thoughts aloud, using a phone or tablet to record.
- This builds self-expression, confidence, and emotional processing.

- Ask them to listen back sometimes: 'What do you notice in your voice or tone?'

2. **Art Journalling**

- Let them draw, colour, or use stickers to show how they're feeling.
- Use simple visuals: A weather map for mood, a tree for growth, or waves for emotional tides.

3. **Role Play or Storytelling**

- Invite them to create a short story with a character feeling what they feel.
- Through storytelling, they externalise emotion in a way that feels safe and imaginative.

4. **Movement or Sound-Based Reflection**

- Children can express their emotional state through dance, instrument play, or body movement (e.g. 'Show me how frustration moves').
- This helps move feelings through the body, just like journalling moves them through the mind.

Final Encouragement for Families

Reflection isn't about perfect grammar, long essays, or even words at all.

It's about:

- Giving children a safe space to meet themselves.
- Helping them feel what they feel without shame.
- Guiding them back to their own truth; gently, regularly, and with love.

Whether it's with a pen, a keyboard, or a paintbrush, reflection becomes a mirror. And through that mirror, our children learn to lead themselves with grace.

REFERENCES

Bandura, A. (1977). Social learning theory. Englewood Cliffs, NJ: Prentice-Hall.

Barrett, L. F. (2017). How emotions are made: The secret life of the brain. Houghton Mifflin Harcourt.

Barshay, J. (2023). The pandemic erased two decades of progress in reading and math. The Hechinger Report. Retrieved from https://hechingerreport.org

Battiste, M. (2013). Decolonizing Education: Nourishing the Learning Spirit.

Beck, A. T. (1976). Cognitive Therapy and the Emotional Disorders. International Universities Press.

Bell, N. (2007). Visualizing and Verbalizing for Language Comprehension and Thinking. Gander Publishing.

Bochner, J., & Pieterse, M. (2021). The cognitive and emotional benefits of expressive writing: A meta-analytic review. British Journal of Psychology, 112(2), 411–434.

Bowlby, J. (1969). Attachment and Loss.

Brinton, B., & Fujiki, M. (2005). Social competence and children with language impairment: Making connections. Seminars in Speech and Language, 26(3), 151–159. https://doi.org/10.1055/s-2005-917120

Bruner, J. (1990). Acts of Meaning. Harvard University Press.

Casey, B. J., Jones, R. M., & Hare, T. A. (2008). The adolescent brain. Developmental Review, 28(1), 62–77. https://doi.org/10.1016/j.dr.2007.08.003

Center on the Developing Child at Harvard University. (2016). Building the brain's "air traffic control" system: How early experiences shape the development of executive function. Retrieved from https://developingchild.harvard.edu

Chouinard, M. M. (2007). Children's questions: A mechanism for cognitive development. Monographs of the Society for Research in Child Development, 72(1), 1–129.

Clark, C., & Teravainen-Goff, A. (2018). Mental wellbeing, reading and writing: How children and young people's mental wellbeing is related to their reading and writing experiences. National Literacy Trust.

Cozolino, L. (2014). The neuroscience of human relationships: Attachment and the developing social brain (2nd ed.). W. W. Norton & Company.

Damasio, A. (1994). Descartes' Error: Emotion, Reason, and the Human Brain. G.P. Putnam's Sons.

Davidson, R. J., & Begley, S. (2012). The Emotional Life of Your Brain. Hudson Street Press.

Deci, E. L., & Ryan, R. M. (1985). Intrinsic motivation and self-determination in human behavior. Springer.

Department of Education, Skills and Employment. (2021). NAPLAN 2021 National Report. Australian Government. Retrieved from https://www.education.gov.au

Dispenza, J. (2017). Becoming Supernatural: How common people are doing the uncommon. Hay House.

Dossey, L. (2009). The Power of Premonitions: How Knowing the Future Can Shape Our Lives. Dutton.

Egan, K. (1986). Teaching as Storytelling: An Alternative Approach to Teaching and Curriculum in the Elementary School. University of Chicago Press.

Einstein, A. (1931). Cosmic Religion: With Other Opinions and Aphorisms. Covici Friede.

Fredrickson, B. L. (2001). The role of positive emotions in positive psychology: The broaden-and-build theory of positive emotions. American Psychologist, 56(3), 218–226.

Fredrickson, B. L. (2009). Positivity: Top-Notch Research Reveals the Upward Spiral That Will Change Your Life. Crown Publishing.

Giedd, J. N. (2004). Structural magnetic resonance imaging of the adolescent brain. Annals of the New York Academy of Sciences, 1021(1), 77–85. https://doi.org/10.1196/annals.1308.009

Gilbert, P. (2010). Compassion Focused Therapy: Distinctive Features. Routledge.

Gottman, J., & DeClaire, J. (1997). Raising an Emotionally Intelligent Child.

Gottschall, J. (2012). The Storytelling Animal: How Stories Make Us Human. Houghton Mifflin Harcourt.

Graham, S., & Perin, D. (2007). Writing next: Effective strategies to improve writing of adolescents in middle and high schools. Carnegie Corporation of New York.

Grof, S. (1992). The Holotropic Mind: The Three Levels of Human Consciousness and How They Shape Our Lives. HarperOne.

Hawkins, D. R. (2002). Power vs. Force: The Hidden Determinants of Human Behavior. Hay House.

Hillman, J. (1996). The Soul's Code: In Search of Character and Calling. Random House.

Holmes, E. A., & Mathews, A. (2005). Mental imagery in emotion and emotional disorders. Clinical Psychology Review, 25(3), 335–361.

Immordino-Yang, M. H. (2016). Emotions, learning, and the

brain: Exploring the educational implications of affective neuroscience. W. W. Norton & Company.

Immordino-Yang, M. H., & Damasio, A. (2007). We Feel, Therefore We Learn: The Relevance of Affective and Social Neuroscience to Education. Mind, Brain, and Education, 1(1), 3–10.

Judith, A. (1996). Eastern Body, Western Mind: Psychology and the Chakra System as a Path to the Self. Celestial Arts.

Kahneman, D. (2011). Thinking, Fast and Slow. Farrar, Straus and Giroux.

Kaufman, J. C., & Beghetto, R. A. (2009). Beyond big and little: The four C model of creativity. Review of General Psychology, 13(1), 1–12.

Koenig, H. G. (2012). Religion, Spirituality, and Health: The Research and Clinical Implications. ISRN Psychiatry, 2012, 278730. https://doi.org/10.5402/2012/278730

Lieberman, M. D. (2000). Intuition: A social cognitive neuroscience approach. Psychological Bulletin, 126(1), 109–137.

Lyons, L. (2003). Reading, writing, and self-regulation: The role of executive function in literacy learning. Journal of Learning Disabilities, 36(6), 493–505.

Mangen, A., & Velmans, A. (2019). Handwriting versus Keyboard Writing: Effect on Word Recall. Trends in Neuroscience and Education, 17, 100119. https://doi.org/10.1016/j.tine.2019.100119

Mangen, A., Walgermo, B. R., & Brønnick, K. (2013). Reading linear texts on paper versus computer screen: Effects on reading comprehension. International Journal of Educational Research, 58, 61–68.

McCraty, R., Atkinson, M., Tomasino, D., & Bradley, R. T. (2009). The coherent heart: Heart–brain interactions, psychophysiological coherence, and the emergence of system-wide order. Integral Review,

5(2), 10–115.

McTaggart, L. (2007). The Intention Experiment: Using your thoughts to change your life and the world. Free Press.

Oschman, J. L. (2000). Energy Medicine: The Scientific Basis. Churchill Livingstone.

Panksepp, J. (1998). Affective Neuroscience: The Foundations of Human and Animal Emotions.

Perry, B. D., & Szalavitz, M. (2017). The boy who was raised as a dog: And other stories from a child psychiatrist's notebook (3rd ed.). Basic Books. (Original work published 2006)

Pinker, S. (1997). How the Mind Works. W. W. Norton & Company.

Pinker, S. (2007). The Stuff of Thought: Language as a Window into Human Nature. Viking.

Porges, S. W. (2011). The Polyvagal Theory: Neurophysiological Foundations of Emotions, Attachment, Communication, and Self-regulation.

Reber, A. S. (1993). Implicit Learning and Tacit Knowledge: An Essay on the Cognitive Unconscious. Oxford University Press.

Rubik, B., et al. (2020). "Biofield Science and Healing: Toward a Transdisciplinary Approach." Global Advances in Health and Medicine.

Runco, M. A., & Acar, S. (2012). Divergent thinking as an indicator of creative potential. Creativity Research Journal, 24(1), 66–75.

Sapolsky, R. M. (2004). Why Zebras Don't Get Ulcers: An Updated Guide to Stress, Stress-Related Diseases, and Coping. Holt Paperbacks.

Shaywitz, S. E. (2003). Overcoming Dyslexia: A New and Complete Science-Based Program for Reading Problems at Any Level. Knopf.

Siegel, D. J. (2012). The developing mind: How relationships and the brain interact to shape who we are (2nd ed.). Guilford Press.

Siegel, D. J., & Bryson, T. P. (2012). The whole-brain child: 12

revolutionary strategies to nurture your child's developing mind. Delacorte Press.

Taylor, S. E., Pham, L. B., Rivkin, I. D., & Armor, D. A. (1998). Harnessing the imagination: Mental simulation, self-regulation, and coping. American Psychologist, 53(4), 429–439.

Ungar, M. (2013). Resilience, trauma, context, and culture. Trauma, Violence, & Abuse, 14(3), 255–266.

Van der Kolk, B. (2014). The Body Keeps the Score. Penguin Books.

van Eeden, F. (1913). A study of dreams. Proceedings of the Society for Psychical Research, 26, 431–461.

Vaughan, F. (1979). Transpersonal Psychology in Psychoanalytic Perspective.

Wineburg, S., McGrew, S., Breakstone, J., & Ortega, T. (2022). Evaluating information: The cornerstone of civic online reasoning (2nd ed.). Stanford History Education Group.

World Economic Forum. (2023). The Future of Jobs Report 2023. Geneva: World Economic Forum

Zak, P. J. (2012). The Moral Molecule: The Source of Love and Prosperity. Dutton.

Zak, P. J. (2015). The Moral Molecule: How Trust Works. Dutton.

Zull, J. E. (2002). The Art of Changing the Brain: Enriching Teaching by Exploring the Biology of Learning. Stylus Publishing.

www.ingramcontent.com/pod-product-compliance
Ingram Content Group UK Ltd.
Pitfield, Milton Keynes, MK11 3LW, UK
UKHW062310290726
14090UKWH00018B/979